BABBLES and BLOGS

of / by

Ajay Ray

Babbles and Blogs

About this book:

The blogs were posted in public domain and covered the period of January 2008 to October 2011 Previous blogs written between October 2005 to December 2007 were published in a separate book **'A Random Journey of Mind'..** The weekly readership ranged from an average of 20 to 40. Some posting had reached a peak of above 600.

ISBN: 978-1-105-63240-2

Babbles and Blogs

Dedicated for pleasure reading to all curious
Readers
&
Shaun, Tejas, Trevor and Kajal

A Few Words like before:

This book (and also previously published book - A RANDOM JOURNEY OF MIND) do not boast as literary gems. It is about our daily lives, living and experiences - written weekly and posted as blogs. As such it is dated as when written. The journey is a random journey of mind. Mind is the master of human existence and it cannot be reined in and subjugated by anybody. But it is also always impacted by people, thoughts and events around. It is the most wonderful thing that we have. Human progress is nothing but products of human minds and implementation of its ideas. So its journey is a very relevant journey that embraces everything and everybody. So is the scope of this book. It is personal- at the same time it is universal. Books are nothing but tools of virtual entertainment. So if it can bring a little joy or a little smile or a little understanding in any reader's mind then it will have its day in the sun. Thank you. – Ajay (May 1, 2013)

Babbles and Blogs

Excerpts from Babbles and Blogs:

My New Year Resolution: "...*Honestly I think we are voyeuristic animals. We always read what others write or think. Thus a writer writes... Is there really anything that matters to anybody else except when it impacts one's daily life...*"

*Power of Tears: "... **What was the genesis of Senator Clinton's tears? The political pundits have termed it as a political tear – probably.. That emotional connection draws us to that smile... Verbal eloquence probably has a limited life, but a touching emotional image has a much longer life... All tears are not therapeutic. Like when a child cries... Tear is a language of silence...**"*

*Nobel's Thoughts on Reading:"... **Doris Lessing (86), who won the Nobel Prize of Literature for 2007 ... lamented the sad and continuing demise of reading as a past time... In short are we advancing intellectually and dying mentally... The Internet is filling our brains with inanities!... I don't see that Shakespeare contributed any benefit to the Chinese people... Reading is a vital part of living – if it dies we all somewhat die...We have to understand first what Literature means, and how it is an essential part of humanity...**"*

*Almost Destroyed by Mold: "... **This happened five years ago, in July 2003 I was shocked and shaken to the core... I never thought a small water-flooding problem would have so much consequence ...**"*

Babbles and Blogs

Excerpts from Babbles and Blogs:

America at Crossroads: "... **Those are new challenges that were not seen two hundred years ago. So, we cannot follow any precedent occurrence.... We need a leadership of mind, heart and intelligence....**"

Remembering Maharishi Mahesh Yogi: "**....My brother who I was very close to was very unhappy at home, and left for Rishikesh without telling anyone about his whereabouts .... This concept is neither new nor unique. In India the practice of meditation has been around for ...**"

When the Pressure is On: "... **the heart did not attack, but has been attacked! No I did not have any heart attack. But the pressure was spiking up like crazy without notice and without regard for time and place...**"

Moolade – A Story of Female Circumcision: "... **a tourist can only see the architecture, infrastructure or geographical uniqueness. It does not tell one about the minds of the people living in the land... Though it is practiced in African cultures mainly, but immigration and globalization have spread the practice worldwide...**"

No More than 33.5 inches: "... **men over 40 will be penalized monetarily and may lose their job if no effort is made to bring it down to 33.5 inches of waistline?...**"

Babbles and Blogs

Excerpts from Babbles and Blogs:

A Story of Eating: "...**To be on the safe side, I have set an arbitrary limit of 5 to everything. That is 5 gm of sugar, 5% Daily Value of sodium, 5% fat cholesterol...**"

What is Time: "...**But why does the day start at middle of the night – never made sense to me.....there is no entity such as time – it is only about movement of sun relative to earth...**"

Somebody Hates Mickey Mouse: " **...probably was that Mickey was trying to spread his corrupt influence (read fun) on this fatwa- issuing cleric when he got alarmed...**"

Sexy! Oh No: "**Sexy' by formal dictionary definition means sexually exciting or interesting. By this definition if one wants to look sexy then the underlying motivation...**"

The Las Vegas Salesman: "...**He said his dad was a top salesman also, and always helped, guided and taught him the lessons of life. He was his best friend all his life...**"

Shame Game: "...**people over the world live in two different cultures - 'Shame Culture' and 'Guilt Culture'...**"

Slap of an Eunuch (Hijra): "... **Probably another Hijra will come someday and slap him again for lying....**"

Babbles and Blogs

Excerpts from Babbles and Blogs:

He Liked Sudoku: "...**But not this gentleman. He had his reading light on, and he was immersed in the book with his pencil in hand...**"

Jia Your Mom is calling you: "...**It is now an internet craze in China. Everybody is talking about Jia and her mother...**"

A Visitor from India: "... **myself had never experienced such big temblor before. I got very nervous, and thought it was prudent to go outdoor for safety. Before going out I frantically....**"

TABLE OF CONTENTS –

BABBLES AND BLOGS

 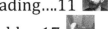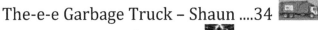

Babbles and Blogs

Babbles and Blogs

My New Year Resolution
(1-4-2008)

Every New Year starts with great hopes in our mind. When we reach the twelfth month of the current jaded year – we start dreaming of a better new year. So we make lot of resolutions. Then mostly we forget that when the New Year is not new anymore (that is when it becomes more than say two weeks old) then we sink back into our old habits, and wait for the next year to make a new resolution. We are always hopeful that like the New Year we shall be new persons. I know how eagerly we waited for the new millennium – and how apprehensive (or hopeful) we were at that time. President Clinton assured us that he would hold our hands to steer us safely to the unknown millennium. There was dour prediction that the world would come to an end – computers would collapse, the power grid would become non-functional, and some people even hided themselves in caves somewhere to shield themselves from the unknown danger of the coming millennium. But the New Year came and passed by like any other year.

It is for sure that the New Year starts with great hopes and expectations, and we all promise ourselves to strive to be a better person at that time. Thus the overweight person wants to get rid of some weights, the person who drinks or smokes too much wants to cut down on his bad habits, etc. If we look at the list of popular New Year's Resolutions, we find that the popular resolutions are - shed some weight, do more exercise, cut down drinking/smoking, spend more time with family, enjoy life more by travel etc, learning a new craft or language, read more books, watch less TV, spend less on junk electronics or cloth or sports equipment, clean up the garage etc. Whatever be it – it seems we want to get rid of some of the bad habits that we have acquired without even knowing how we got into that. I think as 24 carat gold is not durable – so are 24 carat persons. So we have to have some alloys or impurities for our day to day living. Our main job repeatedly is to make a New Year resolution on the New Years Day by promising to upgrade ourselves to become a less alloyed person.

Babbles and Blogs

But my New Year Resolution has nothing to do with making me a better person. It has to do with this blog. Since starting to blog on October 25, 2005 – and contributing to that on a mostly weekly cycle – the number of blogs had become substantial. For a two year span – it had reached more than 200 pages in my computer on pages of 8 ½ x11 or about 7300 lines. I know my blogs don't have any aim or purpose – except to indulge myself in random thoughts. So I thought why not put all the blogs together and publish a book named 'A Random Journey of Mind'. So I was looking at the possibility of publication – do It yourself way. Of course no big publisher will be interested in such things, as they always look for the author's name recognition. Obviously I have no name recognition – and I doubt if the total count will reach even three digits. So sales and marketing effort of this kind of book are not going to be that much.

I also don't want to go to Vanity Publishers, who will publish anything you wish to publish as long as you give them a fat check. But who wants to spend money to read one's own writing? At least I am not of that kind. Then also this is not an academic book or teach you something book that some academic publishers will be interested in. Then naturally nobody is interested or will be interested to read a book called 'A Random Journey of Mind' by an unknown person.

Somebody even asked me why anyone should be interested in what my mind thinks. Honestly I think we are voyeuristic animals. We always read what others write or think. Thus a writer writes a fiction or a non-fiction of crazy people and their lives – basically reweaving the characters that the writer had come across. Some scholar writes about communism, or capitalism or something else. Why anybody should be interested in reading that. He is not the President of the country that we have to know what is in his mind. Is there really anything that matters to anybody else except when it impacts one's daily life? Thus probably a serial killer would be a great writer – as it is very important to know what is in his mind, and nobody would care to read Harry Potter who does not exist except in some body's imagination. But the truth is people like to know what other people think and what other people's experiences are. May be someone will find a symphony there as the world is a very big populous place.

So I will publish this book that will have at least one buyer that is myself. If anybody else wants to read that it will be available through 'print on demand'. There are many publishers who would do this 'print on demand' kind of publication. I short listed the publishers on this field – found some big players there including Amazon, Xlibris, iUniverse, Lulu. I think I shall go for Lulu. I like their approach – no copy right problem, ISBN listing and reasonably priced depending on the volume of the publication. They will even sell it for a small share for their out of pocket cost. The format preferred is 6x9 pages with 30 lines per page. My initial reformatting indicates it will be close to 450 pages. I wanted to add some cartoons too – but that would add to the volume. So I am not thinking along that line.

It seems the editing is a major job in any publication. I am not going to outsource it – I shall do it myself – as I am the one who can follow my thought pattern. But it is a time consuming job. I shall do it in my spare time after doing my regular office work. So it will take some time for sure. Then again there are new skills that I have to learn from how to make TOC (Table of Contents) and many other small details. But learning and doing this project is going to be fun. Hemingway said that a man should do three things in life – one of them is to publish a book. I reflected on that why he said that. And there seems to be a lot of wisdom in that. We are not all Kings or People of Great Importance or Talent – so we cannot leave behind a magnificent structure or a magnificent composition. But we can leave behind our thoughts of the moment, our joys in relationship or travel, our perceptions and feelings of what was going on around while we lived. Nobody knows what the dinosaurs did or thought – as their thoughts were not inscribed on anything for prosperity. So I think a publication is important if not from a commercial point of view, but from the view of an imprint of one's own story of life. And that is my New Year Resolution.

Power of Tears (1-11-2008)

I was intrigued by tears the other day – as I witnessed Hillary Clinton trying to suppress her tears in response to a simple question (while campaigning for herself). Then I read that the tear alone swayed many women voters and raised her support by 10% among the democrats voting in the New Hampshire primary. She ended up beating the other contestant. Initially when I saw the tears on CNN – I thought probably that was a blunder. It could be a political suicide as America wants a strong leader who does not blink, who does not shed any tears of weakness. Curiously I asked a doctor friend – was she ashamed of Hillary's tears? She said – no question of being ashamed, now she supported her more than before! I thought that was strange

– but then I read that actually many voters felt like that. That turned me to ponder about the effect of tears. I know it is a very difficult subject – but no harm in trying to understand tears.

What was the genesis of Senator Clinton's tears? Some woman in the crowd asked her – who did her hair. I would think the response could be – that was nobody's business except that of her hair dresser and herself (sounds rude – politically damaging); or that she had been so busy with her mission to put America on the right track that she had no time to think about that (sounds very serious, but may sound fake); or that – was not the questioner happy with her hair , could not the questioner mind her own business only (sounds very unfriendly); or may be – thanks for asking, I did not get any time to think about that (acknowledging personal well wish) etc. So that question could elicit probable defensive posture, probable angry posture, probable aloofness posture or friendly posture. But swell of tears in her eyes in response to that question? I still do not know what chord that question struck in her. Though I see the political pundits have termed it as a political tear – probably a vote-getting ploy in the drama of the Presidential election. Many even hinted that many presidents had used it success-fully to win public approval – so that must have been a strategically smart move delivered with surgical precision! My ordinary thinking suggests probably the hectic schedule had weakened her! I am not judging anything right or wrong. because in this case – it was a non-verbal response to a query – which could have any meaning. Tear is a non-verbal subliminal language and is more powerful than words.

I have seen many exquisite paintings and sculptures of many countries of different era. They are all trying to say something – but there was no photograph or audio graph of that event and surrounding to explain that particular mood of the painting. Normally if it is a soldier or peasant then it does not depict any emotion but depicts an activity only then we have no problem. But when it portrays an emotion – like sadness, smile, pain etc – then we are in deep trouble. Then we try to understand that subliminal emotion. Then it becomes subject to our interpretation. Take Mona Lisa for example. Why is it so mystic and consequentially so classical? It is because of her expression of an unexplained emotion through a half-smile – which we don't know what that was about. If there was a photograph of that modeling session – we could see probably the artist might have said 'cheese!', or that there was a playful crowd nearby, or probably that she was an extremely shy person nodding acknowledgement to the artist etc. Then we try to understand the emotion expressed in the smile. We imagine many unspoken thing about the emotion of the moment. Basically we try to recreate the unspoken surroundings with our own imagination. Now that emotional connection draws us to that smile and to that picture. Because it is a two-dimensional picture with an emotional overlay, we try to frame that in time, mood and circumstances. So what I am saying really?

What I am saying is that if Clinton answered in so many words – she would have destroyed the mystic by putting the answer in a definitive frame of her mind. By not answering that she allowed the unspoken emotion to be much louder than a spoken answer. That silent tear was an emotional answer and that touched many more people. Somebody thought that she was a relentless warrior without a personal consideration; somebody thought that she had put the country above herself; some people thought that she was very close to all common ordinary people, and that she was on the same wave length as the rest etc. Now what we think is colored by our bias, and the interpretation cannot be definitive. But whatever be it – that tear must have appealed to many hearts. Verbal eloquence probably has a limited life, but a touching emotional image has a much longer life. So could it be that might have contributed her 10% additional support?

I know I am getting into a philosophical pit, but all I was trying to see how a tearful emotion can sway so many people. The actual story of surge in support in this situation could be far from the effect of tears. The actual cause can be a possible mix of misinterpretation, manipulation, inner private bias etc. So what I am saying is totally apolitical. I remember one poem I read in school – probably by Wordsworth. The poem was describing the grief of the widow of a fallen soldier. She did not cry at all at her personal loss, and all others were very worried that she might die if she did not cry. Crying is a shock releaser – that takes away or minimizes the stress in our body and system. I have seen that many tribes in India have professional criers – they come in a group when somebody dies. Their job is to cry and that cry helps to reduce the shock and stress of the loss of the dear ones.

Now all tears are not therapeutic. Like when a child cries – it can be from pain or hunger etc (which can be handled by medicine or food); or for his mother (needed for emotional support). So it seems that tear is a manifestation of pain whether physical or emotional. If the tears are sincerely emotional that is bound to draw others for sympathy. Tear is a language of silence – that has more eloquence than our ability to express ourselves in words. Pundits say our face can express four languages of emotion – sorrow, happiness, apprehension and approval (I may be wrong here). Funny that many people think that tears are signs of weakness – but in reality it might be just the opposite!

Nobel's Thoughts on Reading (1-18-2008)

I am not a student of literature, so am not conversant with the treasures of great minds stored there. But something got my attention about 'Reading'. Doris Lessing (86), who won the Nobel Prize of Literature for 2007, (in her acceptance speech) lamented the sad and continuing demise of reading as a past time and its necessity in the modern computer crazed society. Then I thought why she is saying that. She also said something like - that the Internet has created a generation who dispense countless hours (like addicts?) with the Internet – blogging, e-mailing, searching etc, but all amount to inanities (uselessness – I think that is what she meant). So I thought why not pause a little and ponder what she means. Are we all going forward or backward; are we unlocking the door of the kingdom of information but losing our soul in that quest? Are we getting to be without soul, and thus without any feeling or any possibility of survival?

In short are we advancing intellectually and dying mentally? Something also I read in paper - in South Korea they have started *'computerholic anonymous'*. That support group helps each other to winch away from the addiction of computer and internet. Also I read the story of one mother lamenting that her kids 14 and 16 year olds don't talk with anybody and have alienated themselves in their rooms. She has no idea how to handle the situation. So it looks to me that the computers and Internet have driven away the urge of emotional socializing and reading, and are substituting that with trivia, and transient knowledge. The Internet is filling our brains with inanities! For sure this is a very serious concern about our current and future generations and that was probably what the Nobel Laureate was talking about.

To understand this I went to the web site of the Nobel Prize – just to get a better perspective of what was the thinking of Alfred Nobel, a Swede engineer and philanthropist. He made his fortune in the explosive business (he was a chemical engineer), but left his entire estate to endow prizes to those who, during the preceding year shall have conferred the greatest benefit to

mankind. He died in 1896 and awarded the task

of selecting the prize recipients to Swedish Academy (and Norway Academy for Peace prize recipient). To implement his dream – lot of things had to be straightened out, and the Swedish Academy started Nobel Prizes from 1901. As can be understood- physics, chemistry, medicine etc can really confer great benefits to mankind. But Literature? What possible benefit can the literature give to mankind? It does not make us any safer, does not improve our living, or does not conquer any disease. Then why did Mr. Nobel include literature as a benefactor of mankind? To understand that I read his background, but could not find anything to give me any clue. Only thing that can remotely connect his mind to Literature was that he was a philosopher. (Probably his source of wealth was death and killing – so his inner person clamored to balance that by making contribution to life and living in general). It was kind of strange also because literature is expressed through languages and dialogues - so its appeal and content can relate to a particular segment of world citizens. Thus I don't see that Shakespeare contributed any benefit to the Chinese people, and that any person in Africa cared for Rabindranath in spite of all the beauty and treasure of his contribution. But somehow Mr. Nobel was convinced that Literature could confer great benefit to mankind (not to one particular nation) irrespective of the language in which it is born. I know the English teachers in school or English professors in colleges recite literature, glorify literature, and lament about the poor souls who do not appreciate a great literature. But a non-English, non-teacher person like Mr. Nobel also somehow thought along that line that Literature enriched people and acknowledged its contribution towards mankind's benefit! Now, the present Nobel Laureate is lamenting about the dying passion of Reading. The far-reaching conclusion seems to be Reading is a vital part of living – if it dies we all somewhat die. Very disturbing conclusion – but must be true as it comes from a great and outstanding mind.

I know that we cannot live (or rather live effectively) without reading. We have to read the paper to know what is going around; we have to read the manual and instructions to see how things operate; we have to read the bank statement to know how much money we have; we have to read letters to know how our friends and other people we care about are doing etc. So it is obvious that we did not forget to read – we have to read to live. Actually we now read more than ever before. Because knowledge enters our brain through the activity of reading – and with Internet exploding phenomenally, knowledge is entering our head in much higher number than before. So – how could the Nobel Laureate say that we are forgetting Reading? It is obvious that she is not talking about reading in general, but talking about reading of literature in particular. But what literature has to do with our living? We can live our whole life (and most of us do) without reading a serious piece of literature. I myself have not read the literary creations of the great minds that were honored with Nobel Prizes of Literature year after year for conferring outstanding benefits to mankind. So the answer does not seem obvious.

So I think we have to understand first what Literature means, and how it is an essential part of humanity. Suppose we go to Greece and find some beautiful fallen statues and temples– what could that possibly mean to us? Almost nothing besides that they are just another evidence of life in past in Greece. But suppose we know the statue was of Aristotle – then of course we become interested in the statue. Then also if the statue depicts Aristotle as thinking- then we become more curious as what he was thinking about. When we find that he was a philosopher – we understand that during that time they were very civilized. They did not spend all their time with daily business of living – but they had some time of leisure – that they could devote to other pursuits. Then we become more curious as to what they were thinking, what did they know, what was their problems, what was their happiness, what was their sorrow, what was they proud of, what was their imagination, what was their anxiety etc. Now a whole world of past existence comes to life only because somebody cared to tell us about those people. Of course a historian can keep record of big events, a philosopher can tell us what he thinks, an artist can leave behind a masterpiece sculpture or painting- but does it tell about everybody who lived at that time? No. These remnants of artifacts or statues cannot do that by themselves. They cannot bring themselves back to life. Who can do that? Only literature can do that. Only the literature people can bring out the inner world of emotion, passion and imagination in their literary creation and leave that for others of present and posterity to know. So Literature really is life, it binds lives and can infuse lives in inanimate things, and bring out the inner and outer worlds of the period and the people. And that becomes a treasure to posterity. The past then reveals itself in much more understandable details than what is visible to naked eyes. So if literature is dying – it may also mean that we are dying as a lasting civilization? In fact, literature is our letter to posterity, a narrative content of our inner selves that are partially expressed in our outer activities. It is a virtual world of memory of our moments of leisure, our states of minds- in other words of civilization itself. So Literature really reflects the emotional health of a society. In times of prosperity it dazzles. In times of misery it cries. In happiness it radiates. In captivity it suffocates. In aloofness it dies. Who can bring it all alive for now and for future? Only Literature can. It is a fable of the living, and a link between present and posterity. Today will become yesterday and tomorrow will become today. Time will change, but we will be memorialized. Thus the literature should never die. But it has to be born first. The only way to create, sustain and encourage literary creativity and activity is by creating writers and readers – two sides of the same coin.

So the dying passion for Reading is really a bad omen for literature. In other words if Reading dies, Literature dies, and we all die a little today inside now and will be dead in future. I don't know if that was what the Nobel Laureate was talking about, I just guessed it in my way.

Almost Destroyed by Mold (1-25-2008)

I don't know how many people have been attacked by Mold. We had been and now we are scared of Mold. No, Mold did not attack my body physically or incapacitated me, but it did incapacitate a much larger thing. This happened five years ago, in July 2003. I have forgotten many details, but it was so scary that I remember most of it. So I shall recollect that to the best of my memory and knowledge.

We own a preschool, and my wife runs that. She has been doing that since 1990. In 2003 summer, we thought we would go on a family vacation to Europe. We were looking forward to the vacation for a long time – as mostly we were so strapped for time that we did not think of vacation for some time. But we were determined to have that European vacation no matter what. We had planned in details about the trip - gathered all the information about Paris (West bank, East bank, Notre dame, Versailles, Champs-Elyse, Louvre etc) and all about London (Buckingham Palace, Trafalgar Square, Tower of London, London Bridge etc). Also we had booked for a night show on London's Broadway, booked Eurorail tickets to go under the English Channel. Any way we had planned for the vacation in great details and were looking forward to it.

The flight was on Monday night. Came Monday morning, as we were discussing the fun trip - the person who used to open the school called us frantically that the school was flooded. We had no

idea how there could be a flood in the school as

there was no rain or nothing of that sort at that time. So we ran to the school and found out that there was a plumbing accident. The flexible pipe leading to the toilet sink had snapped, and water was gushing out. Probably it happened during the night time – as no one noticed it , water gushing out of the link had spread all over the building (a medium sized school) and all the classroom carpets were soaking wet, the materials were wet at the bottom. In short it was a scary scene of disaster.

On arriving at the scene of disaster, we turned off the water valve coming into the building. That stopped additional flooding, but the extent of flooding that happened already had turned a nice building into a pitiable mess. I had no idea how to handle it. We had no experience on handling this kind of situation before. First I thought – why not look in the yellow pages to find out if there were any services pertaining to this kind of problem. We were relieved to see that there were companies that dealt with water flooding problems. They call themselves 'water damage and cleaning contractors'. So we called the one that seemed closer to us. They said it was no problem that was their job. In half hour two big vans came with a crew of four or five people. They put out their suction pumps and heavy hoses, and started to suck the standing water out. There was another van full of giant ventilating fans. They placed six or eight of them in the crawl space below the building. All of them started working in unison. I asked them what they were doing with all the fans. They said – it had to be done – otherwise in twenty four to thirty six hours Molds would take over the building, and we would have no choice other than demolishing the building completely. I was shocked and shaken to the core. I never thought a small water-flooding problem would have so much consequence. In short, we had been attacked by Mold, and the war against the Mold had to start in earnest right away. Any lack of effort or delay in taking safety measure would bankrupt us thoroughly that would entail not only loss of the property, but might also lead to multi-million dollar lawsuits for health–related damages due to Mold. Now I realized Mold was no small thing.

Forget about London and Paris. If we did not go that would be a small financial loss. Now we were facing a crisis that had the possibility of ruining us completely. Immediate containment of the Mold was necessary to prevent the calamity. The ventilating fans were operating 24 hours all over and under the building for three or four days. When the contractor thought that the water problem was under control, they took the fans away. Then they put on heavy plastic contain-ments with limited access to each room – so that nobody could get in. And sign was put on to the effect that it was hazardous to go inside the containment without respirators, and only authorized personnel were permitted inside. Now the war against the Mold was on. The workers had to create holes in all the walls so that fresh air could get in, some walls were taken out. The soaked carpets were removed and were to be taken to hazardous landfill. People in space suits with respirators were going inside the contained area. The Testing Lab people came to take air samples every other day to find out if the spore count had come down to an acceptable level.

This went on for two weeks. I am not going to detail here the difficulty we faced of running the school while the school building was closed. Though we did manage that with use of other facilities (creating chaos and inconvenience to parents and teachers,). This writing is about Mold, so I shall limit my jottings to issues related to Mold only. This fight with Mold went on for two weeks. The damage from Mold was brought under control. We had to change some walls, some flooring, all new carpets and sanitizing each and every material with Mold detergents. The repair also took another three weeks. But finally we did win the war against the Molds. The building came back to operation after five weeks. Our financial wipeout had been averted. The Insurance Company usually does not cover Mold damage.

Those who have not been exposed to this kind of Mold scare – might wonder what was the fuss about. So a few words about Molds would not be out of place. Molds are nature's scavengers – they occur everywhere. In fact all Molds are not dangerous – the anti-bacterial drug Penicillin is a Mold itself. It is not all the Molds that all are scared of. There are a few kinds of Molds that are dangerous (mostly they grow indoor) – 'Stachy-botrys' is the most dangerous one. The Molds cause damage externally (athlete's foot etc), internally (pulmonary disease) and most commonly allergic reaction and minor irritation. Usually the infants and senior segments of the population (including pregnant women and immuno-deficient people) are fatal victims of this dangerous Mold. Molds were there as long as there has been life. But the buildings we live in now a day are very dangerous from the Mold point of view. We live in air-tight buildings with porous building materials (like wood floor, wood wall, wood roof, plywood, dry wall etc.). Molds grow with water accumulation on cellulose objects. Thus it can happen in places of leaks in the hidden plumbing lines, air-conditioning drips etc. The word 'Sick Building Syndrome' has been around for some time. That Sick Syndrome includes Molds along with other chemicals released inside the closed building. Usually the symptoms are allergy attacks – so allergy prone people have to be especially careful. Any stains, bulging out of wall indicate water problems. Where there is water problem, there is Mold problem (if it interacts with woods or wood fibers). Most of the Mold problems became publicized when a Texas Jury awarded $32 million (in 2000) judgment against an Insurance company for failing to repair a plumbing problem in a home in Texas (Ballard Residence of 11,000 sq ft – a mansion) - that resulted in mold manifestation. The house became uninhabitable. Now the Insurance Companies have excluded Mold damages from their coverage. The initial damage from Katrina was of water – that turned into a Mold nightmare for the staying-behind population. This writing is getting long—so I shall stop here. Only thing I hope nobody is attacked by Mold like we were, and probably everybody should take caution beforehand. If there is any suspect stains of mold indoor whether below the carpet or behind the wall or any exposed places – it is prudent to get rid of that mold – before it turns on you.

***

**America at Crossroads**

America at Crossroads (2-1-2008)

This week I thought I would write about some quirks in conversation that I noticed. It has to do with 'No Problem'. When you thank the waiter for serving you the food, many times the waiter replies 'No problem'. That confounds me – as if I was creating a problem, and the waiter restored my peace of mind by assuring that it was no problem. I also did not have an inkling of an idea that going to the restaurant and responding to waiter's query as to what I want to eat was going to be a burden on the waiter. But there are more important things to talk about. So I am setting aside that trivia topics.

What is happening now in US seems to be a seminal event - the Presidential Election and people's turn to choose their Leader. This definitely seems to me the most interesting election that I have seen or participated in. America seems to be at cross-roads of history, and American citizens are being tested right now as to what they want really and as to who they trust more. Among the Republicans the choice seems to be between Romney and McCain, and among the Democrats the choice is between Clinton and Obama. So the final choice will be between Romney or McCain versus Obama or Clinton. Now if McCain gets to be the final winner then nothing new has happened – citizens have fallen back on their old habits and chose somebody they were familiar with. But if the final winner is Romney or Clinton or Obama – then America has radically changed their previous mind set. In other words then they would take a bold step that would impact the choice of a whole new generation of would be leaders.

If the contest was between the mind set of Democrats and Republicans – then nothing is there to think of. Behind all the talks of fiscal conservatism or social conservatism or reverse of that (i.e. liberalism) – the whole thing boils down to a few issues – tax cut, pro life, immigration or social entitlement (that is what I see broadly). Based on that I don't think people have to think much. Whatever they want they can vote along that line. Then the election will be based on media savvy consultants, bending of truth in ad (if not total fabrication), and beauty contest among the contenders. Young and dynamic contestant will draw out younger voters; politically seasoned and older contestants will draw out status-quo-preferring people. So basically the result can be predicted easily based on 'blue state' or 'red state' mentality with some minor local variations. The twenty four hour news people and pundits will spin the old yarn till the results can be predicted by opinion poll.

 n this election there are other factors involved. In this new era we have to counter stateless global terrorism, global competition for economic survival, proper response to environmental concerns and a humane solution of millions of illegal people etc. Most of the other issues like tax cut or pro life etc are old issues and the direction changes with time according to the views of the independent voters. But the other issues have nothing to do with party doctrines or old formulae. Those are new challenges that were not seen two hundred years ago. So, we cannot follow any precedent occurrence. It will depend on personal leadership. So it is not the party label only that is good or bad, a lot depends on who we can trust a non-partisan view and a non-myopic view of the world.

If Romney wins then of course that will be a triumph of religious liberalism. If McCain wins then it will be a win for status–quo mentality Though that will be a big boost for older contestants. If Clinton wins then it will be a crushing defeat of sexist mentality (the thinking that only men can lead and the whole leadership game is men's game only). If Obama wins then of course US would show the world that it has conquered racism at the highest level of governance. So no matter what, it is not a ho-hum election with a limited look for the coming four years. Whatever happens will be viewed by a global audience and will influence the American dreams of the posterity.

So this time the voters have to go beyond their own narrow interest and boundary, and choose a leader for themselves and a leader who can also get respect of the entire free world. What happens in America today will vibrate throughout the whole world. Hopes and aspiration of other people beyond America's border will swell or ebb with whom we elect. So it is more than a local election with limited scope. With our global unpopularity and thorny cooperation between western allies, we need a leader who can inspire so that others can aspire, a leader whose move may not coincide with the moves suggested by vested interest. We need a leader who can think for today and tomorrow, a leader who can unite diverse and different ethnic groups, a leader who can show the world that he/she wants the good and welfare of all, a leader who will show the world that he can work and talk with all leaders and take their counsel in account, a leader who can honor the trust people have vested on him.

Yes, for a leader – one does not need twenty or thirty years experience (the elected leader can choose people with experience), or does not have to have military experience (he can access all military knowledge and intelligence); or even does not have to be able to please the party

across the aisle (he can persuade by emphasizing the macro view of benefit), or does not have to be of any particular color or sex (smartness, honesty and leadership are not color or gender dependant). Yes- the bad people or terrorists will try to create problems by staging attacks and planting obstacle to defeat the new leader. But anything can be handled by the collective force of unity, good judgment and goodwill. We already have enough leadership of business style and enough leadership of party politicians. We need a leadership of mind, heart and intelligence. A person who can feel , one who can think , one who has a passion to redress the unjust , one who can restore impartiality, one who can strike a balance between what should be done and how that should be done, one who can see beyond today, one who can inspire the young and the old, one who can rekindle the inherent kindness of the American people, one who can restore sanity in confrontation with enemy, and still be able to stoke the passion of the young and uninitiated to serve the country they love. That is the kind of leader and leadership we are looking for. And I think Mr. Obama can meet that challenge. But let America decide. I think this election is a seminal event, and that is the footprint of time.

***

Remembering Maharishi Mahesh Yogi
(2-15-2008)

Last week I missed writing the blog- probably due to a lack of planning and lack of time. One of the problems in writing weekly is choosing a suitable topic. I try to see what remarkable thing happened in the week - that is important and also excites my interest. Thus I saw in the paper about the Maharishi's death in Holland on February 5 (Tuesday). I thought that would be interesting to think about him a little0 bit. In 1968 I had been to Rishikesh (a place for ascetics at the foothill of the Himalayas). At that time the Beatles were there also. Maharishi was raising a big wave in the western world by his 'Transcendental Meditation'. I was there for some other reasons. At that time I was visiting India also. My brother who I was very close to was very unhappy at home, and left for Rishikesh without telling anyone about his whereabouts. I think he wanted to feel good and wanted a break from the tedious routine of mundane daily life and usual surroundings. Also he had a religious bent of mind. I did find him there. At that time I also saw Maharishi's Ashram (a place where ascetics live). I was neither a follower of Maharishi nor an admirer of him – so I did not go to his Ashram. But he seemed to me a very interesting man.

I don't know how he became to be known as Maharishi. A 'Rishi' is someone who has attained spiritual enlightenment and he who leads an ascetic life. A 'Maharishi' means a Rishi of a very high caliber. But one thing for sure they don't crave for material possession or material pleasure. That is where they stand out from common family people who covet for material pleasure catered by material possession. A true ascetic though was regarded highly in ancient India. But this Maharishi lived in a mansion (of 200 rooms) in a village in Holland, and all the gold and glitters around him do not match the popular concept of a real Maharishi's life style. This Maharishi seemed to me a genius in Marketing – who created a brand name of the age old meditation technique practiced in India for ages. By some estimate his empire is worth close to three billion dollars. How did it all start?

He was born Mahesh Varma. He earned a bachelor's degree in science form Allahabad University. His real age seems to be a guess to his followers. By all calculation it is between 84 to 91 years. In college he was a student of physics. So he had a mind with a respect for discipline in science. Probably he did not pursue any office job after graduation. He became a disciple of

Shankaracharya (one of the four reigning top Hindu spiritual leaders) - Brahmananda Saraswati. Probably there he practiced yoga meditation under the tutelage of the Shankaracharya. In the ashram Mahesh Yogi had to live a disciplined ascetic life of celibacy. I think his guru died in 1952. After that he spent some time discovering himself and to find a true mission in his life. At that time he came up with the concept of Transcendental Meditation – tailored for the instant-pleasure-seeking western world. As the western way of life is hectic and restless – he preached twenty minutes of meditation every day. His idea was that by practice of meditation – the mind would transcend to a level of happiness (or bliss) above daily worries that are always distracting our mind. He marketed meditation with a brand name (Transcendental Meditation) and with good salesmanship amassed enormous fortune.

This concept is neither new nor unique. In India the practice of meditation has been around for more than four thousand years. Even now many common people practice daily meditation routine during their daily worship or obeisance to deity either in morning or in evening; though this practice has been adapted to a western style, Yoga means 'union' in Sanskrit. I think the ancient Hindus thought that to attain the spiritual bliss the body must in good shape and mind disciplined. So they prescribed many flexibility routines and postures for the whole body or different parts of the body. That became the discipline of Yoga. But just a healthy body does not assure a healthy mind – so they prescribed meditation for mental discipline also. This combination (or yoga i.e. union) is an age old method or prescription for healthy body and mind. The net benefit is that body influences mind and mind influences the body.

About more than one hundred years ago – another great Indian yogi ascetic Vivekananda felt that western people could benefit from this age old Indian practice of yoga. He came to America as a representative of Vedic monks to address the World Council of Religions in Chicago in 1993. As he was an impressive speaker and a charismatic personality, he was invited to lecture intensively to teach Vedanta (the philosophy of universal brotherhood) to Americans. He also had other spiritual thoughts of benefits at practical level - which also he preached. He gave many lectures on Yoga and Vedanta. Those lectures are pure gems of a very high caliber. He taught the yoga free to the American students without any fee. If he had the commercial motive like Maharishi Mahesh Yogi then his wealth also would not have any bound. But a yogi is an ascetic, and he is not supposed to have any lust for material prosperity. Thus when I read about Maharishi's opulence that really dumbfounds me. Did he really exploit the western people and their wealth in the guise of a great yogi? I know he did not cheat any one – but should not he had been made the dean of commercial marketing in a university, Instead he got to be revered as a spiritual leader?

Of course we have to lay the credit where it lies. Mahesh Yogi made meditation a mass phenomenon. He encouraged research to find out the true benefits of meditation. Extensive research showed that meditation does have beneficial effects. It calms down a person, lowers the stress, and increases the sense of well being. I think during the sixties America was going through a turbulent time due to the Vietnam War and the youth was looking for a release of stress caused by the unnecessary war. Among his disciples were the Beatles (specially George Harrison) , actresses Mia Farrow, Shirley McLain; director David Lynch , magician Doug Henning, TV personality Merv Griffin, footballer Joe Namath and many more from the entertainment world. He also founded Maharishi University of Management (School of Meditation) in Fairfield, Iowa. He founded his world headquarter in Vlodrop, 120 miles from Amsterdam. He had also been mired in controversy – as he claimed that an advanced yoga could levitate a person though he did not give any physical demonstration. He has been admired as a holy man by many, and scorned by many as huckster.

Beatles

But whatever be it, his legacy has been to bring meditation to mass consciousness. As Al Gore got the Noble Prize of Peace for bringing to our attention the phenomenon of global warming – though he himself was not a pioneer in that field - same way we can think of Maharishi as Al Gore in the meditation field. I hope his successors are as successful as he was in promoting well being of the masses on a global scale.

***

The-e-e Garbage Truck / Shaun *(2-22-2008)*

What is it – Shaun?' – The-e-e Garbage Truck; 'What is its color – Shaun?' - Gre-e-e-n . Those are all Shaun's replies when asked about his favorite toy. The replies are all given with a wide grin showing his all upper four front teeth, and his face glowing with joy. The toy is a green garbage truck. Every Friday morning I take him outside– when he waits eagerly for the big garbage truck coming to pick up our garbage from the black plastic drum. Shaun is all excited when the garbage truck shows up in the corner of the next intersection. The garbage-truck man also becomes very happy – watching a waiting enthusiastic crowd of two, and in recognition gives two honks to Shaun's delight. Shaun sleeps with the green garbage truck toy next to him. His parents say that sometimes during sleep he says g-a-a-a-r bage truck also. When he gets up in the morning – the first thing he looks for is his toy garbage truck. Actually his preference for first sighting in the morning has changed from Jimbo (from his Gymboree), to Doug (a fluffy dog) and to Mickey (a Disneyland character) etc. Those were his favorite bedside companies before – that have been completely overtaken by his new favorite – the-e-e garbage truck. Shaun is only eighteen months old – we all adore his fascination with trucks and toys. If someone wants to experience what a pure joy looks like – then one must see Shaun when the big green garbage truck shows up near our house.

What does the garbage truck do – Shaun? – 'Daa–ank' is his reply. He watches 'baaketball' (basketball) on TV and sees Kobe Bryant of Lakers jump up and dunk the ball in the basket. All 'baaketball' players are Kobe. Now he has learnt the colors. He knows blue, green, red, purple etc. When I take him out on stroller I ask him what color the house is – he promptly answers that. (One house had a color that I could not define, but Shaun assigned it some name). He has a knack of identifying things. He watches the streams of cars swooshing by on the nearby busy street, he watches that with fascination. Th-e-e-e car, another car, another car, he keeps on saying that. Vroom – vroom, vroom. He knows about all the cars and trucks from his picture book with illustrations. He knows his 'mama's car – and he thinks all SUVs probably belong to his mama. He knows the big rig, delivery truck, tractors, fire trucks etc. When he turns to the page of fire trucks – then he starts to make a sound hu..hu..hu..hu. I guess that is how the fire truck siren sounds to him.

He loves his animal book also. Specially the gorilla goodnight book. That particular gorilla steals the cage key from the zoo keeper and sets all other animals free. And all the freed animals go in a procession behind the gorilla to their sleeping den. He knows the procession of those animals – the gorilla, the hyena, the giraffe etc ... even the small armadillo. He calls the gorilla 'goria', armadillo 'armadio'. He calls the frog 'ribbit' – I don't know why. But he has given names to everything that he sees. The monkey with banana catches his attention. That is 'bana'. He also likes oranges – that is 'ana'. He likes strawberry – he calls that 'starbuck', I guess that is a fallout from his mama's adoring patronage of the Starbucks nearby their house.

We have a dinosaur that echoes everything one cares to ask him – like what is your name etc. I kept it as a welcome and friendly dinosaur in the family room. But apparently that bothered Shaun. He said – 'dinosor' 'OUT'. He knows a few operating verbs- and 'out' is one of them. We put the dinosaur in the garage. Now he will not go to the garage any more. Many things he did not like in the house – he sent them to the garage. I guess all the disfavored animals have to wait their time in the garage till Shaun grows up and permits us to welcome them back. Another animal he does not like is cow. We had a toy for him with different animal sounds – one of them was cow's. But whenever the cow makes his pathetic sound Moo...– he cries. I guess he does not like any one to be of a sadness mentality with sad sound. His grandma was saying that they went to a department store – where Shaun started to run around between the aisles of clothes. He loves to play hide and seek (peek-a-boo), and the merchandise aisles are perfect for that kind of play. They tried to divert his attention by saying many things etc – like asking him 'what color is that, Shaun', 'peek-a-boo', 'how does the fire truck go Shaun'... But nothing was of avail. Then his grandma said that she would get Mr. Cow, when Shaun stopped running, and said very sternly to his grandma – NO. But invoking 'Mr. Cow' did stop him from running.

He has a small brother (cousin) Tejas. He is not yet three months old. So when Shaun makes a mess, and we ask Shaun who did it- Shaun passes the blame on to Tejas. When we ask him where is Tejas – Shaun would make his eye very small (to customize the look for a baby) and look for Tejas. One day he was even looking below the sofa for Tejas, and came to tell us there was no Tejas below the sofa.

When eating something – if he likes it, he will say 'I like it'. If he does not like – that food will come out of his mouth in unrecognizable forms and will be scattered in different directions on the floor. Just to make sure that his 'granma' makes that kind of mistakes no more – he says emphatically 'NO'. But he likes chicken and rice and salmon, and is always full of praise for those foods, and one would not miss his high decibel eating and liking of those foods. It was too bad that his parents gave him taste of adult foods too soon and now he won't go back to baby foods. He even likes Ravioli with all that complex Italian masala and spices.

He is always exploring the boundary of his freedom. So he throws things around to see what is permitted or not. Now while his grandma feeds him on the high chair – she makes lot of sounds that do not make any sense to adults. But Shaun understands those sounds and repeats them and breaks out laughing. When his grandma is quiet, he will make those sounds to grandma to provoke her, and breaks out laughing. But now sometimes he hits grandma very affectionately. When his grandma says no – he asks 'why'? I think grandma is caught in the middle – in her school she is well known for getting along with all kinds of children. She does that with disciplined love (probably a 50-50 mix?). Now in case of Shaun is that going to be 50-50 also? Or will love knock out discipline by 20-80, that we have to see. I see Shaun is very adept in understanding the essence of adult attitude, so probably that is a teasing test for his grandma. But the way he giggles and cuddles his grandma – I think he does not like to be limited by any boundary.

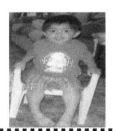

***

Oscar Mania & Debate *(2-29-2008)*

I cannot refrain myself from rambling a bit about the Oscar. But then the debate should come first. Right now the race is for who gets to be the democrats' nominee for the presidency. Now it has entered into a very funny and interesting phase. I always thought that the Clintons with their combined IQs of formidable proportion and a nostalgic heroic record of providing us with a stable and sensible government while providing a good economic health for the country, along with building a towering goodwill beyond our border – would be hard to beat. But lo and behold – a colored man with a Muslim middle name and with no strong family background, and with no financial or diplomatic or party clout is giving her so hard time! She is running around for votes and following the pundits' analysis that the Latinos can only rescue her candidacy! Anyway, the contest is probably between the hope for a change and a desire for status quo – militarily, politically and globally. Definitely it is much more than an ethnic endorsement. Whatever the American voters will decide would be fine.

But what are they debating about (seems eternally – twenty times plus already)? What accusatory arsenals she is hurling at him now – her health plan is 5% better than Obama's. Unfortunately the truth is – whatever good plan they may have – that has to pass the hurdle of consent of four hundred other lawmakers. Her other accusations are that he should have rejected (instead of just denouncing) some unsought support of a Black Muslim leader. Now she is adding another doubt in the voters' mind that she is a better decision maker at 3 o'clock at night! Amazing! Is this a leader's statement or a loser's statement? I am not commenting about that – only thing that tickled me is the funny phase of a serious political contest. Whatever be it – they have the crowd of American voters mesmerized about what next they would hear. Who can beat this Reality Show? Let the fun go on for as long as possible – it is good time for all of us (except those two contestants).

I watched with interest the Oscar award on the TV. It seems to be the super bowl of cinema. The main difference is that the elimination is not by phases here, but by an announcement of a dignitary of the film world. The TV people have vacated the TV landscape of other weeds since morning. The eminent TV commentators are endlessly speculating who will come with whom, what they will wear, what they will say and how they will look. Eager spectators had started to throng at the entrance of the show theater – since a few days before the event. The TV people are asking the crowd what they expect, what will happen – as if a carnival of star parade (like the Tournament of Roses on the new Years Day) will unfold very soon. It is not that they are all movie buffs – but surely they are the people who stoke to star mania.

This is the eightieth anniversary of the academy award. It started in 1929. I read that a few people in the movie making business in the nineteen twenties got together to form a movie club, and thought they would honor the best effort of one among them. So they came up with a 13 ½" statuette with a reel of film in hand and called it Oscar. The whole game started then – who would win Oscar next year. It seems a fantastic success story of a group of dedicated people. That game somehow went beyond the studio corridors and film workers – and reached a worldwide audience of thirty to forty million people.

One thing is for sure that movie-making is a multiple participant sport that can be enjoyed by anybody with no knowledge of predetermined rules and no exotic expertise. But it is so complex and so different from any other sport. In the world of writing – it is a show of individual talent. Same is true for recognition in any other achievement like awards in science, politics or even games like basketball or football. In other games, it is a question of one superstar. But that is not the case for a movie. It will be foolish to give an award to the best actor or bets director only. The academy gives awards in twenty five categories. Besides the best film, best documentary, best animated film, best short subjects – others are about the contributing people in creation of the movie. We can easily guess what that would be – acting, directing, art direction, screenplay, cinematography, music, sound track, visual effects etc. The real artist seems to me is the director who blends all these into an audio-visual magic package that we call a movie. So when I see that the stars show off their glittering dresses or parts of their bodies – and give the impression they are the 'movies' – that kind of pisses me off. Of course they should get their share of the credit – but not that dispropor-tionately large share. But the popular culture is sexist. They look for what is sexy and package everything accordingly. So we just know the stars – but hardly know others that made them so.

Of all the five movies nominated for Oscar I had only seen two of them – 'The Diving Bell and the Butterfly' and 'No Country for Old Men'. I was impressed by both, and strangely thought that the "No Country..." would probably win. This movie is not about love or sentiment. It is the portrait of

Evil at its worst. When the Evil stalks some one – how that game looks like, that was amazing. If the films were to be judged by their content – probably "No Country for Old Men" would be far from a descent choice. But we are not talking about good people or bad people – but about the movie. What I found was a pin drop silence during the show, the gripping moments of the hunter and the hunted etc – the audience was spell bound. It may be a violent portrayal, but it was a rendition only that was done by super direction. The directors were Joel Coen and Ethan Coen. I shall not forget one comment they made during their acceptance speech – '.... we will be happy as long as we can play in the corner of the sandbox. .' Yes the movie is made of many many sands, and let the creative artists play with the sands. That we shall look forward to when we go home and try to transcend reality for a couple of hours in our leisure time. And shall wait for the Oscar till next year.

***

When the Pressure is On

When the Pressure Is On (5-16-2008)

I see the last blog was posted on February 9. The reason that I did not post any blog was because I was not feeling well for the last two months. I was under pressure. I know everybody is under pressure of some kinds or other. But my pressure was not caused by others; it was by my own system. It was that my blood was flowing with high pressure. I guess when that high pressure blood reaches heart, the heart finds it difficult to cope. Then the heart is said to be under attack. In other words the heart did not attack, but has been attacked! No I did not have any heart attack. But the pressure was spiking up like crazy without notice and without regard for time and place. I should not probably talk about this kind of personal thing; then again blog is nothing but a person's mindscape in a particular time. So if it is happening, and it is not mentioned then some part of timescape will be blurred. Actually we are all nothing but specks of dust in the ocean of humanity and we are always buffeted by huge waves of geopolitical and geophysical events. We cannot keep our eyes and ears closed to the outside world. So what is happening now?

I see Asia is rising. China is getting ready for the super quadrennial sport event (Olympic) in

August. Voices that did not object their autocratic policies before – now are jumping on them for not being kind and sensitive to the Tibetans! I see that catastrophic geophysical events happening all around the globe – Myanmar Typhoon, Earthquake in China. That just tells me that Earth is still a work in progress and is not finished yet. Like everything else, our planet Earth must also have a beginning, middle and an end. All the stellar bodies in the sky - were they always dead masses or had they now reached their end of life cycle? So end is inevitable. But are we not hastening its demise by our reckless, inconsiderate behavior? We are fixated on our mobility on high way – and in that pursuit we are doing harm to the health of our planet. By destroying Amazon's rain forest, creating green house umbrella and suffocating our mother planet. Are not all the typhoons, tornadoes etc are signs of atmospheric disturbance? We cannot attribute this atmospheric calamity to other innocent lives that are our fellow cohabitants on this planet. Then again there is the terror and unnecessary loss of lives and belongings, which also again are caused by lack of vision, greed and short-sightedness. It is obvious all problems cannot be solved right away like a magic. But why not everybody try to live with goodwill and strive for peaceful living for all? I know all living beings are timed for self destruction and life is nothing but a journey to death – still if we don't try to change ourselves we will just hasten our demise and will cause demise of other cohabitants on this beautiful planet.

I know I got a little carried away. But with the change in guard going to take place in a few months and with the whole planet looking for our leadership in the right direction – I think this US Presidential election is a very big and important event to all. Now America is trying to choose its leaders among an old man (McCain), a woman (Hillary Clinton) and a black man (Obama). It is too bad that we cannot simply think of them as 'man' with individual attributes and thinking, and pay attention to what they are thinking and what hopes they project for our future. It is not a party contest – which a clever strategist with catchy slogans can turn things to their own advantage. The leaders are always putting their own narcissism on mass display. I don't believe the new leader can transform all of our enemies. I think the leaders should focus on the welfare of all citizens in a patriotic (not partisan) way. Why cannot we choose someone with good ideas, who can dare to take an unbeaten path to a possibly stable prosperity, peace and mutual understanding? I think we have one candidate who can fit the presidential shoe this time, and we should give him a chance. Let us not talk trivia, nonsense and hyperbolic claims of aptitude. One is not tested unless one is put to test. So experience that was previously productive can only count so much. Seniority in experience may also have amassed some mosses that need to be gotten rid of. So I just hope the majority can see the truth. I always believe that the progress of humanity or a nation's progress is fueled by the collective sanity of the majority. That has been the story of civilization and of progress.

I see that I was going to talk about the pressure that stymied posting of blogs – but I am talking about something else. I have gone through spikes of blood pressure, whole body shaking, running to emergency four times, calling 911 for a helping hand, always scared that it is coming, coming... I have also seen that the doctors being perplexed as to why and what causing it. I have gone through all tests – including nuclear scan of kidney, all kinds of ultra sound and cardiograms, MRI etc. They have inserted many needles to get bloods for different kinds of testing to find the culprit- but to no avail. Other disciplines besides my primary physician's (internist) – like nephrologists, cardiologist, neurologist etc were consulted. Though I was carrying on my daily office work for a few hours of the day when I was feeling better- I realized whatever caused it – it had not been caused by a malfunctioning organ. So it must have been caused by some side effects of some medicines, some temporary imbalance in the system caused by some gastrological inputs. I also got all kinds of well-wishers' forecast of my future – ranging from a totally doomed future to a severely disturbed future. I also heard different theories – ranging from dust in my heating system, eating of spoiled fish, artery clogging peanuts (which I am fond of), excessive caffeine etc. I have been cautioned of hyperglycemia, hypoglycemia, too much potassium, too little sodium (as we use No Salt for salt), too much exercise, too little exercise, lack of meditation, no breathing control etc. I received lot of suggestions on changing of lifestyle (which really means how we allocate our 24 hours), monitoring the body on a daily basis etc. Mysteriously whatever caused my problem for the last two months also disappeared mysteriously – leading me to wonder how delicate our system is, and how lucky we are when all the different organs individually and collectively function all right. We should not really do things foolishly that hurt a working system. It is as personal as it is universal.

A Very Good Boy – Tejas (5-23-2008)

His name is Tejas. He has a very bright smile. Whenever I (or anybody else) go near him – he has a greeting of wide smile on his face. Sweetness always envelops his face – and his eyes seem to connect with understanding. He does not say anything funny himself – but he will watch you intently to see the intent of your action and communication. If he senses your intent as trying to be funny – he will give you a few minutes but no laugh. If you pass his test of funniness – he will break into a cackle of laugh unstoppable, hilarious and without abandon. He seems to derive most of the fun from something falling from your hand or from your head. He is a very fun-loving boy. All this funny stuff he would indulge in only if he is not hungry or sleepy. Smartness and connectivity radiate from his face. He does not say clearly why something seems to be so funny with him and why something does not. He is only five and half months old now. He is our grandson.

So he had his first party of his life. That was on May 4. The party was for his first ceremonial tasting of solid food (a creamy rice pudding) that was spoon fed to him by his maternal uncle. That particular ceremony is called *'Annaprasan'* ceremony. This ceremony also signifies his graduation from the newborn to the baby stage. It is an Indian custom regionally practiced among the Bengalis. Bengalis like fun and they invite their friends and families to share any good special moment of everybody in their family. It is not a religious thing (though there are some people who won't do anything without a religious ceremony. Including even buying a new car) – but more of a social thing – so that friends and relatives can come and see the baby (first time for many), and join the festivity amidst an atmosphere of good will and merriment.

Also a fun game is played trying to crystal ball the baby's future. That is a tall task – as the infant has not yet attained a speaking age – let alone all the myriad professional choices that life has to offer. So the game is played in two segments. Like – what is likely to be his goal or mission in life? On one tray – there were four choices: a gold coin (signifying his goal to be a very wealthy man), a book (a learned man), soil (a real estate man or land ownership) and a pen (a man of letters and art). Though we all elders were rooting for the gold coin that he would choose – but after some deliberation he went for the pen! Pen as a first choice disappointed some elders – but then again wealth can come from any medium. We see what a Harry Potter can do to your coffer. And also look at all the writers of stage and screen – some of them pocket a cool million for a script that makes you cry (or close to that).

But goal (or a statement of mission) does not tell us what method or profession he will choose to reach his objective. That was again a tough call – tough even to an adult – not to say that Tejas is only five and half month (not years) now. So, on another tray we had arranged for the many choices that he may go after to achieve his dream. We thought that he would most likely choose his mentor from among his parents, uncles or grandparents – the people who are close to him. So, on another tray we had symbols of many different professions that his loved ones had chosen. That ranged from stethoscope (doctor), gavel (lawyer), calculator (engineer), floppy disk(computer), paper (insurance policy), ruler (teacher), saline solution (optometry), a string (a stringed musical instrument like a sitar). One of us thought that he should be given the option to choose sport as another profession. So a small basketball was also added to the tray. It must be stated that Tejas's elders are a very liberal group (contrary to many conservative Indian families) as they were willing to offer Tejas so many choices! It was again a very difficult choice for Tejas. He looked intently at the colorful basketball on the tray – spent some time – then went for the stetho! A big applause came from the invited guests as according to them Tejas has made a very good choice in going for the medical profession.

Through this game we obtained a peek at his future intention. He wanted to be a physician. As he had chosen pen earlier as his mission – so only way his new move can be translated is that he may want to be a researching medical professional. With all the medical problems that we all go through – I am sure he won't run out of research materials. I am also sure – by that time President Bush and his advisors would be long gone and hopefully the spigot of federal fund will be open for research. So I myself did not see any reason to object or even mildly challenge his decision! The fun part of it all was that all the friends and relatives those who will see him grow in front of their eyes could participate in wishing Tejash a good beginning and a bright future.

As I was saying Tejash is a very fun loving boy. Anything that makes noise will get his attention. If you sneeze he will look at you. If somebody else claps he will turn his head to that. When no body or no toy is making any noise – he will look at things that are moving. Color and movement seem to grab his attention most. He is also a very discriminating eater. Though he is restricted to milks and formula now – he is very choosy as to how he would drink – bottles with right nipples that his mouth can latch to or droppers or spoons. I have seen his grandmas struggle to find out the correct medium of conveyance of food to his mouth. He won't drink unless something interesting is brought to his eye. A two person feeding team is what he wants .He easily gets bored with the same toy or same activity after a short while. It seems his mother has categorized the toys according to his likely span of attention. His method of resting and sleeping is also not so obvious. He sleeps at an angle in elevation, and that has to be accompanied by a swinging motion – level 2 (as I learnt there were 5 levels of swinging). He likes to listen to the same story over and over again. He likes to look at the waterfall in his backyard. We had a freak hail storm yesterday – which Tejas has enjoyed very much.

He is ahead of babies his age in height and in mobility. When lying down – he is always tilting his head up at an angle – as if he would get up and run right now if he could unfasten the seat belt. He is a bundle of energy. At night when things are quiet he quietly enjoys the alarm clock's reflection of time on the ceiling. I saw him eating the rice cereal yesterday. His satisfaction and enjoyment of that cereal were so sonic and enjoyable.

Tejas – you are growing up fast. And very soon will be able to read this blog. This is what I wanted to say – you are a very good boy. You have an understanding and curiosity in your look –

that will propel to a great future for you, and we shall be all very proud of you.

***

Memorial Day Musing (5-30-2008)

Though I don't do anything special on this day, but I feel strongly and sympathetically for the war heroes. The fallen heroes did not fight the war for their own sake or by their own choice, but they fought in a foreign field and fell for sake of all. Sacrificing one's life is the supreme sacrifice that one can make. So when I come to think of the fighters fallen in a war I am humbled and think ourselves as the lucky beneficiaries of their contribution and sacrifice. Though I had to enlist in the draft in the sixties, I was never drafted. I think I got exemption 5A (I actually forgot the number – probably that applied to people who crossed the age of 26)). If I was drafted and had to go Vietnam – I might not see the light of the day today. There was so much turmoil among the college students and the prospective draftees – then many campuses turned into battle fields. I think the Kent College campus protest got the headlines, and protests spread around other campuses. I remember President Johnson could not bear the prospect of sending more young Americans to the war zone, and did not put himself for the Presidential nomination contest with the shadow of Vietnam over him. President Nixon called the war to a halt, and disbanded the draft (or conscription of eligible men for service). Selective Service System was the agency for drafting and recruitment. I think President Carter reinstituted the registration requirements again. Now the Selective Service System is to be used in contingency only – if and only if approved by the Congress.

I know at that time - young people were always under the hanging threat that they might be drafted any time to fight in a war in a foreign land – whose necessity and urgency did not make any sense. The Vietnam War that ensued was a battle of the superpowers in a third country for enforcing their ideology, i.e. Communism versus Capitalism. America was clearly at disadvantage – as one of the proponents of Communism (China) was next door with abundant supply of men and material. The war lasted for 7 years (1964-1973), and cost American combat casualty of 211,000 and Vietnamese casualty of about 3 million people. The environmental degradation caused by war was also enormous, as forests after forests were de-foliaged chemically so that the enemy could be visible. I also read that neighboring country Laos – which was probably used by the Vietcong as staging area – is the most heavily bombed country ever. Even now the ammunitions left over after the war explodes and kill civilians every day.

As I am not a history student or a history buff – my knowledge of war and war-casualties is almost zero. So I had to do some looking into it. It seems America was involved in ten wars besides the current one. Three wars - Mexican-American War, Revolutionary War and War of 1812, Spanish-American War were territorial and independence related. Total casualties were around 40,000.

Civil war lasted for 4 years with a casualty figure of one million. World War one and two cost more than one million American lives (European casualties were more than 40 million). Korean and Vietnam War was ideological war between two super powers – the casualty was around 100,000. Gulf war was in response to aggression. And now we are involved in the war on terror. Actually that term seems very vague - more precisely war in Afghanistan and Iraq. I think the fatality is around 4000. Though we are fond of distilling everything in terms of statistics and numbers, the actual damages to the affected families are much more.

I know during Vietnam War there were many protestors - all of them young college students with a dream of bright future ahead. But instead what they faced was the gloom and doom awaiting them in a foreign land – the cause of which could not sink in general understanding. That probably created a distinct chapter in American culture. The Hippies, drugs and flower generation. Though America has been involved in almost all wars – but American experience of war compared to the Europeans or people in other war zones is not that deep or saddening. When Europeans cry for peace – they don't do that because they lack the macho, but they most probably had experienced the devastation and desolation caused by war – which is hardly ever won decisively by any party. One war or one victory always leaves the seed for future war.

I know mine is only talk and no action. When I filled up the application for citizenship – one item caused a problem inside me. Taking the oath that I shall bear arm if necessary. That is I have to fight a war if necessary? I can hardly stand any killing, how can I be capable of killing others if necessary. I know Mohammed Ali caused uproar – when he objected to bear arm. He was de-crowned from the championship title, and was put in jail for three years. He was so morally courageous that he was to stand behind his belief and ready to bear any consequence. So I had also thought about using the 'Conscientious Objector exemption. Then also I thought that would be a good move as that would also apply to my children in the future if necessary! But after long thinking and counseling by others I did not invoke that clause. So I said I was willing to bear arm. Though I doubted my fitness to be a soldier – but then I thought no matter what if that what everybody else is doing – why could I be so different? Luckily I was not drafted and never had to face any war front. But those who are standing there and risking their own lives for others' lives – I have enormous respect for them.

But I do not see the war heroes being remembered and honored all their lives. I have seen them sinking into helplessness and hopefulness. I also read that the military suicide rate and veteran suicide rate is very high. I don't think that is the way they should suffer; they should be public heroes and role models of the civilian population. We pay so much doting attention to celebrities who have not contributed anything like fighting for the country, whereas the war heroes don't get any societal recognition except on just this day. Only one day per year is reserved for them. I think there should be more recognition than that.

Stars and Stripes Forever

***

Hey George,
Do you remeber
where you put
that old "Misson
Accomplished"
Banner?

A Seminal Event – Obama (6-6-2008)

What I am referring to is Senator Obama's securing Democratic candidacy this week for US Presidency. As I have to record what is in my mind right now, I cannot overlook this event. It has far more meaning than a mundane quadrennial Presidential election. US are now the world's only superpower. That has been acknowledged by the world. The world watched in silence as US waged a unilateral war against Iraq. Whether the world agreed with US or not – the present administration thought that a chessboard move of crippling Iraq will end all the problems of terror – a worldwide menace. As we have seen after eight years it has not done anything good, but created a lot of animosity throughout the world – and almost dealt a fatal blow to US moral leadership. Though it proved

that US could not be challenged militarily by any –
but it also proved that the de-facto moral
leadership crown that US was enjoying had
become tarnished a bit.

So definitely a change is needed. Not in more
arsenal, not in mere troop deployment, not in
more cunning diplomacy, not in mere bartering
deals of concessions – but in more fundamental
issues - Trust, Confidence and Mutual Understanding between people. Of course no fool
expects hundred percent concurrences with
everybody on every issue. With the advent of
internet – people are more global now than
national; they understand each other not through
the eyes of their governments only, but through
their own eyes, and eyes of their fellow citizens of
this planet. They can feel other's sorrow, other's
helplessness and other's motive more easily. But
this understanding means nothing - if their
governments do not care to listen. So a change in
attitude is needed, a change in mindset is
absolutely a necessity. Patriotism cannot be
demonstrated merely by a meek acceptance of
status quo , and also it should not be brandished
as a party logo. All dissents cannot be treated as
threats against national interest all the time. A lot
of change in mindset is needed. So welcome
Senator Obama – hope you win, and get a chance
to try your thinking for a change, and bring back

compassion, honesty and credibility in US leadership.

I know that was an overflow of platitudes for a nominee. But I was reading the world wide reaction to this news. Papers from Azerbaijan to Zimbabwe – had this news on their front pages. I almost get a goose bump when I read how excited the Germans are, how excited the Africans are. It can only happen when they think that it is good for them also. In other words they are welcoming that news and they are also looking forward to the change. It can only happen when they think that US President is world's leader also. That is sort of their leader also.

Why is it possible that Senator Obama could be a little different? Many newspapers compared him to a mix of Kennedy and Martin Luther King. Kennedy is the one who wanted to spread the message of friendship throughout the world by creating Peace Corps. Of course one cannot neglect military leadership – but might is more powerful when restrained rather than when unleashed. I had read that in Vivekananda's speech. Though I don't understand it completely, but it makes sense. When we build a dam, a tremendous amount of energy is created – that can be harnessed for peaceful purposes; but if it breaks loose, it only brings death and destruction. So a message of understanding and a stretching hand of friendship may pull in more people than a scary frown to prove one's might. Martin Luther's legacy was his dream streaming out in his eloquence and oratory. I have read Obama's writing – Audacity of Hope. It gives the impression – that what you see, he can see and see some more. He can see a logical sequence in happenings that shape history. There is an aura of vision – not expressed in a stream of flowery language, but that connects events which seem to reach an inevitable conclusion. I had a hunch of his extra-ordinariness, but never dreamt that he would come so far in so little time.

Why do I think it is a seminal event also? Because he seems a blend of a variety of genes. He is partly black, partly white. He has been brought up in Asia and in US. He had exposure to conflicting faiths. He has been brought up not in a secure and confined environment. He had spent his growing years in US, Indonesia and Hawaii. He was not born with a silver spoon, and he knew that nothing would be given to him – but he has to earn himself. Coming from an ordinary background – he has to have a good ears for common people and their thinking. His family was not privileged and aristocratic – as such he is not expected to have a special soft corner for the uncommonly rich people and their interests. He had experienced hardship – so has to have a good raw understanding of life, its potential and limitation. In other words – he has a global and universal characteristic. No wonder why the people of the world in general seem excited. They think that he will probably listen more, have more compassion for them, and more tuned to their state of affairs. Are all this going to be against the interest of US? Hardly. Human potential unfolds in different stages – personal, national, then global. Good does not confine itself to a privileged few. So he can possibly be a good US president with a global perspective and an empathetic understanding hopefully. That is why this event seems seminal to me.

From another angle, discrimination and racism have been a curse in all societies. And that has been throughout the ages. There is also discrimination based on wealth, based on education etc – but those discriminations are limited to an upper crust and that may or may not affect the whole society. But when the evil of racism is not contained, it affects the whole society. It affects the whole being. It is like a black shadow over a soul – that harbors and perpetuates a sense of inferiority and degrades human dignity. It cannot be cured by itself. It can only be cured by light of education, and it can be cured by acceptance of merit. So when Obama is aspiring to be on top of all – that is achieving to be the number one human on this planet – then others are humbled, and the sense of unearned superiority among many will get a fatal blow. That will be the greatest antidote to racism which stereotypes people based on color only. Martin Luther's dream of a future when a person would not be judged by the color of his skin, but by the content of his character, seems to be getting real now. And that will liberate us all – and elevate us all above any narrow racism. Though some deviates are to be expected, but now it can make us all equal. That is why I think it is a seminal event.

***

A Prince is Born – Trevor (6-13-2008)

Though I am a little late in writing about Trevor, still he is only 2 weeks old. He was born May 28 (Wednesday early morning). We got a chance to see him in the hospital next day. A little cuddly thing – wrapped up in a warm blanket, sleeping quietly in his bassinet next to his mother's bed. He was born 7 lb 6 oz, 19" long. He looked very cute. I also heard his shrill complaint – obviously very hungry. I think his transition from the darkness in the womb to an all lighted world (hospital room) is too traumatic. That's why he decided not to open his eyes fully – but was peeping through a small opening between the eyelids. That is definitely very smart, as too much light is no good for a baby's first exposure to the brightness, and also it is not very conducive to sleep. He seems to be very smart in the art of no-hand held sucking and drinking. His mother is also doing ok. His father is assisting his mother – I don't know how though. Trevor is our grandson. So he is a prince and we welcome him to this new world and our growing family.

He has a little brother Shaun who is one month shy of two years. Shaun was told about the impending arrival of his brother. He seems to know that his brother is too small- so he looks at him through a tiny opening of his eyes. I guess, to see small thing you don't need to open your eyes fully. Though he has acquired an awesome extent of vocabulary for his age, and he knows numbers to 25 and all the twenty six letters of the alphabet, he cannot figure out what Trevor is crying about. To him Trevor can say only ' waaa, waaa'. Trevor will have to grow up under the shadow and guidance of his elder brother. But as Shaun seems to have very tender feeling for the baby brother, he seems to be in good hand. As the parents are very experienced for the second time around, they seem to have everything under control. Of course experience is the greatest teacher in life. Also the ambient atmosphere seems calm and relaxed. During our first child, for first three months our son cried a lot without any apparent reason. We were told by the doctor that was due to colic (an idiopathic diagnosis may be). When asked what colic was – the answer was very vague and round about. But we were told that was mostly stress related. The child senses insecurity, and the crying could be related to that. As the baby grows older and he senses more relaxed parents – he also relaxes more and cries less. So Trevor must be sensing that he is with very experienced parents now; and is not particularly concerned about their ability. So his cry is only need based. Sleep, hunger and inconvenience are the only three factors that prompt him to register displeasure, which comes out as crying. When the pacifier is misplaced or falls off his mouth that definitely makes him unhappy. So crying is the language of need and attention. And everybody can understand that language. Nobody goes to university to find out what crying means.

When Trevor grows up, he might be wondering what the world was like when he was born. This year US is going to have a presidential election – to be fought between a septuagenarian warrior and an ambitious young man who wants to change how politics are conducted in

Washington. In other words he will strive to take the politics out of the presidency and make the democracy like it was envisaged during its formation- viz. the government is to be of the people, by the people and for the people. The brand of democracy being practiced right now is government by the lobbyists, for the donor businesses. That may not benefit the majority of the people. The statement is not really 100% right, but it is not 100% lie either.

The war in Iraq that was launched in 2001 is still going on. The enemy is not always visible, and is adept in hiding in places further away. The war has turned an affluent country into a heap of rubble (not 100% of course), costing thousands and thousands of human lives, made the country go backward by forty or fifty years, creating global discords and nobody knows what lies in future for us and the Iraqis.

We are all facing an energy crisis. The price of gasoline (which is next in importance to food and medicine in America) is reaching close to five dollars a gallon – and the jump took place in one year from three dollars a gallon. The pundits are debating about the method of solution. One thing is for sure that with the rise in global demand, things are not going to get better – unless tackled comprehensively. So when you grow up and drive car, it may be half the size of your parent's car.

The climate in US is changing perceptibly- with more rains, floods and tornadoes. I don't know why though. It may be due to global warming or maybe not. But pattern of climate seems to be changing. Some of the floods and storms occurring seem to be of 500 years frequency. I hope the climate does not get worse when you grow up.

Computer, internet, social networking, cell phone, Wii (sensory games) – all will affect how you grow up. Less human contact may turn the world of reality into a virtual world. That may lead to many cold terminators around. We are seeing that glimpse sporadically now. Hope it does not get worse.

Right now a lot of illegal immigrants are causing chaos among the politicians. It may be that society has to rethink and absorb the illegals to create a bottom layer of service network.

Overall the basic humanity will not change. Courage, hard work and determination will lead to success. Family and community and empathy for others will create happiness. You are in very good hands, to be guided in the right direction by the people who will be around and who love you very much. So Trevor we embrace you on your happy landing, and wish you all the best in your journey of life.

***

Moolade

Moolade – A Story of Female Circumcision
(6--20-2008)

Moolade is a Senegalese movie made in 2004. This is a movie on the stated subject by an activist Senegalese writer-director. Actually my knowledge on the subject was next to nothing, but I had sporadically come across the term many times. Since I became a Netflix subscriber, I noticed Netflix has a good collection of foreign movies. I like travel, and have traveled many different countries as a tourist in my limited way. But a tourist can only see the architecture, infrastructure or geographical uniqueness. It does not tell one about the minds of the people living in the land. Though it is true people and their culture are reflected in the architecture, but even then it is very limited. Like when we go to Rome we see fantastic architectural feat, we know they were great organizers, with good judgments about materials and methods. Also when you see the great Coliseum, you know they enjoyed organized spectator sports - but what can we know about their lives and aspirations? This is where literature and movies come in handy. They can open a window into a culture that we could not get any access to, even if we tried our guts out. They bring out the people, their mind and hearts. And talking about movies - that better be made by the people of that culture. Thus we can see a fantastic Hollywood movie about China (say Good Earth), where we end up appreciating a great acting or great directing – without touching the soul of the subject matter. Anyway, in short I like foreign movies. That is some kind of virtual tourism of a foreign culture.

The movie is about female circumcision but Moolade does not mean female circumcision. It means a magic screen. It shows how a defiant woman challenged the age-old tradition by a magic screen (say mental strength of unyielding resistance), and saved a few young girls from the torture of that primitive practice. As I did not know anything about the subject beyond my exposure to a dictionary – I looked into the subject matter in some more details. Thus I came to know it is a prevalent custom in many African countries- ranging from Senegal (on Atlantic) to Ethiopia (on east coast), and from Egypt in north to Tanzania. It encompasses a culture of about 130 million people. Every year about 4 to 5 million girls are subjected to this horrible practice. It is confined to Muslims mainly – but has nothing to do with a religious indoctrination. It predates Islam, and is known to have been practiced in Egypt about 2000 years ago.As this practice violates basic human rights, UNO got involved in it. The practice of cutting an organ is practiced on young girls aged four to seven years. It is done by a knife, performed by a group of senior female members of the society. It results in excruciating pain, deformity and results in death many times. So the International advocacy group changed the term of female circumcision to Female Genital Mutilation (FGM) to bring attention to an unhealthy practice. In many countries it is banned now. Though it is practiced in African cultures mainly, but immigration and globalization have spread the practice worldwide. Even US had to enact laws prohibiting such practice. In 2006, Khalid Adem became the first man in the United States to be prosecuted for mutilating his daughter.

Though many African countries have outlawed this practice, still it is culturally prevalent in many countries like Sudan, Ethiopia and Egypt. This practice supposedly makes a girl marriageable.

As I was appalled by such brutality still being practiced by one family member to another, I wondered who started all this and why? It is obvious this is something men as cultural leaders – imposed on the weaker members of the society. Their continual schemes to keep the women under control by creating taboos, superstition and myriad other schemes to enforce their control. Why cannot men think that there would be no man if there was no woman? Why cannot they be decent and courteous to other members of the society that nourished them? It is obvious man is a scheming animal without mercy (in general) - they are the ones who should be controlled. Thus they deprive women of education, keep them confined at home, and erect all kinds of social control to subjugate them. Basically they think that is the way to keep themselves and their families out of trouble. By denial and deprivation of human rights? This just tells that education is the only tool that increases awareness and can attack social constraints and taboos. You don't have to be a Feminist to understand all this – but you just have to be a decent human to understand the basic dignity of life.

It is sad that many societies stone their females to death while practicing infidelity themselves. There are many other practices like Foot Binding (among the Chinese) and Breast Ironing (in Cameroon of Africa). The old Chinese tradition was to bind the women's feet so that it could not grow more than 3 to 4 inches. That supposedly made the gait very sexy – a lotus walk. Just for men's pleasure (innuendo of weird method of control over their women folk) – the women were subjected to lifelong deformities of their legs. This practice is not there anymore – but it had a life span of more than thousand years in China till being banned in the early twentieth century.

The Breast Ironing practice is performed by mothers on their daughters – as that makes their daughters less sexually attractive to men – so that they are spared from rapes by men. So the men are at the bottom of all evils. They do the bad things and then they create restrictive social customs, create social taboos, and they prescribe punishment. Why cannot women rise against inhumanity of a part of their own societies?

I have seen that Hindus have bestowed the ultimate honor to womanhood- emphasizing their role as protectors – giving them a duty to nourish and sustain the society. They even made women goddesses – an ultimate honor a human can bestow to another human. Even if we don't go that far, why cannot we be a little more decent and empower the women as the men have empowered themselves?

 Actually I was not thinking about any of this, but the movie 'Moolade' brought it out from my inside. I am glad it is out. Thanks.

***

A Long Voyage Long Ago I
(6-27-2008)

Sometimes people ponder about their past - how and why something happened to them. Every life is nothing but a collection of events in his/her life's journey, experiences and encounters. Many people say life is a safari. That is very true. If life was not a safari – then probably one's life will end at the point where it started like that of a tree. But people move for job, adventure or other interests or problems. I myself moved here long ago in the middle of sixties. I was wondering who I was then that took such a long trip and transplanted myself from one corner of the earth to another corner. It is such opposite that if you pierce a long needle through a globe from the heart of USA – the needle will come out on the other side through the heart of India. It is geographically so opposite. The time hours are also twelve hours difference – that is America's noon is India's midnight. So what was the moving force? When the grandmas used to tell fairy tales – that always started like – once there was a country where the sun rose at night and moon rose in the day. Probably the story location referred to a place where such opposite things happen. As a child I did not believe that. But I see that is true for USA and India. If the world was not divided into 24 time zones, but followed just one time zone – then when sun is at mid sky in US, the moon is at mid sky in India.

In India education is considered a passport to a better life. The more the better. Probably – during British Raj (Raj is short for Raja i.e. king), better life was available by speaking the king's language. And if you spoke the royal language then of course you had access to a better life whatever that means. That was true in the nineteenth century. But when everybody learns or speaks English then learning English alone does not assure a better life. So you need more than a language skill. That is where professional education becomes a key factor to a better life. Then again, when almost everybody is educated in the societal niche you belong then a little education is not enough. You have to go for a higher education. So that was the motivator for sure to a young man (like myself) trying to move ahead in life. Of course if you are a talented performer or player – you already got the key to a better life. But what about people like me – who really do not possess any saleable talent? For that situation – education helps. It raises your capability, consequently your position in life. Good thing about education – if you pay attention and devote some of your time then you can acquire the education that is distributed (free or with fee) to the ordinary people in the colleges through lectures, courses and examination. What I am saying is that if you are not talented enough to stand by yourself, you will be better off with some education. And if possible make that a higher education. So this lure must have baited me when I was done with the Bachelor of Engineering Degree from Calcutta University (1962).

But the question was where should I go? Of course being educated in English medium, I could not choose to go to Germany and France. At that time I highly looked on both the countries for their contribution to science and arts. As I was tempted to go to Germany, I took some German language classes too. Then I thought it was a long shot to gain skill in another language in a short time. So I gave up on German. And French I never attempted – as it seemed to me that the spoken French and written French are two entirely different languages. So France and Germany were out of my thinking horizon. Also looking at the contribution made by Jewish scientists, I did also think of going to Israel for higher education. But then also I learnt they used partly Hebrew and partly English in their curriculum. So that was also out. Of course at that time USA seemed so far away – I had restricted myself to comparatively closer countries. I must also admit that I was not geo-politically conscious then. I did not know that wanting to go some place and being accepted by the host country are two different things.

So my attention shifted to England and USA. At that time the older generation that governed our action advised me to go to England. The logic was simple – England had very good universities, they had a better understanding of Indians they had ruled for so long. England had lot of companies that operated in India or had Indian connection. So looking at the job market, they predicted an English education would fetch higher profession-al salary in India. And of course all the British people I had come across then were people with responsibilities and high authority. Somehow the British looked snobby to me and seemed very condescending to Indians. Also I could sense they looked down on Indians – no matter who they were. I never found fault with them – it is a mindset. If you are the ruler, subconsciously you always feel superior to the people you rule or who serve you. A slave or subjugate can never rise or be equal to the master. On the other hand I had great respect for British. I never understood how a few million of them could rule over hundreds of millions all over the world. Not for one year or ten years, but for hundreds of years. The British had to be fantastically smart, fantastically organized; diplomatically extremely cunning and great risk takers – always outsmarting others in their own arena. Though I had great respect for England – still US allured me more.

US also had great universities. I knew the names of MIT, Harvard, University of Illinois, and University of Wisconsin etc. Also I knew there were many more great universities in all the states, even though I did not know their names. Also American scientists were making clean sweeps of all the Noble prizes in almost all disciplines most of the time. Their might and influence were on the rise. Their movies were everywhere. Though they were Hollywood made and was for entertainment mainly – still somehow the movies made the Americans more approachable, more human than their British counterparts. They also had vanquished the Nazis, saved Europe, devastated and stomped on Japan's arrogance and then rebuilt it again. I had a feeling the future belonged to America. If you looked all around – you saw America in some form or other. Planes in the sky, cars on the road, sophisticated instruments in hospitals and factories - all had American connections. So I thought this was where I must come. Also American standard of living seemed higher than those of other countries (including England) of the world

Of course if I say only ambition was the motivating force, I would not be speaking the whole truth. There was the sense of adventure. Going abroad also would bring more mental freedom. Chances to do new things, to see new places, meet new people. Familiarity and staying in familiar circles of relatives may bring safety – but that takes away the desire to challenge and compete also. Eventually the restricted boundary and familiar circle that brings peace also breeds boredom and suffocates one mentally. Travel I must, see I must the outer world – that was also another motivating factor. So all these different thoughts gelled inside me and somehow strengthened my determination to come to US for higher education. But it was not that easy for someone with no connection to the higher hierarchy. It is getting too long. More on that later.

***

**Patriotism American Style**

Patriotism American Style (7-4-2008)

This week is the long holiday weekend for the Fourth of July. First of all, I have to say that this is my adopted country, and my birth country is India. So by simple logic one may question my patriotism. But truth is I liked this country and I loved this country that is why I adopted it. In case of the birth country you don't choose that yourself –it just happens. But the choice of adopted country is a choice of an adult person. I think that is more serious and more deliberate. Just loving and liking the country may or may not make one a patriot. So that question is eternal – whether just loving a country is patriotic or just being born and brought up in the country is more patriotic? It is a profound question, and does not have an easy answer.

I know that during the Second World War, about a hundred thousand Japanese-American were rounded up and imprisoned or interned, for no fault of their own, without commitment of any crime, let alone betraying the country. Same thing should have happened to the Italian or German immigrants, but I have not heard of any stories of their imprisonment. Apparently they were not suspected to be unpatriotic like the Japanese were. Now in this Presidential election I read about the same kind of mentality that is questioning one Presidential candidate's (Mr. Obama's) patriotism because his background is not white European. I know it is more of a prejudice and bias hard to get rid of and there would still be many people who will not say it but will harbor this suspicion in their hearts.

Some great minds said that politics is the last resort of scoundrels. Though I doubt it very much, but we can be sure that only scoundrels use politics to their advantage. Maligning may be a good game in politics, but I am sure all politicians are not dishonest. It also saddens me to see that one presidential candidate (Senator Obama) is being questioned about patriotism, though he is one hundred percent as American as others. But sadly he has to defend it. It is like defending yourself from a crime that you have no connection with whatever. He did not go to war- so he is less patriotic? Is not that true for three hundred million other Americans who never went to war, are they also non-patriots? Or you can simply show that you are a patriot, just by putting up the flag on the Fourth of July? Actually this subject of patriotism is not very clear-cut to me. Is it just saying, obeying or supporting the ruling party in governing power makes one more patriotic, and any kind of dissent makes you less patriotic?

Just to see what patriotism means I looked in the dictionary and in the quotation book. Dictionary says that Patriotism is 'loving your country'. So

we are all patriots when we love the country –
whether or not one got the chance to defend the
country with arms or attack other countries on
behalf of one's own country. Mark Twain said
'Patriotism is supporting your country all the
time, and supporting your Government when it
deserves it'. Of course it is saying indirectly that a
true patriot always supports the country – and
the government can harness the love when
needed. So if somebody who is a citizen and who
loves the country, he is a patriot. Citizenship itself
incorporates oaths of loyalty, but love is more
fundamental and more deep-rooted. Now
suppose one CEO of a very big company who sets
aside millions of dollars for himself and his
cronies, by depriving live hoods of countless
fellow countrymen – does he really love his
country and the people? If you loved the country
and your countrymen – you could never do that. I
think the great philanthropists like Gates,
Rockefellers, Buffets etc – they are more patriotic
than any others one can think of. Some of them
are also humanists – their love goes beyond the
borders or divisions of countries and humanity.
Contribution to fellow countrymen's happiness
and well being are real acts of patriotism. Mere
slogan of patriotism and brandishing a flag does
not make one more patriot. Also challenging
others whether they really love the country
(when both of them stand on the soil and grew up
inhaling the same air) is really more chauvinism

than patriotism. Actually asking Senator Obama to defend his patriotism was a shame to us all. I may have gone little over-board but that is how I felt.

Now George Bernard Shaw thought that 'Patriotism is your conviction that this country is superior to all other countries because you were born in it'. According to this, patriotism is a patent owned by people born in it. But thinking of being superior to others is not decency, it smacks of Snobbism, not even Nationalism. When you look at many African countries like Zimbabwe, Darfur etc, I am sure the people who were born there love their countries, but their Government is killing them or forcing them out as refugees. These people are definitely patriots (and their Governments are not), and they would like to build the country, but their own Government is their own enemy. So loving Government and clapping everything they do is not equivalent to love of the country or patriotism. But any way...

Senator Obama's speech was very intuitive and instructive. Actually he defined patriotism as loving the values on which the country was founded on. A true patriot is the one who is fighting to keep the values as the controlling mantra of a nation's heart. America's Independence Day is not like Independence Day of many other countries. Many countries like

India became independent when their rulers gave them or granted their independence. But America was not given Independence by the ruling British Empire, America declared Independence. But declaring Independence means nothing unless it is governed properly. So it was to be a govern-ment 'of the people, by the people and for the people'. Government is to exist only 'to secure God-given rights, namely life, liberty and pursuits of happiness'. The Independence (of the country) can be meaningful only when the government's actions reflect the will of the nation, and when actions of the individuals are guaranteed independence. So I also think patriotism is love for the country, loving the people and loving the values that make the country's soul (the Constitution). No one needs to demean others in the contest of patriotism when they equally love the same country.

***

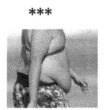

No More than 33.5 inches *(6-18-2008)*

Last week there was no blog as I could not find any time. Because, we had five guests from India who were visiting this country. Hosting is very much a part of Indian tradition. I think my family is an excellent host – though that depth of hospitality nobody expects. Usually people are happy with surface hospitality. A big smile, small food, predetermined duration are all that is needed, but sometimes we overdo it. Anyway that was what it was. The weekend was devoted to the multiple guests and their foods and entertainment.

Anyway, what surprised me last week was a news item that men over 40 will be penalized monetarily and may lose their job if no effort is made to bring it down to 33.5 inches of waistline? But I am no Japanese and I don't live in Japan – so naturally I am exempt. I think when somebody takes away the freedom of food regarding how much we want to eat or what we want to eat that is really tough living. I don't think the US Constitution spells out that freedom or if there is any amendment fortifying that right. But my thoughts are not really about who is the real boss- the individual or the Government, rather the radical changes in our thinking. When I grew up, I thought people looked down at slim people. Usually the background thinking was that the slimness indicated lack of adequate food. Fat people signified exuberance and good living. Even the God Ganesha – the one with an elephant head, who symbolizes success and prosperity, has a big pot belly. All the corpulent businessmen in India worship Lord Ganesha. I don't know about the present generation – but our generation was like that. The Indian mythologists always assigned different animals for different Gods for their transportation.. I see no logic how the small mouse could be assigned to the task of carrying such a heavy and corpulent God! If He was assigned an elephant – that would make some sense to me.

Around the sixties – the western models who got the covers on fashion magazines seldom weighed in three digits. I wondered at that time – whose thinking was that? Was it the designer's, because it was convenient to drape a known slim figure rather than women of unknown dimensions? Or was it the retailer or was it for the male chauvinists who wanted to make women slimmer (as a result much weaker!) - so that men had an easier time to proclaim their supremacy. That was so then. But what happened – models starved themselves, suffered from anorexia, bulimia - and many fainted on the walkways. I am glad that Spain has banned models who are too slim and too light weight. Other European fashion competitions are doing the same. I don't know the guide line, but I think the lower limit is BMI of 18.

I know Japanese are fun loving people. Life is a game to many of them. It has opened up their imagination - I am sure they will come up with games like 'Fatbuster', ' Fatmonster' etc. I am happy with running on treadmills. But the

Japanese have started Bronco machines that will give the fat fighter hell of a ride like riding on broncos. On TV I have seen Japanese Game Shows – and I am aware that they enjoy extreme fun, or Xfun. But if I have to give up my treadmill for a bronco machine, I will rather eat less than fight with the self-created fats.

Talking about BMI – Body Mass Index, it is a handy rule of thumb for measuring body's fat content. Basically it is an index of fat content that was coined by a Belgian doctor. Simply it is a figure of weight (in kg) divided by the square of heights (in meters). If the weight is in pounds and height in inches, then multiply that by 703 to get the metric BMI. That is a 200 pound man with 68 inches height, the BMI is around 30. Normal range of BMI is 18.5-25, Overweight BMI is 25-30, and Obese BMI is greater than 30. Now how did the Japanese translate that to waistline. I don't know exactly, I can only say what I think.

Since human frame is like a flattened cylindrical shape – its variables are weight, height and diameter. Thus, if height does not vary with age or exercise – only thing that can vary is the diameter of the cylinder or the average waist line. So only thing that we can check is the weight and waistline. But weight machines are not that universal – so that cannot be used as a tool for daily use. But waist line is a more convenient parameter. Apparently US approach is a little different. We concentrate more on weights as a measuring tool. I read that American airlines are losing more money because the Americans are more overweight causing more fuel cost to fly the extra tonnage. I also read that they are thinking of adding additional fare for weighing more than 180 pounds. So we are all suffering from the disease of plenty, and have to pay penalty for that.

Many times when I see a problem – I look or try to see what Nature's way is. What is Nature's prescription for weight containment? It is simple – we need food as fuel to generate energy to move. So if we don't move or run much - naturally we should not need much food as fuel. But food is fun and enjoyable – so we eat more of it, and don't really want to cut down our pleasure from food. So eating is all right – but not running or performing much physical labor is a detriment to good health. We need fat as a reserve to ride over fluctuation of food supply. I think – Nature's initial thinking was that everyone should work hard to survive. But our working hard now a day does not mean any physical labor, but more of brain work. Our Automobiles, Supermarkets, Remotes all are making us lazy bums – and we have to pay price for that as a nation and as an individual. So whatever the Japanese are doing seem to be a peek at the future. It may not be accurate, but it raises national consciousness. Even if the plan and implementation is 50%

effective – that will bring tremendous dividend to the quality of national life. So Kudos to the Japanese. But what about the Sumo wrestlers? Are they exempt? I hope so.

***

A Long Voyage Long Ago II *(6-25-2008)*

This week I could not come up with any subject to write about. Then it occurred to me what does it matter if it is not happening now? What happened before in my life is also as important. So I wanted to rewind back to 1964. So this is a continuation of what I started a few weeks ago. This voyage is about my journey to America with a lot of ambition, but with not so much in my pocket. (Unfortunately I cannot boast of my pocket even now – of course relatively speaking). But before that, I like to look around for any event that looks interesting to me. It is senator Obama's speech in Berlin. I know he took a risky step – as it might look very preposterous to many. We can color a canvass any way we want. Then also, I need to ask how many Americans can command such a large audience in a foreign country? May be Rock Stars can do that

– but they do that with some obligation of entertainment in exchange of money. Just because I cannot command such a mass appeal does not mean that I can trash the other guy. The people of Berlin came to see who he was, what he wanted to say and how did it matter to them. I think he succeeded in that. He was saying what he would do – not to make more money, but work together with a message of hope, duty and dedication. When I can find somebody else who can inspire so much then I would say otherwise. I don't know if he would win, because I sense there is an unknown dark force that does not come out in day light. So we have to wait to see how good or great he is to tame that dark force of racism, revenge and collusion. He spoke as an American citizen, and I think everybody is entitled to do that. Whether he deserved that big a stage is a different story. But in no way we can diminish his sincerity and good will as America's good will ambassador to Europe in the common quest of a better destiny for us all.

To go back to what I was saying. Previously I was talking about what motivated me to come to this country. I just wanted to come here for more education and a brighter future. But dreaming and implementing the dream was a different story. I probably was not thinking with a larger overview of college admissions. There was the USIS (United States Information Service) library with all sorts of college catalogs etc. So I had to choose many unknown names from that catalog. I just knew the names of MIT, University of Illinois, Harvard, Wisconsin, Yale – only a few. But I was sure that I would fall short of their admission requirements. It was already month of March - I came to know that foreign students apply for admission almost a year ago. US residents can wait a little longer. So I picked up names of Universities at random –assuming they are all good. Their literature showed great pictures and great achievements by the alumni of the universities. What surprised me was the range of their offering and depth of their staff. I also knew though where you buy merchandise from is important, but then again if the merchandise is authentic you cannot belittle that. After a few rejections and a few good promises from some universities – I at least knew where to apply to for admission.

Then the question came of financing the cost of education for a Master's degree. My personal finance at that age was next to zero, as I was fresh out of college and had only worked for a short time. My family though middle-class, did not have the wherewithal to spend on me. By the way Indian middle class is as not as affluent as American middle class. They have lot less disposable income after maintaining or taking care of their large joint families. Now a day the inflated salaries for young professionals are astronomical compared to those days. Also, as I was too late, the possibility of any scholarship was next to zero. But many institutions promised summertime university jobs, and getting a teacher's assistantship was also a possibility. At that time also I had a very vague idea about how big US is. US is almost three times as big as India with 4 major time zones and two minor ones – whereas India has only one time zone. I also did not know where the different cities and towns were located. I just knew about the big ones. Out of all the applications and some positive responses I had to pick one. So, now came the cost analysis part.

The cost also varied between big cities and small towns. Coming to think of it – education and cost of living was so affordable in those days. I don't remember all the details. But I remember I chose West Virginia University as it looked very good and very affordable. What I remember now the tuition and books were around $400 per semester; housing and meals were around $100 per month, and twenty or thirty dollars per month for miscellaneous expense. It came to around a basic cost of living and education of $3000 per year. The master's degree could be finished in three semesters and a summer – so at most the total cost of getting a master's degree was around $6000. Later on I found out that three students could rent an apartment for $60 per month and share it among themselves. The ticket cost in the bus was a nickel. The ice cream cone was a nickel. The gasoline was 25 cents a gallon. For ten dollars we could fill up two bags full of groceries.

Things had started to change in the early seventies. When I went back to USC for business degree – the tuition cost was $500 / units – so a 40 unit Master's degree came to about $20000. Now that has ballooned to almost $100,000 for a professional or a higher degree. What I am getting at – in those days even $3000 per year seemed a lot. From India that also looked very expensive – as over there at that time $100 could get you through four years of college education. Even I had to scramble around to arrange for that $6000. Finally I collected that money as loan from my brothers – that would finance my journey and education in US. But there were countless other formalities. Foreign travel from India was so bureaucratic and involved so much paper work that is unthinkable. Even to convert the Indian money into dollars – one had to apply to the Reserve Bank. The Reserve Banks permission was also limited by quota. Then also there had to be a guarantor who had to give a guarantee that he would bear all expenses to bring me back if something untoward happened. Then getting the passport was also so involved. The police enquiry to check the background was also horrible and time consuming. The Visa requirement was also tedious. One's health had to be declared fit by the local doctors who were approved by US consulate. So going through all that after lots of sweat and tear – finally I embarked on a French passenger and cargo ship 'Marseilles Mariner' on August 15, 1964. I was so happy to be able to start the journey – I felt a new freedom, and was elated that I would be able to see the larger world. More on it later.

***

A Story of Eating *(8-1-2008)*

We all eat everyday – two times, three times or four times, so that cannot be a story. I can comfort myself that my style of eating varies according to food also. So I am a nibbler, guzzler, one hefty meal, two hefty meals or a big breakfast guy. So I know I end up eating a lot of foods – sometimes from hunger, sometimes from bad habit, sometimes out of temptation. Of course we don't eat like other lives on the planet. We eat what we choose to eat. Also we want to know what we are eating. The name alone is not enough – how much fat, how much trans-fat, how much sugar, how much protein, how much of everything. So everything has to have a label with all details of the properties of the food. Since I am not a food scientist, nor a biologist or a dietician – I have no idea how they figure out all the details. Only thing I can identify as bad food is if it contributes to bulging of the stomach or if it makes me sick. Since I am no number guru, I would prefer everything to be zero. I guess – only plants can do that. They just get by with clean air, clean water. So all the numbers on the labels are puzzles to me.

To be on the safe side, I have set an arbitrary limit of 5 to everything. That is 5 gm of sugar, 5% Daily Value of sodium, 5% fat cholesterol, 5% of almost everything. Also my family is very suspicious of labels on the foreign food. Actually I am suspicious of all labels. I know the food manufacturers want to sell food – they really don't care for our health or abide by their conscience and are not necessarily guided by a strong sense of ethics. I am waiting for the day when the trial lawyers – looking for new pasture - will go after the labels of the food industry. At one time – I thought yellow of the egg was good, that whole milk was good for building bones. Now I have discarded all my previous thinking- because my doctor advised me to stay away from cow or cow derivatives. Sensing that it was a very Spartan advice, he modified his caution by saying everything should be in moderation. Now that is up to me! The ball is in my court.

So if I like something I eat. All I have to do is eat moderately. I also compromise my choosing of portions. Also if those values printed are for daily requirements–then I should get credit for abstaining also. So if I eat something – say 5% DVR of sodium and 3 meals and 2 items – still my consumption cannot exceed 30% DVR. So I should get credit for 60% in reserve. Then also if we overeat one day – the law of average should later bring it down quite a bit! That is the way I guide my indulgence.

But talking about eating is not that exciting. So we have to look around what else and where my story happened and how was it memorable. One of my most memorable eating experiences was in Nairobi – more precisely at Amboseli National Park. They had built lodging and restaurant in the park – open to access by any body including animals. Thus one could find big footprints of elephants next to the lodge in the morning. The lodge management assured us – the animals mostly keep to themselves. They had built the

restaurant on stilts above ground in the silence of the forest, so that animals could pass by. Nearby was a medium sized waterhole. They had also illuminated that area with dim lights – resembling moonlight. The animals get thirsty at night (I guess) when different kinds come in herds. Probably they think it is safer at night – so that the predators cannot see them. It was a memorable sight – many different animals waiting their turn to get to the waterhole. Such discipline is rare in human assemblies. The quality of the food was great. The tropical fruits were great. The settings were great. I would love to repeat that – if I get another chance

Another memorable experience was in Maui. Before that trip – something in a travel magazine (Condo Neste?) caught my attention. They had listed the top 100 (in their opinion) restaurants of the world. It was funny that a very few restaurants from US main land were on that list. Probably they were looking at exotic locations only. Memorable dining experience can probably occur in exotic locations only. Quite a few restaurants from Thailand were on that list. Anyway, one ranked restaurant was located in Maui. So I had made it a point that I find for myself what was so unique – to be ranked in the magazine's list. I forgot the name of the restaurant. It was located in the high rise hotel area of the island. It was located on the second floor with a panoramic view of the ocean nearby. It did not matter to us – as it was dark outside on the ocean. It was a busy place with lots of diners. We were seated on a round table – a party of four.

The waiter greeted us warmly, and seated us.
Then he gave each of us a hard bound glossy book
of 500 pages. I thought probably that was to
promote some book on behalf of some magazine.
Some time passed, we were waiting for the menu.
The waiter was keeping an eye on us. He came
forward on request and asked what we were
looking for. We asked for the menu. He said that
book was the menu! We could choose any dish
out of the five hundred pages – each of us could
choose different menu. I thought he was joking –
but in reality all the diners were leafing through
the many pages of the book to decide. Without an
in depth knowledge of cuisine – we had to tread
the path of familiarity, and chose the colorful
ones. Surprisingly it did not take long for the
foods to be served. I forgot the quality of the food
but surely remember the massive menu book
with lots of glossy pictures.

Another notable experience was in Cairo. We
asked the taxi driver to take us to the best kabob
in Cairo. He was very happy, and took us through
many small streets, finally to a crowded place. It
was full of waiters – though there were not that
many diners. The driver confided to us – the
street vendors made excellent kabobs, but we
should stick to more established places. The
kabobs came after some waiting – it was delicious
no doubt. But we could not be the judge of the
rankings of kabobs. After the lunch – we got the

bill. Per western style, we left a tip of fifteen percent on the table. The driver came running to us and took the money away. He said they (local waiters) are not used to big tips at all. So this rather large amount for tips would cause a scrambling commotion among the waiters. And the situation could get nasty. He told us to go and wait in the taxi, and he would pay and distribute the tips. I guess we were causing turmoil due to our lack of experience in the etiquette of tipping. That experience I remember – not so much for the food, but for the potential tip-riot. A note about tipping – in western hotels and restaurants in Cairo, they are used to large tipping. But I think the locals just like to eat and don't like to spend extra for tipping. I have a few more notable experiences. But this is getting long - so long for this blog.   ***

Dazzling Beijing Olympics *(9-5-2008)*

I have not seen any Olympic in person except the Los Angeles Olympics in 1984. Olympics always overwhelm me–as all the top athletes from all over the world compete in it. This was the 29th Olympiad. This is not a political show, but purely a competition of human excellence and limits. The subject matter is late anyway but the purpose is not writing it as a news item, nor as an item of critical review. This is meant for future recollection mainly. As waves of other events will pound the shore of memory, this particular event and its impression is bound to be wiped out or faded away. Though I attended Los Angeles Olympics 24 years ago – I hardly remember details of any thing that I should have remembered. There are pictures in the album – but who cares to open that album. My memory does not show any sharp image–I can recollect it only as a vague event in the past. So this time I am not letting it go.

Beijing Olympics was very important for the Chinese people as they could show their prowess and their ability to stage the event and compete with the best of other nations on a level field. Lot of skepticism was cast as to their ability to stage such a colorful and complex event. There were criticisms about their nobility, because of their denial of freedom to Tibetan people. There was apprehension about the location suitability as the breath-ability of air was a question mark. How did they stand up to the mark? I would say excellent – as they did their best, with style, finesse and originality. Jacques Rogge, the IOC president, acknowledged it as the best Olympic show ever. The next Olympiad will be in London, and London already confessed that they would not try to match the grandeur and high cost as has been incurred by the Chinese authorities. The Chinese built excellent Olympic facilities like Bird Cage Stadium for Ceremonies and Athletic events. They built another notable structure – Water Cube – for all the swimming events. They closed down all factories in the city to provide clean air for the guest athletes so that they can perform at their peaks. The Tibetan Independence did not happen that was the only omission that could tarnish their clean reputation. I have yet to see a country with a very clean record on everything. So that can come later.

The Olympic opening ceremony started precisely at 8:08 pm on 8-8-2008. I understand 8 is a Chinese lucky number, and so many 8's definitely made it a super lucky day and time. The cast of performers were in the thousands. I think the drum sequence had 11000(?) drummers performing in visual splendor and rhythmic unison. I did not see any dragon dance. The Korean Olympics had one sequence when the priests exorcised all evil spirits on the opening day. Probably the Chinese did not have to do it because their opening ceremony was taking place on a super lucky day which had many 8's! The Olympic Torch Lighting was also spectacular as they did that with a sky-walker with the torch. That was very stylish and elegant. We are all used to procession of nations in alphabetical order in Roman numeral. This time they did that by Chinese alphabet that definitely kept us in suspense as to who was coming when. Thus Argentina was not followed by Australia. At least I was glad that the athletes came on time – without knowing when their turn would come.

I think about 12000 (?) athletes from 205 countries competed in the events. About 100 heads of States were there on the opening ceremony – including President Bush and Russia's President Putin. The athletes' prides were on display. Many of them had gigantic egos- but they were all thrilled to be participating in the sports competition representing their own countries. Some Olympics in early 1900's had also many arts events in the Olympics – they were eliminated later, limiting events to physical skill and endurance. They were 28 sports – with many medal events in many sports. Like Soccer, Hockey etc had one medal only but swimming, tracks and gymnastics had many medals in their categories. I counted the total number of medals given in the Olympics – it came to about 942 medals – so it comes to about 314 events. The total medals won were topped by US at 110, followed by China at 100. But the gold count was higher for the Chinese (51) versus US (36). These achievements are extraordinary – as there are many nations that did not win any. And nations like South

Africa (1), India (3), and Nigeria (4) did not win that many medals at all. There are many nations who never won any medal in any category. But, they all came – it is a competition of goodwill and show of camaraderie. The winners can claim to be the best in the world in their categories. When you think there are more than 5 billion (that is 5 followed by 9 zeroes) people on this planet – then their achievements can be seen in a proper perspective.

On the same note, it can be said that nobody is born with superior abilities – though there may be genetic advantages sometimes. Thus if blacks were better athletes per se – then how come Nigeria and South Africa did not win that many medals ? The most impressive athlete on track was Usain Bolt (Jamaica) as he proved himself to be the fastest human on land. The most impressive athlete in water was Michael Phelps (US) as he proved himself to be the fastest human in water. All the finals were spectacular as one could see that anybody could beat the others. So I cannot even imagine the tension and adrenaline pumping in their blood during the events. They are the best physical specimens as created by

God, shaped by human skill and enhanced by practice and endurance. Another pleaser was the gold medal, won by the US basketball team. They had lost their top ranking before, so US regained it with style and humility. It was also funny to know that Kobe Bryant was the most popular participant in the Olympic. He was even more popular than their homeland heroes. I also shall remember the gymnastics performance of the Chinese girls – they seemed so young. Many suspected them to be 12 years old. I don't want to argue anything – but I think the sixteen year old competitors also had their chances available when they were twelve. Overall, it was a very memorable Olympics. Very well done. I just hope the brotherhood and goodwill among the nations don't end when the Olympics end.

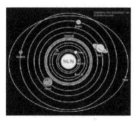

What is Time (9-12-2008)

The other day in a party, I met a long time family friend of mine. To pass away some time before the lunch was served, we were talking about many different things mostly of general nature. One of my questions was how he was handling the time as the retirement had offered him unlimited trove of time to spend anyway he wanted. He said he was enjoying every minute of it – keeping himself busy with so many things to do. Then he was saying he found out many things now that he did not notice before. He paused and asked me if I knew what time meant. I told him why not he think about it and write about it, as we can learn from his finding. He said he did not or could not write. I told him writing is like eating – you don't think just grab the food and chew. Same way you don't think about writing – you just put down on paper what is going through your mind. He told me that was not easy, and asked me why not I write something on this. I told him though I did not have much spare time to think about time, and really knew nothing about time – but I would give it a try to write on a subject even if I did not know anything about it. I told him that is what most everybody does. So this writing is about time. I myself have a gut feeling that time does not exist really, it is nothing. Say, nothing as in Seinfeld series. It is nothing and that is everything. I also think time is not any force, but it is just a measuring tool between two events.

That is my gut feeling, but how does one put that in word? Not that easy. But before that I have to see what others think about time. Everybody knows when one has good time and when one has bad time. It is also obvious that time flies during good time and does not move during bad times. But that is an emotional measurement of time. What is Time really that moves or does not move?

So I have to look at it from a few angles, and get a perspective of time itself before getting back to my gut feeling about time.

First of all we know what the time of the day is – as we all abide by the watch that steers us to the next move. In my house though there are so many clocks and watches , and most of them have different readings of time that always create confusion – as such I have designated the biggest clock in the living room as the 'Chief Clock'. I never understood why there are twenty four hours in a day – we could make it 20 hours a day – with each hour being a little longer than what it is now. But why does the day start at middle of the night – never made sense to me? Why could not we make the early sunrise as zero hour that would be easier to tell time? Whoever designated the starting point of measuring time of the day made a wrong start, and now we are stuck with it. But what then is the time? It is relatively speaking about the location of sun from its noon location (that is at zenith). This concept of time perfectly makes sense to me. But then what is a year? It is also supposedly about the location of sun that we started to measure its movement from relative to planets. So we get roughly about 365 spells of sunlight and darkness during one rotation. Obviously the slant rotational axis and elliptical orbit of earth around the sun deviates it from an ideal circular rotation that would have made our lives much easier. We all live by Solar time. So there is no entity such as time – it is only about movement of sun relative to earth. I understand astronomers don't like solar time as it is imperfect – they would rather go by the relative movement of earth and a fixed star – that is a Sidereal time (watch the word 'real' hidden in the word Sidereal). So I have to come to the conclusion whatever time we talk about, it is about our location on earth in a planetary space. It is just a concept and otherwise does not make any sense. But who cares – if we all agree to make the same mistake then mistakes are no longer mistakes!

Still it does not tell me that time does not exist. What did the greatest brain of the twentieth century say about time? He (Einstein) said that time is a fourth dimension, and we all live in a time –space continuum. That is very heavy – but that is definitely true. Time is really about our location relative to sun. But that location is always shifting as sun is hurtling through space – so its location relative to other bodies is always relatively changing. So? That means there is no fixed time (or deterministic location), but it is an eternally changing time-space continuum. That does not really help us any – but it is obvious that time is a co-ordinate kind of thing like a four dimensional histogram. So my conclusion is same

as before that time does not exist but the movement does.

Still we say that we had good time and we had
bad time. Time is not really good or bad. It is our
location at any moment relative to other things
and people that matter to us – when it gives
pleasure we call that good time. So basically time
is neutral – time does not do anything good or
bad – it is only the surroundings that do us good
or bad. We all know a bad leader can create bad
time for all of us and vice versa. So I can still stick
to my initial thinking that time does not exist.

But we in our daily lives think that time is a
tremendous force – it will knock us down one day
and cheer us up another day. A representation of
such a conceptual theme is hard to portray in a
physical shape. But the Hindus have done it. They
created a black Goddess called Kali. ` Kal` means
'Time'. She is the blessing of life and also the
destruction of death. They have colored her black
as the color of darkness of space or the color of
the vast empty beyond. But she is very loving and
smiling – as there is nothing like a bad time. So it
is all in our understanding and emotional attachment of feeling. In our mind we try to sequence
that. And we can only do that in our frame of time
i.e. solar time.

But in reality – there is nothing like Time. It is a
movement – never backward though, always

forward. Hopefully I have been able to express my gut feeling. I shall ask my friend to check that out.

To end it on a very positive note we have to invoke Rabindranath's description of time. He saw Time as a tremendous force. I shall recourse to one of his poem written late in his life. It is from *Sesher Kabita* (for those who may care to know that). I am giving it in my poor and horrible translation (I hope that is not taken as any insult to Rabindranath):

Do you hear the sound of the Chariot of Time, my friend –

That is always invisible-

Pulsating and palpitating throughout the endless space?

Do you hear the cry of the star cocooned in the embrace of darkness

In the deep gloom of the space?

My friend Time in Its eternal journey

Snared me in its spell –

Picked me up in its chariot

On a journey away from you to a far distance.......

I have nothing to add to what the poet is saying. So as I said - may be Time is nothing, or may be something or may be everything. Who knows? I don't for sure.

***

As The Child Grows *(9-19-2008)*

We are all products of how we grew up. Past is always embedded in the present and future. I have read that the story of life can be viewed as a multi-story building. The previous ten years of life build the foundation for the next ten years. Thus how the child will behave in later years depends on how or what he is learning now and what he is absorbing from the immediate environment. I am not a mother – as such do not have the nursing and survival instincts as nature endows the mother with. But we all walk and live in the real world, so all the tools of experience and observation are there. Some noted author said that common sense is the

most uncommon thing in the world. That is not a tricky one liner – it has some insights. Many times we don't use our common sense – rather than act on only what we hear or see. Thus if we are not vigilant, we shall act according to someone else's thinking and will not be guided by our own common sense. I am not talking about knowledge that needs to be transferred from somebody who has it to somebody who does not have it. Thus what a child should eat , or what medicine to take is not a common sense issue , rather that is a knowledge issue - so we should listen to the doctor or the practitioner in that field of interest. I know it very well that common sense has limited application – but that is the first gear that turns the wheel of life. So we have to judge what is a common sense issue, and when to listen or seek advice and when not. We have to be especially careful when pop culture and pop magazines dictate and trash talks abound.

 I shall not tread the path of knowledge (that is for professionals to dispense with), but look at other daily life issues that we always face. One way to look at a child is that he/she is a man/woman in the making. I think first two years of a baby's life – nature is the builder, protector and provider. Nature provides all the tools to the mother and builds up the baby according to nature's way. Thus the tooth comes out to cope with food needs, words come out to serve the communication needs, nature fills up the baby with love for the mother for security needs, nature provides gut level emotional intelligence to the child to address safety needs etc during the early phase. Nature equips the child so that he/she can meet future needs and challenges to face the real world.

Also I think Nature is more or less done with the basic preparation of the child at the age of two. Now comes the period when the child is facing the world beyond the basic nurturing stage. Now the child is big enough and must get to acquire more skills. He has to learn what is right or wrong, he has to learn through communication and commands. Basically the child's growing up responsibility is handed over to the parents and immediate family. Now the parents are everything in the world to the child. The parent's are the child's playing companion, child's fun, child's love and guide, and everything. The child has to feel the love as that is what glues him/her to the family, not a superficial dutiful love, but a cordial, bonding companionship love. I have seen many cases when the parents are respected public leaders or respected professionals – but were too busy building up their own career, fame or public life and really did not provide enough time to the child to build up the bond that the child would have cherished. We have seen that no matter how great Gandhi was – he showered only dutiful love to his children while they were young, but the children did not get the companionship love. As the bonding element was missing the children felt neglected, and grew up to be a stranger to Gandhi himself. Thus during this precious early time of a child's life the parents should spend as much time as they can as a companion , as a mentor and guide in steering the child's journey of life. Thus goals and careers may have to be modified and focus may have to be adjusted. I have heard of many stories when the parents lamented in later life that they neglected and missed this precious portion of the child's life, and now it was too late to get it back. Life is a forward journey – so 'now' is very important. It is really 'now' or never. The childhood never comes back.

The child is a stranger to this new world of his. Everything is a wonder, everything is unknown; usefulness and relevance of things around are unknown. The child has a huge task of sorting out what is important, what is useful – all this can only be done by the child himself experimenting with unknown. His curiosity is unbounded. So the child needs help and guidance. Toys or abundance of it may mean nothing to the child – as he is not sure whether that has any use at all. Toys are child's temporary companion; it comes to life only when the parents play with him. So playing with the child and spending time playing with him his way is very important in a child's growing up. Through play he learns, has fun, bonds and expands his mental horizon.

Also child is a new member in the community of civilized people. The civilization runs on the wheels of good behavior, good conducts, good manners and implicit rules. Thus a child can go to school in any dress he likes – but there are implicit rules in how one should dress etc. This is just an example to point out that there are rules of conduct when one is in a community of other people. How can a child have any idea of expected conduct whatsoever unless the parents teach him? Take the cloak of civilization away, man is nothing but an animal in the jungle. But we have left the jungle stage long ago. Only the parent can teach the child what is a good behavior, what is bad, harmful and unsafe. The teaching of discipline cannot be taught by lecture method, but can only be transmitted through practice, participation and repetition.

A child wants love that is the bond - so he won't do anything consciously to be deprived of that. He wants to be another person like an adult (I am not talking about his boundless energy, curiosity and desire for fun – that should always be addressed). A child has to be able to conform to accepted code of conduct. A child loves repetition that reinforces the habit. But unless he knows that is the way to do and get along, he will always seem to be disobedient.

Our present president (President Bush) talked about 'no child left behind'. In reality he meant only 'bad teachers to be left behind'. In my thinking a child is truly left behind – if at this early age he does not get the family environment, family companionship, and needed atmosphere of love. He would be lonely with toys or no toys. Nobody transforms his curiosity into learning about things etc. Basically these childhood years are very important in so many ways – these are the years of building the basics of a good person, a noble person, a sharing person and a loving person. The child like everybody else wants to grow up amidst love and fun. Of course all this does not guarantee hundred percent successes. Genes, associations, personal ability, physical and mental acuity – many other factors will come in later life. Even if nobody can guarantee every-thing – at least the parents can give a good start. The first ten years belong to the parents. So I think it is a golden period in a child's life and should not be neglected, wasted or diminished.

***

Unpardonable Accident *(9-26-2008)*

Accidents are something over which a human is taken as having no control. All accidents are not avoidable like a mechanical failure of a system or an incapacitated human being. There is also danger from nature which may be beyond our ability to control. Those kinds of accidents or mishaps are tragic but can be rationalized – and we call those acts of God. But when something is not an act of God, but an act of a careless man, that kind of accident is really unpardonable. I am referring to the commuter rail accident that happened in Los Angeles on September 12. It was a commuter train –route 111- that crashed into a freight train. It happened because the driver (an experienced one) failed to stop at a red light. The reason for that was not mechanical, but that was due to his doing text messaging on his cell. The consequence was that 25 innocent lives were lost and 125 people were injured to various extents. To me it is unpardonable. The driver got his penalty by immediate death in the crash. But it is too bad that many others also became victims of his carelessness.

People in Southern California live on wheels because of a large geographical area of the metropolis and lack of adequate commuter transit system. That creates congestion on highway, delays in commute and also burns nature's reserve of dwindling fossil energy supply and worsens environmental pollution. Not to talk about the stress of driving, inviting road rage from other impatient drivers and loss of valuable personal time that could be used for resting, relaxing or reading. Commuter trains are great that eliminate individual driving and also unlocks valuable personal time. When one rides the commuter train – one always resigns the watch-out responsibility to the driver. Most of the time nobody even knows what the driver is doing. (May be video cameras in every compartment could be a check on his activities or may be another co-driver to assist.) His attention is always needed as there could be danger on the way that may need his intervention. Like - astray animals on the track, malfunctioning signals, or other forms of unanticipated danger. Just because the driver is not pumping pedals or turning steering wheels, does not mean that the train needs no supervision or attention. In other wards he is in charge of safety of 300 or 400 people that are in the train. He is the one who is supposed to guard others from the train going astray. But sadly he was doing his inconsequential text-messaging neglecting his duty. This is definitely being callous to a sad extreme.

It seems in past God and War kept balance between life and death. Virus and bacteria are God's agents of destruction. Mostly we have conquered that front. War seems also unavoidable. Since other animals are no match for man's prowess, Man is the Lord of universe; he has to be his own agent of destruction. The lost passengers were a mosaic of citizens living in this area. They included people from all walks of life - a lawyer, a high school coach, a lover, a grandfather, an aspiring medical student, construction worker, fashion designer, an army veteran etc. They all came from different walks of life, but one thing they had in common. They preferred to leave the commute to the safe attention of the driver. Their loss is not limited to the individual selves, but also leaves a trail of loss and sorrow among their loved ones. That loss is not a statistical count only– but a very real one. They were in the pursuit of their daily activities with joy, enthusiasm or sorrow. The driver should have honored their faith in him and should have reciprocated trust as well. But apparently some individuals are too shallow, and never really know how their activities are connected to others' lives in the larger world. This kind of consciousness is absolutely imperative when doing any work in public or for public.

I have seen reckless individual behaviors in people at work. Recently a friend of mine who was recovering from Leukemia went for a regular check of his blood palette count. The nurse who was suffering from cold forgot to wear safety gloves and other safeguards – as a consequence my friend got infected with a common virus – now he is in a life support system. I had also seen an intoxicated surgeon coming to operate a vital organ. One thing one has to understand that no task is small enough to be taken lightly. A moment's lapse may cause havoc. Thus a security guard sleeping on the job, a sleeping driver of an automobile or even a dozing teacher in a classroom –they all are misbehaving in their jobs. Not only that they are supposed to keep an eye on the safety of others they are indirectly assigned for safekeeping.

I was looking at Wikipedia on the list of human loss in accidents. Of course on top of the list is natural disaster, followed by war and then famine. There are accidents caused by human progress that could not occur in distant uncivilized past. They are explosion, coal mine disaster, aviation accident, ship sinking, industrial accidents, traffic accidents, hospital sickness etc. On top of all is the nuclear threat. The worst industrial accident occurred in Bhopal in India in 1984 when about 20000 people died. That was an industrial accident, but the guard who was supposed to ring sirens was asleep. Thus one individual in most cases stands between danger and safety. This kind of awareness cannot always be enforced, unless the person has a moral conscience. As more and more people seem to be preoccupied with their own little interest - the larger view is often obscured.

One way to teach safety to all – is to instill in everybody that safety is a team work and emphasizing the importance of honoring assigned responsibility. Doing work means fulfillment of a responsibility. Everybody should realize that no work is too small, but everything is somehow inter-related. Thus even if there is no immediate consequence of a simple lapse one day, we are all supposed to look after each other for our own safety. This kind of empathy can grow only when there is more human contact and feelings for others. We are gradually entering into a cold no-feeling technological age – where we live in a virtual world; don't talk to each other, but use electronic means of communication, where social contacts are being replaced by chat room and twitters. The avoidable accident that took 25 lives could not have happened if the driver was conscious that his job was not only to drive the train – but to do that with a sense of commitment, and a sense of duty to others.

***

A Toddler's Delight – Tejas (10-10-2008)

A toddler is somebody who has just learnt to walk. He may be ten months or 18 months. But whatever age be it – it is a fascinating phase. Just think somebody who was lying down most of the time, then started to move by crawling- then slowly lifted the body straight up – and then started to walk. It looks like the evolution of the Homosapien that took million years – a baby just did that in ten months. What a fascinating achievement. The toddler I am now talking about is my grandson. His name is Tejas. He has smart, bright eyes and quick intelligence and it is a joy to see how he has mastered the trick - the art of walking.

He himself is also fascinated by the world of sound. Any small noise that occurs does not escape his attention. Say, he is drinking milk- when somebody opens the door almost silently not to disturb him, but he will turn his head 180 degree to see what that noise was about. If a toy does not make any sound (say the battery is dead), that toy does not interest him. When a plane flies in the sky and he cannot figure out what is that noise from he keeps on looking on all sides. We have a musical fish which sings Reggae music and Tejas cannot stop jumping to the music. Of course somebody has to hold him up so that he can jump vigorously to that Reggae. Now he can make his own babbling noise by stroking his palm over the mouth while saying ba ba ba ba... He enjoys when others make that kind of sound. He plays piano like Rock stars by pounding on the piano vigorously with two hands. He seems to like the sound he makes as he keeps on doing it without getting tired.

He can relate a few words to the objects around. If we say Light – he looks up. When one says mama and papa he looks at the pictures. He can distinguish between funny noise and regular sound of talk. When something tumbles down from top of one's head he cracks up- as if that was one of the funniest thing that he has ever seen. Never mind that things are slipping out of his hand all the time. He has a Cookie Monster toy that when pushed laughs , gets up, falls down again while cracking up and saying 'that was too funny...'. He is amused by that antic.

He seems to judge the worthiness of anything in his own way. First of all, he has to be able to grab it, and then throw it. After the Handling test, he will thrash his palm on the object to see if it makes any sound. That is his Sound test. If it is a flat object he likes it – as then he can thrash his palm on that to check out what kind of sound that object can make. If it passes all the above tests – then he will try to put that in his mouth. That is his Edibility test. When he is having his dinner or lunch – he has to have something in his hand. He pays less attention to what he is eating than what he is playing with. The TV also must be on so that he can watch Elmo doing funny things while he is eating. But he has to approve what he lets in his mouth. Sometimes his grandmas trick him into eating different foods while he is busy watching TV – but he won't open his mouth if he does not like it. His mama makes fresh puree of different kinds of vegetables and fruits with the hope that she would be rewarded by his approval but nobody can predict what he would like at that moment. Thus a high approval rating cannot be predicted even if the food is of top quality. But whatever is lying on the floor seems to him a better food than what is prepared for him. He loves to look inside the refrigerator. I don't think he is looking for food but looking for something that he can play with. He picks up the tiny particles from floor and puts that in his mouth. Any occurrence like that rings alarm to his grandmas. One of the main tasks during baby-sitting is to ensure that he does not eat those things or climb on something.

He loves to climb up the stairs. If there is any pillow lying on the ground – he will climb over it and then puts his cheek to the pillow to experience the softness of the pillow. When he is climbing the stairs (of course with an adult accompanying him) – he is distracted by so many things on the way like a piece of thread, any tear in the carpet, any stain in the carpet , any electrical cover- nothing is beyond his scope of inspection. Sometimes he is barricaded by a heap of pillows while his is sleeping but when he gets up, he loves to climb up the pillow hill.

He does not want to waste any moment doing nothing. Thus changing his diaper is a small battle. The diaper-changer will encounter thrashing of legs, bending of the body and all other kinds of problems and obstruction. That makes the diaper- changer tired and sweaty. The sitters get tired coping with such a bundle of energy unleashed by Tejas. He does not usually cry but if he wakes up prematurely from sleep, he cries in a very pathetic tone. He always has hard time falling asleep. To him sleeping is a waste of time. Sometimes due to his incessant play he gets tired and he falls asleep on his walker. The grandmas also vie among themselves as to who is the better entertainer. He indicates his different degree of approval by a mild smile, big toothy smile or cracking up with a loud laugh. Even a mild acknowledgement from him is a big reward.

All this writing is an attempt to have a snapshot of activities that a toddler enjoys. It is a whole new world to him. I was just reading the other day a family went on a vacation without any toy, (or any CD or DVD or MP3) – they were just experimenting if that would be fun at all. To their surprise they found out it was a whole lot more entertaining than playing with toys. That makes sense. The whole world is full of play things. It is a matter of connection with senses and things. I see Tejas is adept in that. All his surroundings are his play yards - people, things, toys and activities. When we listen to music – we do that with partial connection, but when we are immersed in things and activities it is a total connection. That is a world of enjoyment that we have forgotten when we grew up. But when you are a toddler – you are experiencing all the joy of discovery, involvement and adventure. That is a wonderful sensation of delight - A Toddler's delight.

***

Somebody Hates Mickey Mouse (10-17-2008)

It is hard to believe that somebody hates Mickey Mouse but that is true. The Mickey Mouse –an eternal favorite cartoon character that has entertained children and adults alike for ages all over the world is under fire in the Islamic desert land of the Middle East. One Syrian cleric who preaches Islam in Saudi Arabia recently declared a fatwa on 'Mickey', allegedly because it is spreading a corrupt influence on holy Islam. My question is – all on a sudden how a mouse (abominable to Islam) can be corrupting such a venerable 1500 year old religion practiced by over a billion people (under the guidance of the holiest peace-preaching clerics but advising to kill most other people on earth!?) Mickey has been around since 1958 and millions of Muslims have visited Mickey's Kingdoms all over the world (for fun and entertainment I hope). Probably if Mickey is that powerful he has already corrupted umpteenth billion Muslims all over the world. What happened probably was that Mickey was trying to spread his corrupt influence (read fun) on this fatwa- issuing cleric when he got alarmed, and declared the world wide alert. Even if some of his ardent followers try to follow the dumb cleric (I won't even honor him by printing his name) and kill all the Mickey's around the world, that would entail confiscating billions of T-shirts depicting Mickey and all the children's toys, movies and other play things. Good luck – fatwa loving cleric, I just feel sorry for his congregation. Mickey was probably a ray of sunshine in their hopeless dark existence, now someone tries to steal that also.

This fanaticism cannot be dismissed as wild and innocent either. The Arab TVs have a look-alike Mickey named 'Farfour' that teaches violence and declares an ultimate victory for Islam. Mickey would never do that, he was born out of a creative imagination to entertain us all though he was meant mainly for children. Because in a child's world there is no boundary for imagination, and there reality blends smoothly with imagination. And that is the most natural habitat for Mickey and his pals. The Arab TV producers should not have maligned and made Mickey (an innocent mouse) into another evil character espousing violence and hatred. Why not the oil-rich Sheikhs spend some of their wealth to educate these dark denizens that make everybody uncomfortable all over the world? I have read that according to their preaching –all carnal pleasures are sins in earth, but are profusely practiced in their heaven, where a real martyr will go and enjoy after his death. So summarily – live your life pathetically wait till you die when all carnal pleasures will be awaiting you. I have nothing to add – except to point out that all sermons are probably just one cleric's thoughts, or probably the sermon was a gist of the thoughts and brainwaves of the congregation. I just don't know and fail to understand.

I personally think that concept of cartoons is a superior product of human mind. It does not depict any person in particular – so cannot really offend anyone in particular. If a person's nose is longer or hairs are anti-gravitational – just draw like that which will incorporate some characteristic of the real character but not entirely. I think the famous Aesop (a Greek citizen) used animal characters in his parable so that the message could flow through without human interruption of fatwa, misinterpretation etc. It was a unique concept, as a story could be created without bringing up one's religions, beliefs or affiliation. Also such a creation is eternal and not limited by the frame of time and geography. One of the reasons Islam prohibited any real representation of a persons or prophets in their mosque was an apprehension that the prophets could be depicted unfavorably, and such could be dishonored. Such a thinking is understandable – but prohibiting motion pictures etc as depiction of human figures could be against their beliefs is hard to understand.(I had seen no movie house in Saudi Arabia – though everybody there watches all kinds of movies on their satellite TVs and DVD players at home). This extreme thinking is like banning all arts so that nobody can do any graffiti. The Greeks on the other hand were not shy about showcasing their figures as the human figures are nothing but unique perfection and divine art. Anyway back to cartoon characters and Mickey.

Walter Disney came up with the idea of a cartoon character which looks like a mouse. The year was 1928. I don't know why he chose a mouse. He himself was not that fond of this furry rodent. One thing for sure – the mouse though an irritant to many – is cuddly, small and furry and always hiding and doing mischief, shy and seems beyond the reach of most. Such ability was important so that it could run, jump and hide into small spaces. Most of the initial cartoons were depicting the mouse's pranks. Why he named it after Mickey – I don't know. I read that Mickey Rooney was a good friend of Mr. Disney and was of small stature, and Mr. Rooney thinks that name was adopted from his name. In the thirties Mickey had lot of competitors like Donald Ducks, Roger Rabbits, Bugs Bunny etc. They were all innocent characters that titillate the imagination of the child, but somehow Mickey stood over them as more ingenious and lovable.

Mr. Disney came up with an idea of a children's fun theme park. Who could really be the king of the park? Who else but the most lovable Mickey Mouse? He is all fun and has no enemy. Though those surly cats are running after him all the time but they end up embarrassing themselves. Though Mickey Mouse was all fun all the time – still no body would take its antics seriously. Mickey also came into the vocabulary as indicating something trivial. Like if somebody derides something he/she may be apt to say that is Mickey Mouse. (No offense to Mickey). I myself have been to Disneyland many many times – never got tired of it. It is a fun place – the kingdom of laugh, joy and happiness. It is where reality ends and imagination takes over. Thus Mickey will always be living amidst us as long as the imagination lives.

So I was really sad to see that such an icon of fun and joy could be subject to one cleric's vile allegation of a corrupting influence. The cleric wants to kill the icon of fun and sirens a holy call of jihad against fun and imagination. Yes when the imagination dies, Mickey dies. So the cleric does not have to worry about Mickey – as the world of the clerics has no imagination. Fun is dead there so Mickey does not fit there. Too bad Mr. Cleric. Mickey is the king of our hearts no matter who says what. He will always be with us as long as we all live. Mickey is not an icon of corrupting pleasure, but an icon of pure fun.

***

The Las Vegas Salesman *(10-24-2008)*

I admire salesmen. They are the ones who make the final deal to marry a product and a customer. Even in big companies where people proudly display their professional accomplishments, they would be no where really if somebody did not sell their accomplishments. The end objective of any company's efforts is to sell its products to potential customers. In any big company salesmen are the customer interface. No sale no job. On a broader panorama we are all salesmen. We sell our physical ability or professional ability on a time share basis to employers who hire us. Even for the job of Presidency – the candidate has to sell himself. Sale does not only mean paying money in exchange of ownership. It also means that somebody has to be taken in confidence (i.e. sold) to accept what he sees. Thus an able candidate if he/she cannot convince others about his/her ability has no chance to succeed. I read that the dour Nixon (when he was a vice president to Eisenhower) should have been a shoo-in, but he could not sell his touted experience to the voting public. The voters were more impressed with the charisma of the young senator John Kennedy. Then how did Nixon comeback? He hired Hollywood image makers and improved his packaging to make himself a better saleable product. In short ultimately if you can sell yourself then only you can win. All this leads me to think that salesmanship is an art and only the gifted and the determined can do it better. Lee Iacocca was a celebrity who turned sick Chrysler around, used to introduce himself as a salesman. I have digressed too much, so back to what I started with – the Las Vegas salesman.

It was an ordinary weekend trip to Las Vegas. We (me and my wife) had booked accommodation in Tropicana Resort through an internet web site. We arrived in Las Vegas and were walking in the lobby to hotel guest registration. Then some young lady accosted us and gave us a flyer, told us that there was an offer of free night shows, fifty dollar poker chips, free gifts etc. So we could not resist that. That seemed a free value of close to $200. In this tight economy – even a ten dollar savings looks good to me. All we had to do in return was to listen to a free presentation (one hour) that would also serve fruits, coffee and a hefty breakfast.

That presentation was about time-sharing condo ownership in Las Vegas. The resort was called Tahiti Leisure International Resort and was located close to the strip. The free presentation offer with goodies was not bad as that would also help us to spend some time with other people and keep ourselves away from the slot machines or other mindless window shopping for a few hours. There was another counter –where another gentleman was waiting to give us the goodies and book us for the presentation. I have a habit of making light conversations with people who seem responsive and positive. He asked us how we were enjoying in Las Vegas. I jokingly said so far so good, only hoped that we would not be robbed after the presentation. He laughingly assured us that possibility was remote as they were licensed, reputed and very good people. Indeed good people they were - in looks and in behavior.

Actually that question was in jest. We have been to many time-sharing presentations. I knew they were good people, trying to pitch their products with fun, allure and entertainment. Our first time-sharing experience was in 1968. That was also in Las Vegas. Coincidentally that was in Hacienda, which was razed down later for the Mandalay

Resort. So I had no apprehension at all about these folks. I knew they were honest, hard-working people – trying to make a sale when people are supposedly happy in a vacation city. Some people are paranoid about sales people. Even I read that in people's survey the salesmen ranked lowest in credibility next to politicians. But I have no qualm. To me it is another way of living – honest sweat for honest bucks.

Next morning we went to the place where a bus was waiting to pick up the people who were waiting to attend the presentation. A few detours and a few more stops to pick up more people – then the bus took us to the resort - only five minutes away – south of the strip. Luxurious foliage, Pacific style palm trees, streams and miniature waterfall – all beckoned us to an oasis that looked more like South Pacific (sans Pacific Ocean) than a blistering desert. A happy crowd of receptionists with tropical outfits and happy gaits greeted the downloaded passengers. They took us to a big waiting room where we were told to wait for twenty minutes so that they could get the presentation room ready. All the wall monitors were showing happy people frolicking in pools amidst upscale luxurious environments- with drinks being offered by waitresses under big umbrellas creating large area of shades. The frolickers were family people of all ages - kids, parents and grandparents. Some people were in wheelchairs and they also were part of the happy crowd.

Then we were all ushered to a big presentation room on the second floor. There were many round tables with a podium and screen in the center. We were greeted enthusiastically by an elderly person, who seated with us on one table. There were probably twenty round tables like ours. Each table was chaired by a salesman with other potential customer couples. Then a super enthusiast salesman (an ex-TV weatherman) took the podium- and thanked us for coming etc. He indicated they were a Fortune 500 company with worldwide resorts like this. They had thousands of customers who were vacationing at spots of their choices in the Pacific, Riviera, Europe, Mexico and Hawaii etc. He was also spinning a big wheel with lucky numbers winning surprising vacation packages. Every time the podium salesman cracked any jokes – all the salesmen clapped and thumped with loud roars of laughter. In between our salesman cracked so many jokes, agreed with everything that I said, gave many advices, and described the happiness he got out of making people like us happy. As a matter of fact he was cracking so many philosophical one liners – that I was impressed and even asked him how he could have such a bagful.

He said his dad was a top salesman also, and always helped, guided and taught him the lessons of life. He was his best friend all his life. Now he surely missed him. He was a Harley-Davidson guy – his wife did not like that, but changed her mind after they spent a vacation in Hawaii on Harley-Davidson. He said he had an accident, broke his knee and he had to quit biking. Since then his health is going down. He smoked a lot etc. His health was slowly going downhill. He appreciated when he got such willing ears as we had. His wife did not like the job he was doing now. But he loved the job. He thought there was happiness in selling happiness. From the glints in his eyes I had the impression that he was happy that he had won a sale.

We would also have been happy – if we could oblige for $55000. But with plunging economy and uncertain future we were not ready-but could not say no to this kind salesman. We told him we would think it over when we go back to Los Angeles, and asked for his number. He said he knew we would not call him when we get back to LA. He had heard so many promises like that before. His face could not hide his disappoint-ment. Very reluctantly and with sadness in heart we took leave of him and went downstairs. Another bus full load of new passengers came in. The good salesman was waiting there and greeted the new people with big smile. I realized that the job of a salesman is full of hopes and dashed hopes. But they keep up their happy, smiling faces every day with every potential customer. So I silently admired him and was happy that we did not fall into the trap of buying a time-sharing condo in Las Vegas.

Annaprasan–Trevor *(11-21-2008)*

Last week there was no blog, as it was the 'Annaprasan Day' for Trevor, who is six months old now. Six months ago we had one for Tejas, and about one year ago for Shaun. They are a young brigade who will be our future team of wheelers and dealers. But for the present we have to know what they are up to. For those who may not know what 'Annaprasan' is–a little explanation is in order. In some parts of India, this custom of 'Annaprasan' is celebrated. This is held around the baby's age of six months. Basically the custom is to feed the baby a little spoon of 'payas' that is similar to rice pudding.

This signifies that the newborn has now grown up and is entering the stage of infancy. Actually this also is meant to introduce the child to many friends and relatives who had not seen the baby before. So it is a social cultural custom. The whole idea is to have a party celebrating the baby's arrival in the family and celebrating his smooth transition to the next stage of growth. It was not a very big party, about eighty to nine people were invited–friends and relatives. Of course many elders got a chance for the first time to see the baby and shower him with their love and affection. So all of these arranging takes some preparation, as such there was no time for blog last week.

A game is also played for fun – to crystal ball what the baby wants to be when he grows up. This crystal-ball game is also played in two parts. The first part is the discovery of intent. So on a platter are laid out four choices –a book (Knowledge), a gold bangle (Wealth), a little earthen toy (Real Estate) and a pen (Professional Learning). Fortunately for us, Trevor did not waste much time to pick up his first choice. The gold bangle was shining from the stage light that must have impressed him. This desire of Wealth is a common human phenomenon–so it is not so specific, also wealth comes from many different ways. So there is a game number two. This assumes that he has to choose a profession to attain his goal and to find out what profession he might have in his mind! So on a bigger platter- are laid out the tools of the profession that his immediate family members are engaged in. That includes the field of medicine, law, engineering, teaching, computer technology and nursing. Not to exclude the possibility that he might want to be a super star like Kobe Bryant, we also put a colorful ball on the platter. This time also, Trevor did not waste much time – he picked up the stethoscope. We have no idea what was his decision process–but many speculated that toy looked interesting and different to him. Some of his well-wishers prodded him towards the colorful ball – to that he showed some disdain. His dad was happy that he will have at least one successor to his profession in the family. His choice was applauded by the assembly, and we were all happy that we have a young and smart boy who already knows how to make the right choice, and do that well on his own.

To snapshoot the time frame what is going on at this time, a little narration of what is happening now is in order. Later on Trevor may want to know that. We just had a Presidential election between the Republican candidate Senator McCain (73) and the Democratic candidate Senator Obama (47). The first one is a war hero, prisoner of war, been in senate for a long time. His opponent is a man of color, of international upbringing (as opposed to vintage American upbringing) but with a very cohesive, cognitive and cerebral approach to nation's problems and with an astounding oratorical capability of delivering the message of hope and change. The nation is now steeped in deep recession – big vaunted financial institutions that acted like wheels of the mighty American Economic engine are in disarray. Banks are failing, houses are being foreclosed, jobs are being lost in all sectors and in large numbers, the international goodwill on which the American leadership used to ride is tarnished, the mighty American empire seems to be tottering – the future does not seem too rosy for America. It seems Obama promised a change, for better, challenged the direction and predicted the recovery of American pride and moral leadership. Mr. Obama won the election in a landslide fashion on the wings of the messages of hope.

The Congress just bailed out many financial institutions, took over controls of some major failing banks, infused billions of dollars in economy. Two wars are going on – one in Iraq and one in Afghanistan. None of those are settled yet. The war is being waged against an enemy which seems to be elusive, and their exact capability and strength seem unknown. America was acting solo –without much help from other western powers. The environment is neglected and damaged, medical research is stymied by religious morality, poor and middle class are suffering and neglected while Capitalism is showing its heartless ugly side by showering the conniving rich with more largess and generous government assistance. The whole world seems to be roiling through a dark period of recession. Everybody is looking forward to the new President to steer things around to the right direction and fix the problems that ail the nation.

The Beijing Olympics took place a few months ago. Lakers have come back to glory and got back their golden touch. Football season is in full swing. Tiger Woods is resting for a year. The Xmas is coming soon. But the stores are not selling much. There are no big Boxing heroes- Oscar De La Hoya (one name) still seems to be the big star. People are not traveling much-not for reasons of security but as flights are less frequent and ticket prices are high. Analog era of television is coming to an end. Windows Vista is the current platform – it seems plagued with problems and not very popular. Satellites, Cables, Internet and Telephone companies are vying for transmission of movies. Nintendo has taken lead in the Games world with their Wii sensorial games. People are abandoning their gas-guzzling SUVs and going for hybrid. Car companies are investing huge amount of money in battery technology to cut down consumption of gasoline. Everybody is talking about alternate energy and conservation. It seems the era of wastage that thrived American economy is coming to an end.

In other words, Trevor – we are now going through challenging times. The future does not seem rosy for the time being. But I hope when you grow up – the leaders will be more circumspect, more comprehensive thinkers, more compassionate and more practical with an overall understanding of history. It is said that history repeats itself. It is always doing that – it has to – the earth goes round the Sun in the same path. The passage may be new, but the message is old and eternal. Fate follows action, so it can always be predicted. Good luck and best wishes as you grow up.

Story of an Immigrant I *(11-28-2008)*

This week was supposed to be restful and enjoyment of Thanksgiving. But some idiots of some fanatic faith shattered peace for all by terrorizing the innocent tourists in a foreign land (Mumbai, India). I don't know what these creatures want. Why not UN mandates some inhabitable area of the globe and confine these people in a reservation where they can practice their barbaric killing, covering up their women with dark clothing, stoning them to death for doing things against God's wishes – while they themselves merrily go on killing others supposedly on God's instruction and approval through their godly spokesmen. At the same time proclaiming themselves as very moral, religious and peace loving people. Enough is enough. The world should get united to root these evils out. Conceding to their demands is like appeasing wolves with meat, hoping that will be end of their appetite. History has shown that lunatics when combine with idiocy become a fatal combination of gasoline and a matchstick. It is obvious these fanatics are nurtured by evil leaders and evil rich with their evil money. Neither do they know how to live, and won't let others live in peace.

But I was reminiscing about something else on this peaceful day of Thanksgiving. Why not we stop thinking big and start looking around and think at ground's level. Talking about Bush or Obama may be interesting, but history will take care of them. But small people like us would get wiped out without any trail unless we talk about small people like us. Because when I look at a person I see lot of stories and histories in him or her either expressed or suppressed, loud or silent, frozen or thawed. I know what Rabindranath once said in his inimitable style – *I have looked around many capitals of the world, magnificence of nature and beauty in the horizon- but I really never cared to look at the beauty of the dews on the small grasses in my backyard with an open eye...* So we are basically blind at a short distance unless we choose the other way.

This is about a person who runs a medium sized Montessori preschool and kindergarten. She runs it very efficiently and with admiration of the parents, students and the staff. She gets calls from Taiwan or Minnesota when somebody with a preschool-aged child moves to her school's vicinity. She does not give any print ad or colorful brochures about the excellence of her school – considered elite by the professional parents that attend the school. Her students' parents belong to the upper middle class–very educated and professional–ranging from doctors, scientists, engineers, academicians and company owners. Most of them seek her advice how to raise a good child. The nervous parents become confident with her advice and then become proud of the achievement of their kids. She thinks life's learning has no boundary. The job of teaching does not end with solving a few math problems or learning words, but a real teaching means making a good human being–to make a small child a good person with good behavior and good habits, to instill a passion for learning and cooperation that will do well to others and to himself. She works hard and expects others to do the same. She does not like any child to fail, and she takes up challenges when a parent with a low-achieving kid comes to her for help. She does not brag, she does not complain, she expects her staff to have a focus in their jobs and not to be a mere show-up with pretension of working etc. But was she like this all the time? I don't think so, because I know this person very well.

Rewind back to 1968. I see a bewildered shy immigrant landing in this country to join her husband to start a new life together in a foreign land with no friend and with very little money. She knows her husband a little bit, not a whole lot, knows him to be very successful academically. She also knows that her husband has no friends in the foreign land-only has a job in a small prestigious architectural firm. She comes from a middle class family–but a family of very high-achievers. She comes from an Indian joint family where about thirty people sit together at dinner time. The family's achievement is kind of jaw-dropping. An University Dean, one High Court Judge, one State Labor Secretary, one very well-known author of numerous novels and block-buster movie hits, one income tax auditor , one engineer, one Superintendent of Education in pre-partition India. Their achievements did not pamper or isolate them as they believed in happiness in togetherness. Her grandma when out on street would be surrounded by admirers who envied her as being mother of so many successful children. She herself had a master's degree in Bengali (one of the major Indian languages) Literature and another Master's degree in Rabindranath (from Viswa Bharati University). She was a person born in the world of many and raised in laughter, chatter and encompassing goodwill of all. Here she was all by herself alone with her husband in a distant soil with no known family member nor any acquaintance for that matter.

She had not boarded a plane before her journey to the United States. She sometimes used to go to airports to get a look at the real plane. In those days airplane travel was out of the reach for the ordinary, and was meant only for rich and powerful. When she boarded the plane–there were about fifty or sixty relatives at the airport to say her goodbye. Some in tears, some in envy, but everybody in anxiety. How would she manage the long flight to America–a long journey, no friend, a difficult to understand language? She gathered inside all the strength she had. The plane soared into the sky–away to the other side of the globe. Stopped in Tokyo, then to Honolulu. Honolulu was the port of entry in those days–as the airlines in those days could not hop the Pacific in one leap. Did not quite understand what the pilot was saying on the intercom and what the airhostess was talking about. She went to English Medium Missionary School–but they talked in British English with Scottish accent. She lost her glasses in the plane. She was looking for it all over without saying anything as she was sure nobody would understand her language. Then one gentleman took the initiative and spoke with her. She said 'I have lost my spectacle'. At first he did not understand–then realized probably she was talking about her glass. The British English that she had learnt in school failed her in the plane in America. She did not know where to get a drink from. She had no body to ask. Her husband was not there. She was all by herself, all alone. A distant way–a long journey…. This writing is getting long; I shall come back to it later.

***

English Language Patient

English Language Patient (12-5-2008)

Last week much did not happen. Mumbai was recuperating from the brazen attacks by fanatic Muslims; India's pride was wounded and the nation shocked again; the world wondering how to shackle these fanatics. Probably these pests are here to stay widening the chasm between civilized and uncivilized. Anyway to return to normal life here. We saw one movie 'Slumdog Millionaire'. A movie of coincidental lucks–of a slum dog (a homeless urchin in shanties) eventually winning twenty million dollars in an Indian version of a contest show 'Who wants to be a Millionaire'. Though uneducated and living on life's edges in the underbelly of a big city, the slum dog urchin manages to answer all questions to the bewilderment of all. It is a feel- good, if it- could happen kind of movie. An American movie in an Indian background.

Thinking about what to write–I thought why not write about the English language of which I had become a victim sometimes. I know Americans find it hard to understand Indian English. When one gets used to American accent, the native Indian accent may go away, but in the beginning there have to be problems. There are many jokes about Indians not understanding English spoken by an Englishman. In a joke – one Indian sheik was going to meet the British queen. As he was sure he won't understand the Queen's English – he asked for some advice from experienced people. The advisers told him – the queen would ask his name first, then she would ask if he was married and then ask how old he was. So when the sheikh shook hands with the queen, the queen politely asked him his name- he said it right. Then she asked if he was married – he said yes as he was married. Then instead of asking his age the queen asked him how many children he had. But thinking the queen queried him about his age, the sheikh said thirty six (his age)!

I have seen such guffaw myself. One young bright Indian student goes to a restaurant; the waiter asked him what he would like to order. He said his own name, because in India the prevalent mode of conversation starts with asking the other person's name. In my experience it happened also. I was giving a presentation in a graduate class (as a student). The topic had to be well researched and it was to be critiqued by fellow students after the presentation. So I was nervous. But since I had done my homework I thought my presentation was good. My presentation was followed by silence – nobody had any question! I thought it must had been a flawless presentation. The Irish professor who was familiar with Indian accent took me aside. He said he had lot of questions on my presentation! I asked him why did not other students raise hands to discuss any disagreement – he said they could not because they did not understand at all what I was saying. Of course I became very conscious about spoken American English and gradually tried to improve myself.

In college as a student I went to the college book store to buy some school supplies. In India they call the erasers as 'rubbers'. So I asked the clerk – do you have rubbers here? She was surprised that I would ask for rubbers in a book store! She advised me to go to a drug store where such condoms are sold! I was totally nonplused why should a drug store (that should carry medicines only) carry rubbers (erasers) instead of a book store?

Once I saw on TV the Indian Prime Minister visiting US was delivering a speech to the Congress. He spoke in fluent and elegant English, but CNN was subtitling the whole speech as he was delivering it. (I guess that was to make sure that American listeners can understand his English) I know English language takes different shapes and sounds in different countries as modified by local speech habits. Thus when an Australian gets excited – his language deviates quite a bit from American English. Even British English is different from American English in its content and delivery. Thus America follows

Webster for American-English dictionary, and British follows Oxford dictionary. In modern ages the American English has become the lingua-franca of the world in commerce, science and international communication. The Internet age has given birth to so many different terms that the French people are now ready to give up their challenges to English in world domination.

I find I am not getting any fluency in what I am trying to say–because I am looking for funny incidents instead of looking at a broader picture. The accent in any language comes from the nature – the natural surroundings of the inhabitants. Spoken Indian English is more vowel-oriented as the nature is soft there. So the language blends with the rivers and so do their songs. But Western language was born in harsher climate-as such it is more consonant oriented. Consonants get more emphasis. Also the Indian language has fifty two consonants and thirteen vowels. As such even the vowels have different sound depending on its delivery length. Also it is subdivided into groups of five depending on its origin- like where does the tongue touch. It may be guttural, dental, mixed origin etc.

Another problem is lack of accents (that is emphasis on particular syllables in any word.)In Indian languages all the characters get equal emphasis in pronunciation. So when an Indian speaks English – it is mostly accent less. When the vowels dominate a language it gets a singing up and down intonation. So, many Americans find it hard to understand English in an accentless monotone delivered in a tilting tone. When Americans try to speak Indian language they falter as they are used to a language which contains only twenty six sounds (vowels and consonants combined). With that limitation American would falter at most other languages as the others have so many different sounds incorporated in their languages.

The accent also came from upper strata in the society. As the upper class must have a superior air – they speak with style or accents. Even though the written English has some spelling for some word, but the ruling society accented it differently confusing the lower classes further. I think the accent grew with imperial ambition and bossy mentality. It is clear that only British English have words spoken with accented syllables (even Germans and Scandinavians have less accented syllables). The French went one step further by using nasal output with their speeches generated by tongue. So all these problems may be land-related and status-related. Sanskrit (Mother lode of all North Indian Languages) is also an elegant language with different accents on different portions of words. That was done probably to make it the master language and not a language of the illiterate masses. In common conversation between folks there need be no accents, but when bossing you have to emphasize. That is probably how accents crept in. So when the master's language becomes a language of all, the built in accents makes it a speed bump for foreign tongues. That makes us (foreign born) victims or patients of the English language.

***

Sexy! Oh No *(12-12-2008)*

I heard the story, but I do believe it. She had worn a beautiful dress and she came to her workplace (a preschool) in that dress. She was complimented by her fellow workers and one of them went more extravagant in her praise and said she looked sexy (rather than pretty or cute). Instead of taking it as a compliment, she was thrown off balance. What did the praise mean? Was she dressed sexy–that was something she could not think of? Though she was told it was a compliment, she thought the joke went beyond her boundary of taste. She was a mother of two who were in their twenties now, and a very respectable person who rules her family with no nonsense devotion! That was her image of herself. And now somebody with a very low taste dared to call her sexy! She was devastated and had a minor breakdown that needed psychiatric consultation and also a medical check to see her breakdown went to what length. She recovered that took her a few weeks. She dropped the idea of suing the workplace on better counseling as she was thinking it was a form of sexual harassment.

In the jungle of the judges and lawyers I have no idea what is what, because anybody who tips the balance on anything one is in trouble. If there is a touch between two humans (regardless of age difference) it may be described as having a sexual intent. Then there are the advocacy groups, entitlement groups, ACLU and other morality groups who are always watching like hawks if anybody's pursuit of peace has been stymied. If so then it is a constitutional violation, and as such punishable by the judges in the shrine of justice. Since I am so confused I cannot even judge what is appropriate or not. Even if there is no physical contact–just a few sound bytes in the air can be interpreted as a verbal insult, mental assault or an attempt to steal somebody's happiness or peace of mind. So in this jungle of laws I am never sure what is right or wrong. So I have no idea whether that employee's breakdown was laughable or defensible or whatever. So I am not going to be the judge or jury on this.

By the way the person in the story is an Indian middle-aged lady of an older generation, and brought up in a prudent Indian social tradition. Now, the present generation Indians are more globalized and understand nuances of different culture whether they agree or not. That prompted me to think what does that 'sexy' really mean. 'Sexy' by formal dictionary definition means sexually exciting or interesting. By this definition if one wants to look sexy then the underlying motivation has to be along the same line! It makes sense and 'sexy' has to be a great compliment. From what I see, God's creation model is prioritized on maintenance and reproduction. Other activities (like great literature or music) are secondary and do not leave any lasting impact on creation. They are of very limited value to sustain life on this planet. So I am presuming that man's continued existence is possible due to its creative or reproductive endeavor. (No gays or other groups need be offended at this—I am looking at God's business model only.) In that thinking, the more is the better as long as it is maintainable. So man's supreme task is to perform as a reproduction machine. In this task who gets to be selected ahead of others? Of course one who is sexy, that is who looks sexually exciting! Does that mean all good dresses or grooming have to have the subliminal motivation of sexual attraction? I don't know. I shall leave it to more knowledgeable (than I am) people.

Culturally also there seems be a wide range of perceptions. Look at Muslims. They are very obedient to God in complying with their reproductive role–as they have harems i.e. stables of multiple wives etc. So one will tend to think that the so called sex-games should play a large part in their lives and living. But no, they are very strict that their woman should not look sexy! But a woman (no matter what) always looks sexy to men. (It need not be to all men, but any woman will have some following regardless of looks). So their religious leaders stipulated covering of bodies of all women from head to toe. In the Middle East they think it keeps the women safe and keep the men moral. Foreign women don't need to cover themselves up hundred percent. The moral policemen there want some body parts of women that are too sexy to them to be covered up. Like hair, bare hands, exposed legs etc. All these are proclaimed as moral propriety so that their men folks who are so aggressive reproductively can be restrained from going amok.

I remember in the seventies when we were there – American wives would prefer to jog in the open air around their camps. And that they were doing in jogger's shorts. So! It meant a huge expanse of human skin was open to view. The local security guards were so overwhelmed by the scene that many of them fainted on their jobs. So authorities proclaimed jogging should be done in jogging pants and not shorts! Then peace prevailed. One thing still I don't understand is that nobody forced them to look at the joggers–they could read the Koran instead. But they had to look at the ladies and they had to collapse! So it is a society that seems to grapple with their drives and restraint. So they have all kinds of social taboos to handle the conflicts of instinct, behavior and moral duties. Being sexy to them is a sin.

In Indian and Chinese societies, it is obvious they take their prescriptive procreation roles very seriously–as they have contributed close to fifty percent of human lives on this planet. So this sex game is a very serious game there. Then looking sexy must be a model behavior in their procreation game. But they also prescribe non-sexy looks. As a matter of fact the Indian women were used to cover themselves with saris–that meant covering up all their physical attributes, hiding body contours and shapes. So in these societies' sex game sexy looks are not allowed! Instead they have glorified motherhood (restrained sexiness-relegating sex for procreation only).There a woman's ultimate achievement is attaining motherhood, and once married she is out of the sex game. Then she is a venerable mother. Now I see why that Indian lady whom I started the blog about, was so upset when being called sexy. She is married, no more in the sex game and has no intention to be in it–still somebody dared to insinuate her intent so offensively!

Now how does the western society look at this sex game? They have lessened their God's scripted roles of procreation and substituted that to a game of pleasure. In this society women are pleasure partners or sex objects also. To many the ultimate in womanhood has to be good looking objects of pleasure. So in this society whoever looks sexy is ahead in the game, and is applauded by all. That is why here anything good, or good-looking is most desirable and is termed sexy. Thus we have sexy drinks, sexy perfumes and even sexy beast...

So long on someone being called 'sexy'. I don't know if this blog can be called sexy!

***

Story of an Immigrant II (12-26-2008)

A few weeks ago I started to write about a person who has found the mission of her life without much help or much backing. She turned herself into a successful parent and a well-respected mentor to many parents who trusted their kids to her supervision. She probably did not have any well-written agenda or a lifelong dream of scaling to that height of admiration. Everything happened as if by whims of nature, by turns of circumstances and probably by not abandoning herself to a state of ease and leisure. So I thought Christmas day is a good time when we can look at small things, count life's blessings, appreciate life and empathize with other's toils and trouble in their journey of life. One need not be famous to be glorified and nobody is too small to be ignored. But how one does that is also a problem. To see the flowers in a garden you cannot run or jog in the garden, you have to have a slow walk. If life is a storybook of many pages, every page leads to another new page. You cannot skip too many pages. That is also how life unfolds;

every activity leads to another and that to another, and all together it becomes a story. So though it sounds simple, it is not an easy task. But I shall give it a try.

Last time I was writing about her background when she came to this country. Her journey was full of bewilderment. Also there was her determination to adjust and understand. That takes guts and grits, especially in a foreign culture and a foreign country. Last time I stopped when her plane finally landed at Honolulu International Airport. Getting down from the aircraft, one has to go to the Customs first. But where is the Customs? There were signs advising passengers to follow the yellow lines. But where are the yellow lines? Is it on the wall, on the ground or where? No body to ask there, everybody seems to know what they are doing or where they had to go. So it was safe to follow some exiting passengers who looked confident to their destined routes. Finally she arrived at the Customs with the unwieldy suitcase she had. The Customs people in those days were more concerned with foreign fruits and vegetables than terrorists or anything else. After minor questioning, she was advised to go to the passport counter. Luckily she already had the Green Card (permanent US residence permits). Her husband had arranged for that before leaving India. A long journey, unfamiliar food, no sleep and a big luggage - she was exhausted. But at least she had reached US, now only a five-hour flight to Los Angeles, her final destination. The travel agent (Hari Singh) in India who always pretended that he knew everything (though he himself never went anywhere) told everybody that as soon as she would get down from the plane, she would see her husband waiting at the airport. She told me later that she did curse that ignorant bigmouth travel agent when she had to disembark at Honolulu. But the travel agents in India are warehouses of improbable words, and always come up with some beguiling excuses when challenged. More or less all Indians are gifted with words infused with hyperboles and pathos.

Finally she arrived in Los Angeles. By this time she knew where to get her luggage, no more hassle to go through all the different checkpoints of government control. Her husband was indeed waiting when she arrived. They got the luggage and got into their small Renault that he had bought in Pittsburgh, and had it transported by a transport carrier agency. Actually that was a very small car and all that her husband could afford. He had bought the cheapest new car in the market at $1500.00. Many people liked Volkswagen, which he could get for $1550, but he did not like the soldier-like look of Volkswagen and also it cost fifty dollar more. That Renault took them one and half-hour from the airport to their apartment. He did not trust the Renault on the freeway as it had the habit of stopping without any warning. Her husband had been mad at the smooth-talking salesman, because he did not disclose that Renault was being withdrawn from the US market at that time, as it was not fit for US highway. Also that salesman had a peculiar look with his square head imposed on his square torso without any neck whatsoever. From that point on her husband did not trust anybody who had a square head (including in cartoons).

They finally arrived to their apartment around eight o'clock. What a relief now–end of the long journey of many stops, many regulations and unknown foods. Their apartment was in the Los Feliz area of Los Angeles. Los Feliz was a green and woody neighborhood near the famed Griffith Park with its renowned telescope and planet-arium. (Later on they weighed themselves as if on Moon, and found that they weighed only twenty pounds like a baby on Moon). The apartment was in a two story complex with a cluster of buildings around a velvety green expanse of grassy lawn. Her husband had chosen that area, as it was not that far from the downtown office area that was only four miles away. The apartment looked big and expansive, about one thousand square foot, carpeted but not furnished. They grew up in a crowded household, where many people crowded together in a small place. So this place looked unbelievably big to her.

The apartment though unfurnished had a big refrigerator, oven and well heated. The apartment manager had told him that was pretty standard, and any rental unit without heat was against law. He had prepared rice and chicken curry. Some butter and French fries were there as a prelude to the main menu. Her husband was not a good cook, but was very big-mouthed about his achievement in the kitchen. His so-called expertise came from his student day's experience in cooking. He confided that he was no cooking genius, but discovered many wonders in the kitchen. The egg was a miraculous food item; it could be eaten in so many different ways to suit the different time of the day and moods. It could be eaten scrambled, poached, toasted, boiled, made into omelets, and also when boiled with water and curry powder it turned into egg curry. The other thing he learnt was how to boil rice. (He had confided that the easiest meal he had found was soup). At first he was frustrated with the excess water left after the rice was cooked, then he discovered that adding some butter made that excess water disappear. He had shared that tricks with other starving and kitchen-skill-lacking Indian student friends like him. He had also discovered the adaptability of chicken. Cover it with some readymade powder and put in the oven, it turned itself into a delicious food. His chicken curry was not universally acclaimed, but somehow he was proud that it was quite eatable. And he had prepared that with great care. So that was her first meal in US. She was very tired in the long trip, almost exhausted after listening to all the instructions on the way–go there, follow that line, get that and come back again–all kinds of gobble de gook. Exhausted though she tried to eat that meal. He was surprised that she was not as excited as he was about the preparation he had concocted. ... This writing is getting long; I shall come back to it later.

Adieu 2008 *(1-9-2009)*

There was no blog last week, as I was trying to meet a few dead lines of project submittals. So I am kind of late in saying goodbye to the past year. Usually people don't think much about the year that passed by, but 2008 was an unusual year–good and bad, a year that cannot be easily forgotten. What is important and what is not is so personal that any two people may not agree on the same thing. But I shall review in my way what I think was memorable. A few memorable things happened in our family. We welcomed the addition of Trevor (now age 6 months) to our family and celebrated *Annaprasan* ceremonies for Trevor and Tejas (now age 14 months) and saw enrollment of Shaun (now 30 months) in preschool. Now I shall look around the larger world where each happening has some direct or indirect influence on our lives.

The first thing to remember will be the economic meltdown of the vaunted western financial system. Is it a crack in the wheel of capitalism, or an enactment of a Greek tragedy of the consequence of greed and hedonism of the people in power? This meltdown should make us all humble a little bit and dispel the notion that American way is infallible. Has Consumerism reached the limit? We should be humble to acknowledge that no one is strong enough to defeat all enemies and no one is rich enough to feed all hungry mouths. What we saw was the tumbling down of the humongous financial institutions and mega banks-the chariots of capitalism's wagon. Then we saw the invincible and venerable auto industry almost biting dust; other industries crying in despair and mired in deep troubles, the future for all of us looking bleak. Unemployment rising–the future seems to be on hold. May be it was part of the system that adjusts itself in a cyclical fashion. But one thing for sure it was not God made (as GM used to stand for). It was the greed of the people in power who are to blame.

When some CEOs (i.e. drivers of the companies) take away millions in bonuses while their ships are sinking–that is really deplorable. Their unconscionable and unpardonable pocket gains led to deprivation of decent living to millions of citizens and destruction of millions of families. A nation can stand up straight only when its back bones are strong. But when the bone marrows are infected with shameless greed there is no chance. The culprit CEOs have no shame in their systems, are ruthless in their arrogance and merciless in their predatory activities. In Japan if somebody does something unethical and immoral, and when he cannot face the shame he commits suicide. It is good for the system. The system gets balanced again. Shame is like dirt on our conscience, when it clouds the conscience, the objectives seem unclear – then the soul is possessed by the devil. When devils rule then disaster follows. It is all in the leadership. Either it is human and humane, or it is devil and insane. This year should be remembered as when the bell tolled. If we have not heard the bell now, we are heading to God knows where.

But bad is always offset by good. The cloud also has silver lining. We also saw the rise of Obama and his message of hope. Obama's rise to power was very significant. It is not about an achievement of a black American. It was the reflection of changes in America's psyche. The country built on slave labor, finally acknowledged one as their leader. It was a gut wrenching and soul searching decision for all citizens. It was the apprehension of treading in unknown water. He had already won two big battles. He defeated the mighty Clintons for the party's mantle, and then defeated the entrenched Republicans in power for the country's crown. He won the hearts of the young and educated, won the confidence of the veterans and the experienced.

He inspired the youth- the workers that can harbinger a new era with their involvement and enthusiasm. We hope he is as humble and empathetic as he is charismatic. I don't know how he will fare with all the problems facing him-like terrorism, unprecedented deficits, lapses of incompetent prior leadership and cronymanship, environmental neglect, globalization, rising of other economic powers in different parts of the world and a host of other problems. He seems deliberate, open minded and fair in decision making. His job is to lead. He will have all the help from the country's best, because his job is to steer the nation in the right direction, in the sustainable future, fair to all and compassionate globally. He promised changes-changes in our thinking and ways of doing things. He encouraged us to think of the whole, just not a small part of oneself. America's color and thinking is changing, a new generation wants to lead with new enthusiasm towards a brighter future. He heralds the future with no color bar. That was a very welcome event in 2008.

The other memorable event was the Beijing Olympic. It was not just a quadrennial event like other Olympics. We saw the Chinese coming to the world stage and got a glimpse of its potential. Personally I was overwhelmed by the opening ceremony- when ten thousand (!?) drummers beat the same tune at the same time with the same rhythm- that was awesome. Also athletically they were no body a decade back. But by sheer perseverance and determination now they won the highest number of gold medals. That shows how a nation can rise to greater heights by sheer determination and dedication of its people. I know somebody will say they were ruthless communists and forcing their own to perform or else. But the truth is no body can turn a donkey into a horse by beating or coercion or by any special isms. So kudos to the Chinese. I don't know if the people are unhappy for what they have done. I just hope they become a benevolent world power and cooperate with others to achieve welfare of all.

The other sadly memorable event to me was the

Mumbai attacks planned and launched from a foreign soil. It showed all that evil is lurking everywhere. It also showed clearly where the evils are nurtured. No matter how much innocence Pakistan claims–we have no choice but to blame the country where they are trained and planned to cause destruction in another country. It is true if there is one murderer in the family that does not mean all in the family are murderers. Then again pretension of innocence of the murderers' presence cannot be cheered as a responsible behavior of any good citizens of this world. What they are doing to others can easily be done towards them by others and then take the path of pretended innocence. Innocence has a limit but a recurrence of the same mischief can hardly be called oversight.

Also another note on China's fortitude. They suffered an incomprehensible disaster from a natural calamity. An earthquake of magnitude 8.0 leveled a whole city (Sichuan) with 90000 losses of lives, half a million injured and eleven million homeless. That happened just three months ago the much anticipated Olympics in Beijing in August. That also showed China's maturity in handling its own problems and carrying on with other responsibilities and commitments. While we saw the rise of responsibilities, we also saw the economic destruction of Zimbabwe-the consequence of greed, power grabbing and total callousness to its own people. We just pray that there is a more powerful U.N that can do more to help the helpless and redress torture and suffering of the innocent. So adieu 2008 – welcome 2009.

***

Shame Game (1-16-2009)

I was piqued by the bizarre incident of an Arab journalist throwing his shoes at George Bush last month. Then I thought why did that Arab journalist do it? To achieve what? Was it draw attention to himself by a heroic action in limelight? Or to make Bush feel ashamed really? I don't think any of that happened. But I shall come to that a little later. It was definitely a shame game and the Arab journalist was a shame showman.

Since my blog is topical that is related to current happening or thought, I cannot refrain from stating my happy feeling about the miraculous save of lives by a courageous pilot on the Hudson River in New York. We always hear the tragic news of loss of lives by a suicide bomber or due to some natural calamities–so this was very heartwarming. It was another routine domestic flight by US Air (carrying around one hundred and fifty passengers) that conflicted with the flight path of the seagulls on the river. It was like any land traffic accident at an intersection–say between stray dogs and a speeding automobile. Only difference for a land based accident is where the paramedics, fire engines and other helps are immediately forthcoming. Also the car could probably apply the brake or honk to scare the dogs. But for an airborne aircraft no such safeguard or immediate help is available. Any air collision between two flying objects is instantaneous downfall and consequent death. Apparently the birds have no brain (like the idiom 'birdbrain') and as such are stupid, and cannot learn the ways of safe traffic crossing. So the onus is on the pilot to avoid any air accident. But when it happens, then what you do? You are doomed. But not so in this case, so many lives were saved by the stoic professional handling of the situation by an experienced pilot and an extremely cool and decent person. I cannot but praise and thank God for giving us such a decent and capable person-he is pilot 'Sully' Sullenberger of Danville, California.

Coming back to the shoe-throwing incident, last month President Bush was on a stealth visit to Iraq to say farewell to the Iraqi people, whom he liberated from Saddam Hussein's satanic regime. Since he had toiled so hard for the last five years to transform the look of the Middle East, he definitely did not want to walk away silently. So he went there to praise his own achievement and say goodbye to the Iraqi people at the end of the term of his Presidency. But lo and behold instead of thunderous claps he got a pair of worn shoes thrown at him! It was shown on the media many times. It showed a defense-offense contest between an athletic Bush and a 'un- athletic' journalist. The Arab world is in frenzy about the video of shoe-throwing game, and one Egyptian billionaire bought the shoe for a hefty six figure sum as the shoe had become a celebrity there! The President was very agile and had a very sharp eye. Even while the shoe whizzed by him, he determined it was a size ten shoe. It was a shameful behavior by an invited journalist, but I don't think he inflicted any shame on the president. So what was it – which an Arab thought a shameful act and an American did not think so?

What is Shame really - who knows? I know it is a difficult subject and so subjective - but I shall see what I think of it. I know people over the world live in two different cultures - 'Shame Culture' and 'Guilt Culture'. Basically Shame culture is practiced in Eastern Hemisphere, and Guilt culture is more so in Western Hemisphere. Both are really devices for maintaining social norm. I was born in India in a Shame culture. Over there the elders inculcate a feeling of shame (for any kind of deficiency) to the children as they grow up. The traditional approach to stop a child from misbehaving is to remind the child that his misbehavior will be disapproved by others and nobody would like him. Since disliking by others is same as social ostracism, the threat of a friendless and joyless future of the child would be adequate from misbehaving. Thus the child growing up will more likely be a shy person as he is discouraged from doing anything different that will be criticized. It is not like a guilty feeling where you think that you may have done something wrong to others. Shame is more about doing wrong to yourself, failing the norm test of society or peers. It may be a good and working device, but then it stunts the child from experimenting and being independent and daring. Thus it creates a culture of subservience, where obedience to others is inculcated in the system and wired in the brain from childhood. Of course there will be people who won't abide by the norm – but they cannot be in majority. Thus a Shame society would not be producing daring out-of-the-box thinkers. The Western society possibly gained ground by not following the Shame culture.

The Shame culture is more prevalent among the Japanese, Chinese, Indians and the Arabs. The Japanese cultivated the feeling of shame to a higher level – where any defeat or subjugation would subject them to shame. Thus they would be failing to themselves – they don't care what others think really. I have read that some Japanese business men committed suicide as they brought shame to themselves by failing to others' expectations. Many Japanese students commit suicide when they don't do well academically. Thus the Shame feeling may be powerful. I think the Islamic people use this Shame feeling to create suicide-bombers who are inculcated in the feeling of shame about their inferior status to western powers. They also use that widely to subjugate their women folks. If some woman is accused of infidelity, she is pelted with stones by others – supposedly to bring shame (Lajja) to themselves.

The western culture puts more emphasis on guilt, less on shame. Thus to the western mind there is no shameful behavior, but only illegal behavior. If somebody admits guilt (that is, shows obedience to the societal norm of feeling guilty), then the punishment is diminished. Thus nudity is a shameful behavior in east, and not so at all in west. Only thing to be judged is whether that broke any law. Thus every concept of morality, family responsibility and respect to parents – the norms are set by law, not by peers. The judges rule as the final custodian of defining a proper behavior. All one has to do is to prove or disprove one's guilt to be accepted in the society – thus societal issues become judicial contests in the court of law, where the society is a silent spectator. As such broadly speaking the west has less working feeling of shame – but mostly a standard for guilt.

Now I see why the Arab journalist thought he had shown his ultimate disapproval of Bush by his missile shoes. But did it really have the same shame effect on Bush? I don't know, but what I saw was that the commentators took it as an extremely inappropriate or improper behavior. In Muslim society probably that shoe would have caused another war between the offense and defense. No more on this, but now I seem to see what was that really about.

Crowning of Obama *(1-23-2009)*

This week (January 20) the country celebrated the coronation of Obama. Most of the world also joined the celebration. It was probably a seminal moment in US racial history amidst a crucial time of world crisis. It was very clear that US was losing popularity abroad and at the same time failing at home. The incumbent administration seemed to have no clue what to do and what to say, the future of US and the world looked bleak. When it looked like the future is lost, at that time US rose again and reinvented herself in the form of Obama, took on a fresh face, sounded very different and declared its determination and commitment loud and clear. The odds are formidable - but it seemed we have not yet run out of hope and zeal. So everybody was really looking forward to Obama's inaugural speech. Actually inaugural speech is more than a stump speech; it is a mission statement of the administration. It is an oath of missionary zeal to confront the demon in front and bring it under control.

I was saddened to see that many readers in writing letters to Editor (in newspapers) commented that it was a vapid speech and the spark of Obama oratory was lacking. I did not think so. That's why I thought I express my thoughts also. One must not forget what one is talking about, about whom and when. The speech during campaign has to have some substance (but need not be conclusive). Basically the campaign tone has to show confidence, capability and grasp of the issues. It has to inspire, appeal to voter's emotion and point out the stark difference between contestants. One has to be very methodical and logical, dissecting past failures and doing post-mortem analysis. So what we had seen Obama so far was in that campaign mode that inspired the voters to choose him as more competent among the candidates to meet the challenges of our time. But now it is a new role. Now he has been given the crown with responsibility for action. So it has to be more cautious; he also has to close the sore wound of the losers and not lose credibility, build up friendships and has to raise high hopes with regard to reality. That is why we saw President Obama more restrained than candidate Obama. But that is not the only point I wanted to make.

I also read Kennedy's inaugural speech. It was so inspiring, so flying and so grandiose oratory written by very gifted pens. But the basic issues he was referring to was not that complex. The nation was in good health. He declared determination to face Russian challenges in cold war, declared commitment of a new generation to scale new heights and embrace new challenges. It was a mesmerizing oratory from a new leader of a new generation, whom he exhorted to lend a helping hand to the undeveloped and underdeveloped world. Peace with friendship, progress with empathy. The moral tone was set.

Obama's inaugural speech has gone much deeper than that. He, not only, has declared his intent to meet the challenges of supremacy and benevolent leadership, but he also has to rebuild a broken diffident nation, fix an economy in disarray, and inspire a nation suffering in silent agony. The compass of morality has been shifted by greed and corruption of its own leaders. He saw a failure of the inner man in the failure of the administration, failure of the present. So it is obvious that current tools need be changed and sharpened, thinking has to be modified and the sapping zeal needs to be bolstered. So it is much more than a President's political speech of a new administration. It is also a nation-building appeal, an appeal to reform of the inner man, to set the moral compass using guidance of history and adhering to philosophy of the founding fathers. Such an arduous speech can hardly be called vapid by any standard.

The task of building a nation, task of reforming the inner man in disarray is not a political task - it is a nation building task. As far as I know only Gandhi had combined political leadership with nation-building leadership. Throughout the ages when man failed, he reorganized and reformed himself and rose back again. The strength of a nation is not confined to a few, nor can it be dictated by a few in the high post of an administration. When the inner man fails, the society he built fails- the successes he achieved falters, and if the ills are not addressed the system turns into a shamble. That is why it is very important that a true leader just does not address a few changes in policy – that can only go so far. The strength of any nation comes from its own people. The American people are still vibrant and valiant – so failure cannot be their fate. Success has to come – but just one has to reform internally so that the inner man can rise to his full potential.

Basically America was failing not because of its people, but because of the leadership. Economy is a mess, but economy is an engine of progress invented by man himself. It is not a natural calamity or an explosion of a distant star. The economy that was functioning so well for so long – how can it get wrong all on a sudden in the span of a few years? The system cannot be bad, but the people running that had been corrupt and negligent. They just cared to enrich themselves – forgetting that they are a part of a much bigger whole. Their survival needs sustenance from others. Thus when a so-called 'smart' business leader (without having the requisite competence) acquires other companies and then sacks thousands to show profit is not only disgustingly selfish, but it is also highly immoral. Tears of the fallen thousands or millions cannot bless the predator - the predators along with its preys are bound to fall. That was what happened. The greed and complacency grew sky high, overlooked and sometimes blessed by an incompetent, short-sighted leader- that was eating away the nation's bone marrow. So the task of reform is not only political, but on it depends our survival also. When Obama was talking about 'change' he was talking about reforming the inner man. But you cannot say that bluntly and win votes. So you couch the message in a much sweeter term – that was his campaign theme of 'change'. This he cannot do it by himself, those who have done the wrongs must also reform themselves.

Thus Obama addresses the nation '...Our challenges may be new. The instruments with which we meet them may be new. But those values upon which our success depends – honesty and hard work, courage and fair play, tolerance and curiosity, loyalty and patriotism – these things are old. These things are true. They have been the quiet force of progress throughout our history ...' When I heard the speech, it seemed it transcended politics and the mundane; it appealed to reform the inner man. So it was a great inaugural address to me. ... So much on this.

***

I

Story of an Immigrant III *(1-30-2009)*

I am neither a writer nor an artist with any skill to paint any portrait. I am curious when an artist starts to draw a figure where does he start? Is it the face, leg or what? Is dress more important than face? I guess nobody expects any accuracy from the artist. His job is just to bring out the essence. That just shows how clueless I am. But let me go back to 'Story of an Immigrant II' where I stopped when she arrived in US and had her first meal in US. Probably politeness or sheer tiredness was behind her lack of appreciation for the chicken curry! One reader commented that my chicken curry was for the soul (not for the taste buds). Probably that is true – when our taste bud does not make comment. the soul gratefully accepts it. That is also because the soul is formless and has no taste bud.

When she arrived in Los Angeles it was very tough, a major factor being loneliness. Where was the glamour of high standard of western living; where was the affluence that Hollywood portrayed on the silver screen? The entire apartment had – well nothing almost. A few utensils in the kitchen, a lounge chair and a small 15" black and white TV. It was no fault of her husband, as he did not want to make any purchase before she arrived here. They used to sleep on the floor over bedding. The western style of lighting does not depend on any ceiling light that lightens up the whole room. Area lamps lighten a designated area only. Probably it is a culture of privacy that does not want to light up everything. So they had to buy a few standing lamps as soon as possible. Later on when they reminisced about how they started their life in the states, they never forgot to mention that they had nothing in the beginning. When they made some friends that became a support group for the culturally uprooted `lonelies'– an oasis in a foreign land of non-acquaintances. The story of zero beginning was not wholly untrue, but somehow when they met – they all used to share their story of loneliness and sought some kind of acknowledgement and solace in their stories of pathetic zero beginning.

Well one has to understand the time period of the sixties. It was not like what it is now. At that time only foreigners US allowed to immigrate were who had professional qualifications. The whole idea of the hospitality was to enhance the pool of qualified professionals. Also US had just abandoned the practice of allowing only the immigrants from Europe to come here. At that time they revised the immigration policy that was earlier confined to a few limited countries and was replaced by selection based on professional qualifications. As such prior to the seventies the color of America was mainly black (African-American) and white (European-American). The attitudes were European also. Europeans were still colonial powers and maintained their colonial air of stiff superiority by isolating themselves from people of other colors. Discrimination was not open, but discreet. In census, Indians were counted as Caucasians (now it is much more detailed, and Indians are South Asians, not Caucasians). But the general public did not look at Indians the same way they looked at the blacks. Indians were more or less treated as foreigners. So at that time yes USA was an isolated nation, not a nation of many colors. Blacks were treated badly – many Indians who did not look fair were also treated as blacks.

Sixties was an age of transition for US. The Vietnam War and its agony had the whole younger generation in rebellion. The campuses were on fire. Young people were being drafted to serve the country and asked to bear arms against enemies in a far away land. Her husband also had to enroll in Selective Service as a prerequisite to permanent residency status (i.e. a sort of citizenship in waiting). Luckily he just turned 26 at that time that elevated his selective service classification to type V and that made him exempt from battle field duties. He had contemplated to move to Canada, but had taken some potential risk of being drafted to stay in US till the age of exemption Young President Kennedy had come up with a new voice and a new message, declared peace abroad with friendship for all, inspired US youths to be benevolent ambassadors and be beacons of progress and cooperation to the undeveloped and backward countries. Martin Luther King had his famous dream speech that inspired the young generation and challenged the artificial barrier of color. In other words – it was the dawn of the Age of Aquarius. The term was contained in a popular song at that time by Fifth Dimension (?). So it was not really a peaceful time as such.

The general public had very little or no idea and knowledge of India. They had heard about Gandhi. Some looked at him as a noble man and many looked at him as a leader of the poor. They wondered how come Indians did not eat beef. Many people thought the reason being that meat was costly and Indians were vegetarians as they had little money to eat beef. Indian women were not used to wearing western clothes and used to stick to their dress of saris. (So in any party the Indian woman would attract many curious stares, and `how wonderful the dress' was a staple and stale conversation piece.) From America's angle Indian people were more viewed with curiosity than by anything else. At that time the jeans were not in fashion and even western girls who wore that kind of dress were strongly disapproved by others. I don't think the shorts and bikinis were much in vogue at that time. Hollywood films about India (like Gungadins, Distant Pavilion) were mostly from British colonial angle, though it must be said that British had accepted the fact that they had left India but still had a fondness for India and the Indians. The image that Americans had of India was of an exotic land of exotic people, a land of snake charmers, elephants and swamis. The Beatles had come on world stage, and somehow heralded a different melody and a different attitude of a new generation. Maharishi Mahesh Yogi had become their gurus; Ravi Shankar was their sitar guru and some other lesser guru figures like Guru Rajneesh were also popular. Yoga and Tajmahal (as a tourist attraction) were iconic symbols of India. Hare Krishna movement had reached America – the cult of free love had become popular. American youths disillusioned by war resorted to uninhibited love and shifted their attention to alternate pleasure through LSD and other psychedelic drugs. It was an age of turmoil. America was restless.

Going back to Story of an Immigrant, she saw all this in fragments. Her mind and soul was in India though her physical address was US. The letters that she got from India were wafts of fresh air. She would read the letters again and again. They were her companions of loneliness. Most of the times many people don't understand the importance of letters – but letters are really transcendental forms of communication, an embrace between the parties, a stretching of hands to connect, a bridge between past and now. Her parents used to write her almost every week. She also wrote them. They were so dear, but so far. International phone calls were not easy to make. She would treasure each letter and read them again and again. She would also look out of the window to see when the mail man was coming. The mail man would put the letters in a locked mail box – she was afraid to go out alone downstairs. Her husband would return from work after five. ... I also noticed that isolation and loneliness have been stressed so far in this writing. But there was also another side. Adventure side I shall come back to it later.

**

Unconstitutional Oath (2-13-2009)

L ast week there was no blog as I did not get any time. It usually takes about three to four hours of uninterrupted time and concentration. Another problem is to figure out

what to write about. Picking up and deciding on a topic is very hard sometimes though it may sound simple. Sometimes I wonder what is the essential difference between talking and writing. Talking is mostly about things that matter to us right now or for some other time in future. But the purpose of writing is something else. Talking has a brief span of life, whereas writing is supposed to have a longer life span. We write down things so that we remember and recollect in future. So I picked up a topic this time that lasted a little time but that will last for a long time in our memory. That topic is what we witnessed during the presidential oath ceremony on January 20.

Chief Justice John Roberts was saying something wrong in the wording of the oath! The constitutional oath was 'I solemnly swear that I will faithfully execute the office of president'. Instead Justice Roberts dictated to Obama to take the oath as 'I solemnly swear that I will execute the office of president faithfully'. The mistake was probably minor – a grammar teacher would have subtracted one point only. But Obama was aware that his opponents may bring that up in the future saying that oath was unconstitutional and retook the oath as worded by the Constitution. Justice Roberts' oath was not unconstitutional but the wording of the oath was unconstitutional. Actually what Justice Roberts said was more correct grammatically. But who was he to judge the grammar of the oath as worded in the constitution? It was not his courtroom that he could give a judgment! Also even in the Supreme Court ruling no judgment is given by one person, but by a collective majority opinion of a panel of Justices. Suppose the President wants to live in a yellow house – not the White House (which is a President's official residence). There is nothing wrong there as everybody has freedom to choose where one wants to live. For that matter where does Chief Justice Roberts go to give his judgment – the Supreme Court or any other place of his convenience? See there is a tradition that may be right or wrong – but you need to follow that. Tradition is what brings uniformity and what has been accepted by time. There is nothing to judge – whether that sentence is right or wrong. It is a traditional oath as solemnized by usage by earlier generations. Seldom do we get a chance to judge or criticize a Judge, but this time we got a chance and nobody should mind if I use that slip to lecture a judge (who is not any ordinary mortal).

One thing is funny – before the oath Obama was not the President so he had to abide by whatever Justice Roberts dictated. Though Obama knew it was a mistake he did not correct him or took the words of the oath as prescribed in the constitution. It was obvious in his chuckle while taking the oath. (Read – I know you made a mistake your honor, but I won't embarrass you by correcting you while the whole nation and the world are watching.) But after the oath he became the President so he ordered Justice Roberts next day to dictate the oath correctly. (Some body commented that Obama did not vote for Judge Roberts during Senate confirmation hearing and Roberts did not vote for Obama during the election). Now I did not see Jay Leno or other late night comics to make fun of Justice Roberts. Nobody makes fun of a Judge – who knows when one is going to land in his court. Once I tried to argue with a traffic judge that the traffic violation I committed was beyond my control – he doubled my fine for even trying to argue with him. Since then I never tried to argue or criticize a judge whether in court or off court. Similar prudence we all apply to police officers and IRS agents. You don't joke with them or make fun of them – God knows what that will lead to. If you try to share a joke with a Police officer – you may be in trouble. Nobody is supposed to question a Judge or Police officer while they are on duty. Suppose that guffaw was committed by President Bush then the whole population would have jumped on him – ridiculing his knowledge of English, tradition and what not. Another thing to note is that public speaking or talking under the glare is not an easy job – though the politicians may make it look easy. Another advice I am tempted to give is that everybody should rehearse before performing. That is what everybody does even in the school. I said all this in fun – seldom do we get a chance to lecture on such a solemn subject! Since I got the chance – I could not restrain myself! Hope nobody minds.

But what was the fuss about? It was about the grammatical rule (or advice) never to split a verb. An adverb is an add-on to a verb and should take its place after the verb is expressed. Though in case of adjective it should precede the noun it is associated with. So, English language has different rules for nouns and verbs. The controversy over split-verbs is raging over a long time. Though the grammarians want to prescribe the position of all elements of any sentence in order – poets and orators don't follow that rule. Though it is understood that without a set of rules the whole language will fall into pieces and all the elements will have anarchical whims – still in common conversations we alter the structure for emphasis. Also as usage becomes more common (even though inconsistent with rules of grammar) the deviation becomes more popular and is accepted as idiomatic. I know the noun should start a sentence and a verb should finish it in the end – but I myself would not worry too much about whether the adverb is ahead of a verb and whether it is splitting any verb. Thus a song lyric that became famous as 'I will always love you' – probably would not have been as catchy as 'I will love you always'. The things that we can learn from this incident are – rehearse and perform; popular usage takes precedence over rules; respect the tradition. Was it too serious? No, but it was fun to talk on this issue.

***

Plight of an Octumom *(2-20-2009)*

I was debating whether I should write on this topic. This is a very current thing going on – but it is bizarre and somewhat twisted.

I thought while this news is current, probably I should memorialize it in the blog so that it is not lost from memory in time. Incidentally and it seems very bizarre that as the new Obama era started, lot of phony people with their mischievous accomplishments are being exposed. I am referring to Berney Madoff scandal (a looting scandal of 50 billion dollars) – a multi-billionaire with a` Ponzi' scheme ripped of so many people and these people are no ordinary people! They run mammoth pension funds, institutional funds. They are rich themselves, just the greed of making more money snared them into this trap. I always thought that the rich have resources and they are more diligent in keeping and managing their money. Same thing happened with 'Sanford' scandal - another tycoon (and a cricket promoter) with a false financial facade. And in this case also the rich also had laid their guards down when they played golf together and drank together. Also we are now waging not only a war on terror but also a war on our survival. All the people who contributed to the financial meltdown (that has all the country and world gasping for oxygen) were basically people with no morals but were in positions of great power. It seems all these years the bad and unscrupulous were having a great party while the nation was sinking in deep trouble. Was it like Nero playing his fiddle while Rome was burning? What was game to them brought on total ruin to many of us? I just hope more evils are exposed and the nation cleanses itself of all the evils that were having a mayhem unnoticed, unpunished and unbothered.

The term 'Octumom' is a new term that will probably go into the new English dictionary. It refers to the mother who gave birth to an octuplet (six boys and two girls) last month in a local hospital in Southern California. When the news came out – the doctors (neonatalist- doctors specializing in delivering immature and not properly formed babies) were all beaming ear to ear and rightly so as that was a splendid accomplishment. They thought they were delivering seven babies but there was one more unnoticed between the seven. For most of the multiple births that the world has witnessed – mostly all the delivered babies did not survive. Actually Guinness Book of Records indicates that the record belongs to an Australian woman, who gave birth to nine children in 1971. (But two were still born.) Another Nigerian woman in US gave birth to living octuplet in 1998 (one of the girls died a week later). Among the cases of surviving septuplets are the McCaugheys born in 1998 in Iowa. They are ten years old now and they had a big birthday bash for the team recently.

Actually the news of babies are always very refreshing news. Babies are the continuation of human race – what is there to frown on? But in this particular case about seventy percent people surveyed had very negative emotion on this mom (whom New York Post dubbed as *'octumom'*). Why? Because the eight babies were not accidents or freaks of nature thrust on the unsuspecting mother. It was done by planning and in consultation with Fertility Specialists and by 'In-vitro fertilization'. It is not like other normal births where there is a father and a mother, and their happy union in love culminating in new lives. These children have no father – only some male sperm that is standing for father. In modern time raising even one child properly needs so much care and so much planning, and is mostly an expensive proposition. Most people are happy with two or three. As more than that is mostly out of financial and physical capacities of an average family. This woman has no job and has already six more at home. So she must be a psycho, it is not craving for motherhood or anything else of that noble nature. She does not have lot of money to take care of even one; she cannot physically attend to the needs of her children. So what is she? Is she a psycho or a case of planning gone wild?

In this particular case the mother already had six children (born twins and triplets). She was unemployed. But she had her face done like a famous Hollywood actress (Angelina Jolie) who loves babies and adopts many. Then she had consulted with fertility specialists and persuaded one dubious practitioner. Now we came to know that medicine has made great progress with fertility treatment. But the whole idea of fertility treatment is to help out women who failed to have babies on their own. The whole purpose of medicine is to help mankind, not to abuse. It is so innate and fundamental concept that no Board of Regulations cared to set up any guideline on the use and abuse of the fertility drugs. Now if a general practitioner prescribes medicine that hastens death will be quite contrary to the principle and purpose of medicine. Then also there is the issue of how many child one can have. I was listening on CNN to an interview with a couple in Iowa who were raising eighteen children. They know it is hard, but they did not ask for any state handout or public mercy. But this lady even before the birth of octuplets was on state handout for three of her current children. Now what was she possibly thinking? That the generous state will take over and provide whatever needs the babies had and she will glow in media limelight as an exceptional supermom!

So it must be a strange mentality. She is of Arab background. And she knew that if her name is flashed on the front page of newspapers – she would be a famous and marketable commodity. She would get book deal, TV deal, ad deal and she would be a celebrity with an easy life. But nobody seems pleased with her manipulation of the system. I had read a memoir of a foreign lady in Afghanistan. Living amidst them she was disgusted with the parental mentality there. They don't care how many children they have – more the better. At the age of two they let out the kids to the outside world – where they usually get gritty and learn hardship of life. In a civilized society the children are the future of a nation, who need be raised properly so that the fate of the nation can be passed on to future responsible hands. Otherwise the kids will be like animals in the jungle. The society cannot ignore them or reject them. Society has to bear the cost for their welfare. In this case the general public seems to be mad at her for her wanton behavior of adding to the burden of society.

Now in many European countries they reward and provide financial help when one has more than two babies. Two babies are breakeven, that will substitute the death of the parents. So that does not help population growth. In Russia they called mothers of many babies as heroes of the nation. So Nadia seems to have played this trick in a wrong place at a wrong time. Though her action proves that there was a meticulous planning on her part, it seems her planning has gone wild. Mothers are caretakers of the babies and raise their children as best as they can. But Octumom seems to be a mere baby-producer– an opposite persona of a loving mother. Probably she should seek asylum in countries that want to increase their population. There they can make her the chief contributor of a baby factory.

Story of an Immigrant IV *(2-27-2009)*

Last month when I wrote about Story of an Immigrant III, it was mostly about the turmoil that the younger generation was going through at that time in the shadow of the Vietnam War. Though it was a tumultuous period – it also heralded a new attitude of a new generation that wanted to live in peace and love. That I detailed before, as it was the decade of transformation for US as I see now. Whether we accept or deny it, the fact remains that we are all products of history and geography. Geography dictates our living habits. History dictates our genre of activities and mental attitudes. I also heard some suggestions that as the sequences were written a few weeks apart it somewhat lose its coherence. That is true, but blog is also not just a memoir. It is more like capturing thoughts and events that impact our mind and steer our personal lives, our national lives and our destinies. That also cannot be neglected. So I shall try to balance the two.

As I was narrating - her loneliness was crushing. But slowly she got acquainted with her apartment neighbors. The first one that I remember most was Mrs. Anderson. She was a lady in her late seventies. Mrs. A felt her loneliness and spent lot of time talking with her. Mrs. A used to talk about herself and her family, about life in America and

American thinking. She told her that Americans liked privacy and freedom. The kids mostly leave their parents when eighteen and start building their own lives and own families (after they have done their duties of raising their children). Parents also don't interfere in their kids' lives. Everybody wants to spend lives as one wants, and that is the basic pleasure of freedom that one cherishes in life. The children don't want to be shadowed by their parents and the parents also want to recapture the freedom lost. This kind of relationship does not need constant mingling but encourages more limited contacts.

That was a cultural shock. She herself came from a large family. In that family there was no I, but all we. She is used to say they are ten sisters (actually that includes her own one and rest are other cousin sisters).Anything she had done at home or in college would be subject to scrutiny leading to either praise or censure. As if everything was to be judged, juried and decreed on, and then broadcast around. Another thing also bothered her–that when someone in the family did anything good on anything, the bar to merit praise would go higher up instantly. It is not that the critics themselves met or exceeded that bar, but they would start to judge others by that new standard. She herself was kind of a private person and did not want this kind of constant comparison and evaluation. She also felt that her mother and aunts (when they moved to the new household of their husbands) sacrificed their own freedom with smile. She never thought whether that was right or wrong – but it was the system. So the right thing to do was just get along with it. She herself did not have any buffered personal space when growing, and she was not sure whether the new freedom in the new country was a curse or a boon. Though she grew with many in joy – she had no freedom to do much anything on her own.

Another neighbor she met was Mrs. Johnson (I forgot her real name). Mrs. J lived with her husband and a monkey pet. She had never before seen that people can live with a monkey or any animal at all. But she found out that Mrs. J loved that monkey as much as her own child. It was not just having a pet - but they would spend much time entertaining, nourishing and taking care of their pets in sickness also. Also in the pet store they visited – the stores seemed to cater to all kinds of pets besides dogs and cats (like birds, snakes, dragons, crickets and many kinds of reptiles that one would shudder at). But she was never comfortable with any pet - so she did not get too close with Mrs. J.

Another neighbor that she and her husband got friendly with was Mr. Cohen. He was a bachelor in his forties – very open, jovial and talkative. He was living by himself, but always had lady companions on the weekends. Mr. C also told them that marrying a woman and getting shackled rest of the life was not his cup of tea. She never knew before that anybody could cherish such kind of loneliness and interpret that as freedom. She had found that in India people get less lonely as they grow older. From two – the family expands to four and then to eight. She always thought that Family was like a tree – it always grows more and more with people as time goes by. She used to think that was probably the way of the world. But in America she got another cultural shock, where the family never grows beyond two.

Another neighbor she got friendly with was a young housewife named Sally. Sally said she was Italian and asked her where she was from. When she replied that she was from India - Sally asked her where it was. She used to think that India was a big and old country (and full of so many well known great men) and everybody in the world knew where India was. Most of the other people she met always admired India as a country because it had Mount Everest and Tajmahal. Many of them said that during the Second World War they were deployed in combat mission in the eastern theater (meaning Asia) and they were briefly stationed in Calcutta. Also they always said that they wanted to see Tajmahal at least once as it was the most glorious romantic structure in the world. Later on she found out that not all Americans knew much geography beyond their small boundaries. She thought that was in contrast to the most Indians she knew – who seemed to know so much about the larger world, and seemed so interested in all things they had not seen.

Another neighbor was the landlord Mr. Haines. Mr. H was in his sixties – lived with his dog. The dog was his constant companion. He would read the newspaper and that dog would lie at his feet. Mr. H would go out for a walk that dog also would go with him. Mr. H would go to the stores, parks and everywhere- that dog would always go with him, as if the dog was his bosom buddy. She never knew any animal could be so devoted to one person even though they don't share the same language. The dog alone had a full shelf of different kinds of foods (just like another human being!). She and her husband had to go to his apartment on the first day of each month to pay the rent. Mr. H was a very friendly person and led a much disciplined life.

Another surprising couple they met by chance was Dr. and Mrs. Griffith. They were Methodists. Dr. and Mrs. Griffith were very learned people. Dr. Griffith was an outside examiner of the doctoral thesis in Calcutta University. Mrs. Griffith had Masters in Education. They were principals of

Missionary Schools in Calcutta. They had stayed in Calcutta for forty years on a mission from their church. Dr. and Mrs. G got married in a village in India and had their honeymoon in Hooghly (a place they had not visited before). Dr. Griffith had written a few poetry books and gave them one of the books. The poems were wonderful – kind of romantic about nature, love and other finer aspects of human lives. They could speak broken Bengali and would always speak with them in broken Bengali when they were invited to the Griffith residence for dinner. Jokingly Dr. G called their own residence as the Elephant house (because they had collected all kinds of miniature elephant replicas from India and decorated their house with same). Mrs. G was a very grandma like person. Mrs. Griffith used to recollect their experiences in India. She said that when she went to India she was very young and she used to look down on many Indian customs. But as days went on she gradually came to understand and appreciate the beauty and the wisdom of the Indian customs. One example was the manner in which the younger ones greet their parents or other respected elders. Instead of shaking their hands – they touch the elders' feet in reverence and intimacy. At an older age she appreciated the beauty of that manner of greeting – it was so humble, so respectful yet so personal.

But in India she was not used to stay at home and do nothing. Before marriage she used to be a teacher in a Girl's High school. That also she gave up under pressure when she got married in India. But the problem is now what to do with the huge idle time during day? She could not go out, did not know many people except some acquaintances. Probably she would learn to drive, but that would also take some time and one needed to know the places around. At first she thought she would get a translator's job in Berlitz School of Languages. She went there, but they said there was no job for Bengali translation, but would call her when such needs occurred. I think over a three month period there was only a small translation job which also did not mean much.

Then she conferred with her husband and they agreed that a receptionist job might be much easier to obtain. She traveled by buses to some offices with her resume- but they all said that a receptionist had to have some typing skill. So she joined a typing school. She learned some typing and her speed rose to 40 (something like that). Armed with her new skill she again started to look for a receptionist job. Still there was no luck. Finally one office was frank with her and told her for a receptionist's job they preferred locals not foreigners as there was the accent issue. She had accents and she might not understand others' accents. So back to square one. What to do with the time? All her education, degrees and accomplishments did not mean anything in a foreign land.

Anyway, gradually they met more people and she got used to that loneliness. When they went t o downtown fish market, they would meet other Bengali couples and they would become instant close friends. Also the foods in the Restaurant (there were almost no Indian Restaurants) were not what they liked or loved. But they consoled themselves that when in Rome do what the Romans do. The groceries and *masallas* (Indian condiments) she needed for cooking were available only in one Armenian grocery store in Hollywood. They loved goat meat. Luckily there were some ranches not far and some ranch-owners tended herds of goats. They used to go there occasionally. The owner would show his dog which one we liked, the dog would run after that goat and bring it to the owner. The owner would cut and dress the meat and give that to them. Then they would share that large amount of meat with other young Bengali couples, they had become friends with.

Occasionally there would be visitors from India. They would take them around, show them different tourist attractions. The prime attractions were Disneyland, Universal Studio, Lion Country Safari, Marineland, Alligator Farm, Deer Park, SeaWorld, Busch Garden and many other smaller attractions. They used to think that every visitor must be shown Disneyland because that was unlike anything they had seen anywhere. Los Angeles was a growing metropolis and it was extending all around with new developments and suburban facilities.

 Gradually she got used to her life without a daily job. Of course there were things to do at home, read letters from India many times, take care of household chores, cooking etc and she would eagerly wait for weekend. Though she was a journeyman cook, but somehow they liked whatever she cooked. Her husband had been a student, lived alone for three years, and rarely had decent meals, so it did not take much to please his palate. Her husband had confided that canned chili bean soup with heap of crushed crackers was his staple dinner menu. As soon as her husband would come home after work, they would plan what to do etc. If nothing to do – then at least there was Thrifty's Baskin Robins (31 unbelievable flavors) and there were drive-in theaters. Drive-in Theaters were novelties –on Fridays they would drive the car to a huge field where people would park their cars at microphone stands of their choice and watched the movie on a huge screen. They would buy popcorns and hotdogs while watching the movie and return home after midnight. Next two days they would go to sightseeing around town. Even driving around was fun. Freeways were not crowded. People would measure distances in minutes (that is how much freeway time it takes to commute). Then there was the Pacific Ocean with beautiful beaches. The mountains were nearby. Las Vegas was not that far. So gradually she got used to the new world and its attractions. This is getting long, I shall comeback later.

***

Tucson Trip *(3-13-2009)*

Last week there was no blog as we went to Tucson (Arizona) to attend the wedding of the daughter of an old friend of ours. We were very excited when we got the invitation card to attend the marriage. Sadly our friend had passed away in Alabama while teaching in Auburn University some time ago. We could not attend his funeral and a guilt feeling bugged us all the time. His wife (an awesome cook and a mathematics doctorate) was also a dear friend of us and we have seen their daughter grow up from her infancy. Now she is a mature woman, an MD and practicing child psychiatry. They had moved to Alabama in late seventies when our friend got a teaching position in Auburn University. So many memories we have of them – we looked forward to meet them again in such a joyous occasion. We were really happy. Also we had never gone to Arizona though it is an adjacent state of California. So it was an opportunity to settle with our guilt also.

We had our tickets (South West Airlines) and hotel (through Hotels.com) arranged. We chose an accommodation that would be close to the wedding venue. The wedding was to take place in a luxury resort in the northeast corner of the town. We got a last minute request from the bride's mother to get the marriage garlands (two - to be used in the garland exchange ceremony during the Hindu marriage rituals) from Los Angeles – as there was a last minute snafu in that regard. We were excited to play such an important role also. We had the garlands made of carnation flowers by an Indian wedding specialist lady. Apart from the worry as to how to keep the flowers fresh during the journey, we were also worried that the security people might give us hard time if we carried that as a carry-on in the plane. But the Airlines people assured us no problem – as lot of people take bouquet on planes. (I just wondered why I did not think of that!).

I don't get much chance to travel by South West, but it is a very popular commuter airline with 3200 daily flights in the continental US. They have two lines in the ticket counter – one 'experienced' meaning someone who always travel by South West and others 'casual' – we being that kind. They allow the passengers to board like a commuter bus. There is no seat assignment – but they assign boarding pass with designated queuing position during boarding. So the first assigned people get all the choice window seats. I had heard of all kinds of tricks the airlines play to make a few extra bucks. (Like charging additional money for sandwiches, soda, pillows etc). But South West ads proclaimed in their terminal they were a no-fee airline. Water and soda are free – but carbonated bottled water and beer would cost money. To impress their free hospitality they gave us a small packet of peanuts. I read their In-flight magazine that they distribute over 32 million packets of peanuts to their passengers per year! (Thus I was very happy that at least one airline did not want to raid our pockets for peanuts).

The flight to Phoenix was short and smooth. We had the rental car from Alamo. I was worried that Arizona (like California) might have the law that GPS could not be mounted on the front wind-shield. But luckily they did not care as long as the GPS did not obstruct the front view. Tucson is about 120 miles south east of Phoenix. It is near the southeast region of the state 25 miles from the Mexican border. I was surprised that there was no populated area between Phoenix and Tucson (except one very small town of Eloy). The highway did not offer any spectacular view. It was mostly desert – but not as barren as the desert in Nevada. It had tall cactus trees all over though. The trouble with GPS is that it directs you the shortest path without any knowledge of traffic closure. As it happened that all main eight exits to Tucson were closed for repair (I don't know if that was President Obama's stimulus package or what). So we had to take the help of locals for direction. But finally we arrived at the destination – 12 miles from the freeway.

Our friend had arranged for somebody to pick us up from our hotel. We went to their residence. It was the night before the marriage. They had lot of guests from India and from all over US. We knew a few of them only, and made acquaintance with the rest. It was a festive mood. They had *Mehendi* (a removable skin decoration ceremony- like temporary tattoos) and songs (which we missed). One of the essential features of any Indian marriage party is a noisy atmosphere with everybody talking and its associated noise. That is interpreted as the real atmosphere of the house of marriage. So any American who is used to organized non-chaotic silent gathering will be disappointed (but will be amused). We were very happy to meet the guests. The groom was from Houston and they had come to the marriage party in large numbers also. We were very happy to see so many happy relatives and friends were there to participate in the ceremony.

The next morning also we were invited. They had some *puja* (religious rituals by a priest) and '*Gaye- Halud*' ceremony, when the turmeric paste touched by the groom comes to the bride's house. Then the bride's parties smear that paste on the forehead of the bride and the married women smear each other's face with the turmeric paste. I don't know the meaning of the ritual – except that probably it was a fun-filled hazing initiation by the married for the newly to-be-married bride. Or may be, it was an indirect touch ceremony between the marriage partners who will be so close to each other in their life henceforth.

The wedding ceremony was to be at five pm at the resort. The area was a secluded area near the wilderness. The ceremony was supposed to start at five – but after every body's arrival and getting prepared for the priest - the ceremony started around six fifteen. The Sun was about to set – and darkness was about to set in. Being in partial wilderness – the place was primitively dark with dim outdoor lighting and was getting chilly. But the attendees braved that little chill and dimly lighted surroundings. All seemed to have a good time. The priest's chanting of ritual created an atmosphere of religious solemnity.

After that the reception took place in a banquet hall. About one hundred twenty people (friends and relatives) attended the reception. It was a good reception party with the DJ creating a festive atmosphere by playing popular tunes. The bride and groom cut cakes, and there was dance. But we did not stay that long as we had to return to Phoenix next day early morning. It was a brief trip, but was very enjoyable. We wished the newly married couple good time, happiness and prosperity, and parted the party. In short that was our Tucson trip.

***

Caaaar and King / Tejas *(3-20-2009)*

What is that Tejas? - A very soft prolonged endearing sound 'Caaaar'- comes out as his reply. When he gets up from sleep (am or pm) the first thing he would say is – caaar, caaar. What he is referring to is 'car' that he seems to love so much. He probably saw cars in his dream or maybe he wants his favorite toy – a car. He has numerous teeth that sparkle when he says something. His spoken vocabulary is limited now. So anything he likes – he may refer to as car. But he can understand what others are saying or referring to. When asked where moon is – he looks up in the sky. It does not matter whether it is day or night. When he cannot see the moon – he expresses disappointment and turns his both palms up indicating he could not find the moon. Thus you ask him about water or grass or tree or bird – he knows exactly what you are talking about. He is very attentive and in complete communication with you. Tejas is only fifteen months old. He is my grandson. All the different sounds are coming out of his mouth incessantly – mam mam mam, da da da, ga ga ga etc – a continuous flow of vowel-suffixed consonants.

He also acts like a king. His whole house is his play domain or kingdom. He has numerous toys that move, jump, run, giggle, sing – he knows the functions of each one of them. He knows the duty of the garbage can (i.e. to collect all unnecessary things). In his estimation most of the things probably are garbage. Once he is done playing with it, he then proceeds to the garbage can with whatever he has in his hand (to the dismay of nearby adults). When he enters a room – he straight goes to the waste paper baskets and turns them upside down. That happens to be the fate of all the waste paper baskets and all the chairs - anything and everything that he is able to dislodge or turn upside down. Before he comes to our house (Dadai and Namma's house) we make sure that the waste paper baskets have real good clean papers because we know he will flip them all upside down. It is not that he is looking for something or he is disappointed - he thinks they are all his subordinates and must lie at his feet, because he is the king.

He also thinks all remotes (of TV or anything else) are his exclusive properties and subject to his handling. He will straight go to the remote basket and take two remotes in his hand. He uses them as phone also. He always has one remote near one of his ears and another one in right hand. His Namma (grandma) kept a few old discarded phones so that Tejas can walk with those in his hand (and spare the real phones from his ruthless treatment). He has an uncanny sense of which one is real and which one is not working. He will press the buttons on the phone receiver console and listen to all messages. Some buttons say 'no messages'; some buttons say 'please hang up and try again' and some buttons emit peep peep signals. He listens to all and then goes to his next thing of interest. One day in the early morning (he gets up at 5:30 am most days as he thinks sleeping is a waste of time) - he pressed a speed dial button and woke up his uncle at the other end. As his uncle is a medical doctor – he thought that was an emergency call from his sister and got very much worried. We are afraid his random phone dialing may bring the 911 people to our house any day.

His mother believes in avant-garde baby foods and exotic fruit medley puree, and has introduced him to the world of the adult foods. He likes adult foods – a little spicy is more enjoyable to him. His mom and grandmas will make fresh purees of different fruits and berries – sometimes he shows great liking of some day's preparation. But next day he will show no interest in that food, forcing his mother to reevaluate what Tejas likes really.

He likes (on different days) Mexican tacos, quesadilla, burritos, Hawaiian breads, Indian chapattis, nuns, pizza, yogurts and chicken nuggets. When he eats he must watch his favorite show – Elmo and his gang. He cracks up when Mr. Noodles fall down. His eyes are usually riveted to the TV screen and whoever is feeding him has to be outside his line of sight to TV and must do it in between the interesting activities Elmo and his gang are engaged in. Sometimes I have seen his grandma trying to push in some food in his mouth, which if given at inappropriate time will be sent to the floor immediately for grandma to clean up. His message is probably – did not you notice that I was busy?

He does not cry if he does not get what he wants. He shows diplomacy and maturity in handling disappointments. But if his mom and grandmas do anything he does not like – he gets angry. Like sometimes his grand ma would fold the blanket thinking he has finished his nap – he gets angry and protests loudly; because he enjoys the pleasure of hugging the blankets and pillows till his nappy mood has trailed off. He goes to the library with his mom for story time. While other kids seem to cling to their mother's arms - Tejas is busy discovering things around. His mom said one day the Librarian gave him a stare. His curiosity is unbounded. If he sees me drinking soda – he will need the straw right away and touch the side of the cold cup, and say 'co co' (meaning cold). Then when he gets the paper cup with lid – he tries to put that straw through the hole in the lid. If he cannot do that by himself – he will hold your finger and bring your finger to the lid to help him. He knows when to ask for help.

He has very sensitive ears. Any sound (does not have to be loud) will have his immediate attention. He will try to figure out that noise himself. If he knows the sound – he will ignore it. If that origin of sound is not known – he will cling to you. When the gardener comes, he has to watch the gardener's activities (though in a scared mode) very intently from your lap. When the blender makes noise – somebody has to hold him, though he knows it is from the blender that is preparing his food. He is also a great fan of the garbage trucks when it comes around weekly to the curb near his house. He likes to go to park and play with sand. He is afraid to get on swing and slide. He is more interested in observing things and people around. But sometimes while playing when he thinks nobody is paying attention – he will eat some sand upsetting all the adults around him. He knows that was a no no and does not object to other's efforts to clean his mouth of the sands. Then when everybody is relaxed – he will do it again. That way he keeps everybody attentive to his activity.

All this narrative is to take a snapshot of Tejas's activities at this tender age. It seems a child grows with time leaving the childhood behind – but the basic nature or personality stays unchanged. Thus what I see in Tejas is a very attentive, curious boy who will know how to work around things if any problem, gifted with smartness, intelligence and an intense curiosity for the tools of this technical era. A very serious yet very playful boy - a loving, caring human being in the making. These are the wonder years of his life – a very precious and sweet childhood. Love and care will make him a kind and noble person. Habits form very early from observation, curiosity needs to be cultivated all the time, love and understanding have to envelope the child. Nobody teaches no body anything – everybody learns by himself others only assist. Later on in school he will learn through seeing and listening, but at this age learning is subliminal. Every sight, sound and action is wiring the child's brain. He is seeing people with much sharper eyes than an adult can. All this is subliminal. The emotional intelligence is at work. So it is a joy to see him growing up as a loving, attentive and connected child. That is why the *caar, caar* sound comes so sweet to my ears, and I cannot explain it adequately, and just tried to explain that in this blog.

***

So You Don't Like Easter Eggs? *(3/27/2009)*

Easter Sunday is the most important holy day for the Christians. This blog is not about religiosity or holiness. But it also coincides with spring breaks and Easter eggs. That is where the problem was. But to have a foot print of time I need to see what is happening around. It seems President Obama is in full swing. He is fighting a hydra-headed dragon – economic crisis, stimulus, his mandate for green revolution, his push for education, trying to grasp the real reach and capacity of terrorism and at the same time keeping up hopes of ordinary people. He is also conducting Internet conference with the common citizens to keep them up to speed and create a sense of participation in governance. He is making time to chat light-heartedly on Jay Leno (to the chagrin of many pundits). He is also fighting off Republican nihilism, non-cooperation and road blocks to recovery. I heard very vocal Rush L. wishing Obama's failure. He had to do that because (according to him) he is the greatest champion of free thinking and is not afraid like others to speak his mind! What I heard indirectly was his wish for the sinking of the American ship with all people (like us) on board (because Rush hates Obama as the commander). I see the whole world is watching if Obama is the real dragon-slayer. Let us hope so. If he cannot chop off all the heads – let us hope he can slay most of its heads. It seems the old adage is true–United we stand and Divided we fall. The future will be as we choose. Back to what I was saying.

What I was referring before was -aster eggs. I did not know that it could create problem to anybody. But apparently it bothered somebody in my wife's preschool. She runs a preschool with children from all backgrounds. Many things happen in the school that throws light on different thought waves that are in circulation. Most of the stories I hear are about inconsiderate parents, over-eager parents, too much laid-back parents, funny staff stories, parent's confusion, children's funny stories etc. All of that is very important because it is about human mind in all its variation and shades. I wish some times that those experiences be shared with others. But I am afraid that its transmission through another person may be distorted and bias tinted. So it can happen also to the Easter egg story that my wife narrated.

This parent happens to be of a different religion than Christianity. The pre-school has students that come from different backgrounds including Christians, Hindus, Buddhists, Muslims etc.

(Though I have not heard of any Jewish enrollment). The school is not supposed to teach religion; does not teach religion or anything like that. But it does observe whatever major popular events are celebrated in the society as a whole. Thus its activities include all the common celebrations traditionally observed in a school environment – like raising American Flag in the morning, everyone taking pledge of allegiance to the flag everyday etc. The school also does projects that include different themes in different months like Valentine's day, Cinco de Mayo, St Patrick's day, Martin Luther King's day, Presidents day, Easter Egg hunting, Mother's Day, Memorial day, Independence day, Labor day, Columbus day, Halloween, Christmas trees and gift exchange, Chinese New Year etc. The idea is not to show any preference, but make the kids aware of what events are celebrated in the society of which they are parts of. Not only that, they watch space mission, listen to President's speech (whether they understand or not), discuss elections, discuss their trips to Las Vegas or any other special holidays they had. When they go to Disneyland they bring back toys, share their fun and stories with others. They celebrate their own birthdays with other kids and exchange gifts on occasions. They give presents to each other, to the teacher. They make field trips to post office, pet shops, go to senior centers in Halloween with colorful costumes and go to special events in

Sports Arena etc. In other words the school is a small replica of the larger world outside. By doing all these activities they learn about each other, become friends with each other, learn to like and love each other and become fully integrated and functional parts of the society.

This parent though educated (an engineer) objected to let his kid participate in Easter fun projects like coloring of eggs etc. He objected that his kid was doing this project without their expressed consent! Not only that - the father said that the pre-school should not teach Christianity to his kids. That really burst my wife's dam of patience. He not only was denying his own kid the fun of coloring eggs but also blaming the school for playing religion in the school. She really got irritated and wanted to give him a mouthful of advice regarding raising a child. She asked him what he really wanted – did he want to isolate his child from rest of the students and surroundings? Who said to him or where did he learn from -that Easter eggs are symbols of Christianity? Eggs are symbols of new lives. When spring comes, the nature celebrates with new leafs, colors and lives that the rigor of winter is over, come everybody enjoy life; enjoy the advent of spring and happiness all around. US being so politically conscious and so careful not to tip the balance in favor of any religion – even Easter Holidays are called Spring Breaks. Even the Spring Breaks don't happen on the same day in all school districts. Did this parent smell any Christianity or any other religion in that plastic colored eggs that the kids enjoy coloring?

The parent asked why the school does not celebrate Eid (a Muslim holiday) in school. Thus the parent seemed all confused what is religion, what is social and what is what. He smells religion in everything. This mind set never makes a child an open member of the society – but isolates the child and keeps him ignorant and builds barriers. Religion is faith that tells one how to commune with the Creator and you keep that to yourself. Of course you congregate, aggregate and practice what you want with the same kind to promote bonds – but cannot force others to do same. I thought Religion was a bridge to Divinity. Very few people can cross the bridge to experience divinity. Those who did – like Christ, Buddha etc had experienced something that most others did not. They had vision, they had seen how it is all put together, and they got a glimpse of the path to harmony and happiness. Even they were not really partisans but they themselves were gifts to mankind for letting their wisdom to be shared. They just spread their message and experience for others to benefit. They never taught intolerance. They all preached compassion, harmony, honesty and openness. Religion is faith and strengthens inner values. Only fanatics fan separation and enmity with others to promote their own agenda. Where did the parent see all this in the Easter egg coloring? A person that creates a separation wall really is building a prison for himself. All the comments are my comments, not my wife's. Because she runs a school her job is to keep cool, steer and move forward. She said if you want to isolate your child and teach your religion you have to do that at home. The school is a place of learning and its duty is to teach the children about the world and its surroundings.

***

Dubai Sightseeing I *(4/17/2009)*

Last two weeks there was no blog – as we went on a vacation for a short trip to India to meet our relatives. On the way we stopped for a day in Dubai and did some sightseeing there. We flew by Emirates Airlines that operates out of Dubai. (Dubai is a non-stop flight of sixteen hours from Los Angeles). Dubai has come up on the world map very prominently. The Emirates logo has become ubiquitous in the venues of all international cricket and soccer games. It is a small gas and oil country but is bristling with new construction. They also now boast of the world's tallest building known as Dubai World Trade Center. That surpasses the ones in Taipei and in Malaysia.

Actually I was itching to see the Arabian Desert again. We were in Saudi Arabia with a construction management team for four years. That was in the late seventies. The task was to build a port city and the associated infrastructure on the west coast of Saudi Arabia – 250 kilometer north of Jeddah. It was a wonderful experience to see a city taking shape from a blank on the barren desert. Even the initial soil exploration had to be conducted from a station on an anchored ship on Red Sea. Roads, housing, schools, port, desalination plant, power plant, retail infrastructure, recreational facilities – all the amenities that are needed for urban living. When we left there were a few highways and those were not crowded at all. We could travel 250 km in two and half hours. Now thanks to the globe-cast satellite I have, I get many international channels free. Now I see those highways are now jammed with cars like any other busy metropolitan area. So lot of transformation has taken place there. I also hear that they have turned to stricter Islamic code there. Saudi Arabia also does not grant visitor visa except for Hajj to Muslims and we are not Muslims. So there is no way we could visit back to Saudi Arabia to see what we built. But Dubai, though a Muslim country, is kind of liberal and grant visitor visa to tourists. Also they have a lot of western and eastern expatriate population base there. And any travel magazine that you pick up has glowing descriptions of the myriad construction there that is transforming a barren Arabian desert into a glittering gathering place for world's trade and tourism. So we stopped in Dubai.

The non-stop flight of sixteen hours (8400 miles) in an economy class is not a joke and not for people with low threshold of complaint. But I was surprised to see that the passengers (the plane was all full) were not bored at all. They had an ICE entertainment system with a monitor in every seat. That ICE system carried hundreds of movies from all over, live news feeds, different kinds of sports, TV shows, variety shows, all kinds of music from all over, audio-video games etc. So it seemed nobody wanted to sleep except the extremely wearied. I myself saw four cricket games, two soccer games, two movies, three TV episodes and listened to all kinds of pop and classical music. Most people were no different than me.

To give a little background of Dubai and its location for those who may not be all that familiar. Dubai is a capital city of United Arab

Emirates. They have other capital cities in Abu Dhabi, Doha and Sharjah etc. It is located on the south-east corner of the Arabian Peninsula on Persian Gulf. At one time it was known as Pirates Coast. It is a loose confederate of seven Emirates or sheikhdoms. The size of UAE is about the size of Maine. It is a very small area. But in 1970 gas and oil was explored in abundance there. The British had some kind of truce with the sheikhs and the terms of the truce ended in the seventies. When the American oil companies took over oil and gas exploration - the area boomed in prosperity. UAE is governed jointly by the seven sheikhdoms that elect a president and vice president among themselves. The present ruler is Sheikh Mohammed (in his fifties) of Dubai Emirate with a very progressive outlook. He is inviting all businesses from all over and giving them free development zone. There are about 3000 International companies that operate from of there. It has a population of about four and half million people, of which fifty percent are foreigners. They are more liberal than other neighboring Muslim countries. They allow women to drive and also permit alcohol (I don't know if they allow other western vices). They also encourage foreign ownership of residential units (in exchange of 99 years visa – as I heard). They are also very hospitable to western and eastern foreigners and everything written outside are in English and Arabic.

Though Dubai has many 5-star and luxurious hotels I was not sure of the city layout and the locations of the hotels with respect to the airport. To play it safe we had booked an accommodation in a 4-star hotel through an internet booking agency. It was fifteen minutes from the airport. Thanks to modern technology of course, we could take a virtual tour of the hotel before booking and we liked it. The cost was modest also compared to many hotels charging $400 per night. Anyway, the hotel van picked us up at the airport on our arrival after clearing through customs and immigration. One thing need to be said here – the terminal (terminal 3) was huge to say the least. It is all glass and steel, and housed inside huge arches. It was sparkling, shining and expansive. We went down the escalators, followed this arrow that arrow, then walked on many people-movers, then more arrows and more turns, and finally cleared all the regulations to see the exit area of the terminal.

We were apprehensive that nobody might show up – but there was a Korean man with our name on a sign looking for us. We were relieved. The hotel fee included the airport pickup. It was 8 pm in the evening. All the shops on the way were open. As they are closed during the heat of the day their operating hours are from 10 to 12 in daytime and 5 to 11 at night. Their local currency was Dirham (valued at 3.6 Dirham to one US

Dollar). We had exchanged some dollars at the airport just in case. At least we had some tipping money for the good services of the driver. The hotel had 3 restaurants and a night club on roof (on 7th floor). I was curious what the night club might look like in an Arab land, and was surprised to see it was filled with young men and women in smart and sexy outfits. The music was loud. As a matter of fact we were on fourth floor and slept through the noise of the drum till three in the morning. I presume that was when the night club closed.

We had set aside the next day for sightseeing. I did know they had all kinds of tour packages – city tour, golf tour, desert safari, dune buggy adventure, sunset cruise on dhow (Arabian sail boat) and other kinds of tours of different lengths and different interest – but we decided on simple city tour as we just wanted to see how Dubai (a modern desert city) looked and how it did contrast to our earlier experience of Jeddah. So we picked up a private limo tour (6 hours) and oriented ourselves with the points of interest and their approximate locations on the map. The driver showed up at ten with his car. A well-dressed Pakistani man with ties. He said he would show us around. He seemed very respectable, friendly and had big smile. He said he spoke four languages (Farsi, Urdu, Arabic and Hindi). I am hardly familiar with two languages, so I was awed by his language skill. We felt we were in good hands. ... This writing is getting too long. I shall come back to it later.

***

Dubai Sightseeing II *(4-24-2009)*

Last week I started a blog on Dubai sightseeing and ended with our tour selection. Now I find it very hard to write on sightseeing. I am no poet – so I cannot have a flight of imagination; nor do I want it to be a boring narrative of we did this and did that; nor is it a fact finding or adventurous sightseeing description that might tickle the reader's interest; nor is it a photo narrative like an album. So what do I want it to be? I will just narrate as interpreted by the driver. Of course I was asking lot of questions of general nature – some curious and some just for information. Sometimes we shared some jokes too.

Our driver (Rasoul) said he was originally from the Iranian border of Pakistan. So he was familiar with the local languages including Farsi and Urdu. He learnt Arabic for job reasons. Hindi was similar to Urdu – and he learnt it through his acquaintances. And there were many street signs outside of Dubai in Hindi and Urdu. He had learnt English in school. When we wanted to stop for lunch, we offered him some lunch money so that he could also have lunch while we were eating. He politely declined that saying that he ate lunch at 9 am before starting the job and he was not hungry. Along with his clean attire and the tie, I realized that he was on official duty with his clients (us). It was not a vacation or goof time for him. So I admired his work ethics.

He said this was his second time in Dubai. Before, he was the driver for a prince – who was also an engineer on a development project. This time he worked for two hotel chains and was salaried as a limo driver for the tourists. He said he enjoyed the job. Also he said that white people usually ask lot of questions about local history so he had to learn that also. He jokingly said that the Dubai people did not care for history but the Sheikh built one Dubai museum anyway to satisfy the curious white people. We also wanted to see the Dubai museum – but unfortunately it was closed on Fridays (which was the mosque day for the Muslims). As it was a Friday and it was a rest day (like Sunday), the traffic on the road was light. The driver told us that if it was an office day we would be sitting in traffic without much sightseeing. He also said many tourists, who stayed at new luxurious hotels (40 km from the airport), usually miscalculate the time required to go to the airport in office day traffic and miss their connecting flights.

He said about one million people lived in Dubai. I checked that out later on and found that was right. The seven emirates had total population of 5 million. With all the high rise residential apartments all over and so many new under construction – I was just wondering who would be living there as the population base was fixed and half of it foreigners. He said the government was giving 99 years visa to any foreigner who would buy apartment or property there. With tax-free living and crime-free society. he said many foreigners liked it there. Also about three thousand international corporations had bases there – some with headquarters and more coming. I know for sure that the world cricket governing body moved their Headquarter from London to Dubai to a much larger complex and a new modern cricket stadium. And Dubai was also hosting International tennis, cricket, soccer and golf tournaments. Tiger Woods was there just recently. Michael Jackson was living as a guest of the king in Dubai for a considerable length of time to stay out of public limelight. Dubai also hosted many other sporting events.

I was just curious and asked if the Royal families were conceited and kept distance from the common people. He said not at all. When a Royal family member visited any shopping mall, all they have is a body guard and they talk with ordinary people. This king Sheikh Mohammed was very modern in outlook. He wanted to perpetuate Dubai's fortunes even after the oil revenues eventually go down. He wanted to make Dubai a commercial hub of world commerce. He introduced Emirates Air, scrapping the old Gulf Air, and established air links with all continents to Dubai. He promoted tourism and built lot of western amenities. His father Sheikh Zaid in the eighties brought about the changes in traditional thinking to a more International thinking. The king was also highly visible among people.

That reminded me of one incident in Saudi Arabia. Ceremonially to open the project we were working on. The Royal Commission in charge of the projects, invited the King once. The King's arrival date was proclaimed an official holiday so that we could all give the King a big welcome ovation. So we lined up the King's parade routes in the morning. No photography was allowed. We saw caravans of limousines with Royal emblems coming on the road, followed by many ordinary buses. We thought the buses were loaded with royal correspondents and support people. We waited for two hours till the caravan followed through. But we did not see the king at all. Later on we came to know the King was in one of the buses – not in any limousine! Probably the buses were full of security people and King was with them. I could appreciate now that the King of Dubai was very people friendly.

On the question how the world recession affected Dubai now. He said it affected Dubai very much so. Many of the projects are abandoned now as the credit squeeze was affecting the developers. He also said it would not last long. On questions where do the manual labors come from - he said they are mostly Indians and Pakistanis, though Thais and Filipinos were there also. In the management level there were people from all over the world. I agreed with him as I noticed so many varieties of ethnic restaurants catering to Dubai people. In our stay in Dubai we had four main meals – we ate Thai, Sri Lankan, American and European. We were impressed by the sincerity of the waiters in each restaurant. On the question if the laborers were any problem anytime - he said about a year ago many laborers staged strikes on the job, prompting the King to look at the labor problems. Now all the contractors are held accountable for timely pay and strict adherence to their agreements with imported labor.

On the question if the local Arabs discriminated against Indians and Pakistanis - he said on the contrary they were much respected and were in great demand. I was surprised as my Saudi experience told me that the Arabs discriminated heavily against the Indian and Pakistani laborers. They were cheated many times and exploited by the unscrupulous employers. He said in contrast to Abu Dhabi and other Emirates – Indian and Pakistanis are more welcome here. The king had given explicit orders that Indian and Pakistani workers to be treated fairly. I could sense the present king had very advanced thinking – as the Emirates would turn back to desert if the Indian workers stopped coming to Dubai, and also from a commerce point of view India was its big trade collaborator.

The driver while explaining various points of interest on the way also said the King had about twenty seven wives and thirty seven children. I had no idea how he could know such private information. The King had all kinds of wives – Arabic, American, Indian, Pakistani etc. Usually he lets each wife to raise her family in different palaces. I got a sense that Rasoul was probably crossing the boundary of his knowledge. He said women are allowed to do almost everything – including driving and walking around unescorted as they wished. There were numerous malls all over; they were much bigger than most American malls. We visited one Emirates Mall for our lunch. Our feet were tired from walking in the mall. There were many upscale stores, including high end Ladies Fashion stores.

The driver said different area of Dubai are referred to by its neighborhood (rather than by names of roads). Dubai had set aside new development zones for new businesses and its rising population. He took us to the Dubai Marina. The marina is located in a still water harbor off the Arabian Gulf. Many yachts as well as traditional Arabian boats were anchored there. They had evening dinner parties in the dhow. Al Jemeirah area is the latest development zone. It is on the coastal area about 30 kilo meters from downtown. They have American University there along with numerous residential towers. This area seemed to be full of western expatriates, western shops and eateries and pedestrian promenades.

In Umm Suqeim area on the coast was the icon of Dubai viz. Burj Al Arabia (Tower of Arabia). It is about a twenty story building in the form of an Arabian sail boat. The admission was $30 – which we thought was very high. Then in the Jumeirah Heights there were numerous new high rise office towers. The Dubai World Trade Center was also located there. I don't know the statistics – but I heard it was now the tallest building on earth. The whole area was brand new with sparkling looks. But what attracted our interest most was Palm Jumeirah. This was something to see to believe. They had created an artificial island in the form of a palm tree in the water of Arabian

Gulf. It is very large and contains a few hundred buildings along with a resort hotel. The truck of the palm is the passage way from land. All the residential towers were located in the leaf regions of the palm shape. The streets were wide with fast moving traffic. A few more similar and of much larger complexes were also being planned.

We did not see any police anywhere to give traffic tickets. The driver said there were police men but not that many. He said before the Iraq war – even the Army was full of Indian and Pakistani soldiers on their payroll. When Emirates wanted to join America in the fight against Saddam Hussein – most of the Indians and Pakistanis took leave of absence and the Emirates did not have much army at all. Then US assured security for the King and stationed a few warships in the Arabian Gulf. The king abandoned the army completely. Now there was a token police force that took care of minor security needs required for administration. When the King was assured of safety by US – then the king poured all the resources in development. Now I understood what the reason behind the prosperity of the Emirates was. So it seemed friendliness with the west and other big powers had to be the cornerstone of the King's foreign policy theme.

This writing is getting long, so I shall stop here. Any travelogue is not complete without some visual counterparts. So attached are some photographs with brief narratives.

Dubai World Trade Center

Palm Shaped Island

Gold Souk

A Food Court in the Emirates

Terminal of the Dubai International Airport

***

Slap of an Eunuch (Hijra) *(5-1-2009)*

I heard about the slap, but I don't know whether it was something funny or something sad. In our recent trip to India we stayed at our brother-in-law (B) and sister-in-law's (S) house in Calcutta. B and S are excellent hosts and very jovial type. They were our constant companions also. We were kind of immersed in what was happening around there while talking with them. We heard about the family trivia, family drama, associated tensions and frustrations. We heard about the big stories, big problems, small stories and small problems. The slap I am talking about was just a small event that they almost forgot. But it came back alive in discussion as it happened to a security guard they had. Every day we saw the guard (the ignoble recipient of the unfortunate slap) on our way out and coming in, the slap came back alive to me. Somehow I got interested in more details. Every time S told the story she giggled.

B and S own a fourth story condominium flat in a very decent and respected neighborhood in South Calcutta. Their building has four stories with two condominiums in each floor except in ground floor. The cars are parked on the ground floor with a provision of toilet and a small cabin for the security guards. The condo-owners have security arrangements with a security company that provides guards. These kinds of services are also highly affordable there. The company provides security guards on a rotating basis, with each guard working for a twelve-hour shift around the clock. It is not that it is a crime infested or dangerous neighborhood, but over there it is the norm to have a security guard for any condominium complex. India is not a button-operated, closed-circuit camera, no-man land like over here. Over there, there are plenty of people who would be happy to work in this kind of relaxing jobs. The guard's duty mostly consists of making sure that unauthorized persons don't trespass the premises. They don't carry any gun and also they are not gym-toned hunks to tackle real rough intruders. They mostly spend their work time sitting on a chair and listening to songs in the radio. When any owner (their master or 'babu' as they call the owners) comes in or go out, they open the front gate wide for the car. Sometimes if the owners have any luggage they help to carry it inside, press the button of the elevator and make sure the master and his family have safely entered their unit. They are attentive and always on their feet when the owners are nearby. They are there to serve. They talk only when somebody talks with them.

I did not know the name of the guard. I was never sure whether to ask for his name was proper - as I was not familiar with the master-servant protocol there. But I did ask him where he lived. He said he commuted daily from Baruipur (about 30 km from job site), but originally he came from East Bengal. He also said a few other details. I gathered he had a family and he was a very respectable and dependable bread-earner of his family. Some-times we saw him sleeping in the chair during daytime. Probably it was too hot the night before and probably he did not get any chance for a nap. But when he knew that somebody saw him sleeping, he blushed and seemed to say sorry silently for his unintentional snooze. Also we saw him once coming from a public shower place; he was again very ashamed that we saw him away from his job duty. He was well shaven with a brushy moustache. That moustache seemed to tell me that he was a very proud and respectable man, proud of the service he was offering and he was very diligent in his duty. So I was sorry to hear that an eunuch (hijra) slapped this honorable guard on duty.

Somebody may as well question who these eunuchs (hijras) are. Well, eunuchs and hijras are not really same. The West has precise terms for every kind of sexual appearance, preference or orientation. In India the terms are not precise and generally misunderstood. Eunuchs are castrated males. But in India all kinds of sexual deviation and behavior are lumped together and called 'hijra'. I don't know where the term came from, but I have a strong hunch that it was a derogatory word used by locals for the invading Muslims. The term 'hijra' encompasses all kinds of deviate from normal genders and also includes eunuchs, people with ambiguous genitalia, transvestites (male posing as females), transsexuals (people with gender transformation) and feminine males (She-males), though most of them are homosexuals. In other words they are not specifically gender described. In India from ancient time they are considered as third gender. In Mahabharata they are described as 'Kinnara'. Arjun, the great Pandava warrior took disguise as a Kinnara in that epic. In the Middle Ages the eunuchs (castrated males) were security guards for the emperor's harems. But in modern days they have fallen in public disfavor. They had become untouchables. They live on the margin in the Indian society. Consequently they have formed their own groups, have their own rituals of acceptance in their society, and are usually looked down and avoided by the rest of the society. They cannot have normal jobs like other people.

Thanks to Gandhi who erased the stigma of the Untouchables, now the Hijras are very vocal, demanding and also belong to well organized groups. Shabnam Mausi (the movie people made a film on him) was elected the first Hijra MLA (member of the Lower House in Parliament) in 1999. A few other Hijras had also become politically prominent in Gujarat and Madhya Pradesh. But on the whole Hijras have to resort to other means for living. They make their living by annoying people by posing as nuisance or pest. So when a newborn comes home and the family is happily celebrating the event – the Hijras come, and perform some dance (sometimes obscene) in front of the house. Then they ask for money from the family. As their presence embarrasses the family – usually the family pays them off handsomely to prevent further embarrassment. If not paid handsomely the Hijras curse the family and everybody is afraid of the Hijra's curse. This is a very common phenomenon in India. (I read that Government of India employs them as tax collectors in some regions to collect tax from stubborn tax-evaders. And that tactics have been very successful.)

Recently B and S had their first grandchild. That was also one reason for us to go there to see our newest grandchild. As expected a few days later the Hijras came to their residence and enquired to the guard as to who had a baby. To save embarrassing dances to be performed near his master's premises – the guard lied to the Hijras and said nobody had a baby there. That enraged the Hijras as they had news from very reliable sources (the maternity department of the local hospital) that a newborn girl had been discharged to the family who lived in that address. So they slapped the guard and rebuked him for lying. The guard had to say yes to prevent more slaps from the Hijras. So the Hijras finally identified the family and did their dance routine and left with a hefty fee. While leaving, the Hijras told the guard never to lie to them again like that.

I guess the guard listened to the rebuke and was at a loss as to what he should have done. All he was doing was trying to save his masters from the embarrassment of the Hijra dance and blackmails by the Hijras. Instead he was embarrassed himself with a slap. I guess he took it as part of his job and as an unavoidable risk of his trade. I was somewhat sympathetic to him when I heard how he was embarrassed. While leaving he helped us with our luggage in the trunk. In appreciation I wanted to give him some tips. But he said 'No – my babu (master) will get angry.' But I gave him the tips anyway. I guess after we left he went back silently to his chair to do his silent job. Probably another Hijra will come someday and slap him again for lying.

***

Mother's Day in the Park *(5/15/2009)*

Last week there was no blog as it was Mother's Day and as a participating parent I also joined Mother's Day party, when the kids and parents assembled in the park and got together in a spirit of togetherness. This year things were a little different. The kids having their own families and living in different cities, it is a real hard chore to stage a Mother's Day assembling everybody. On top of that there are multiple sets of parents and there are grand kids ranging in age from one to three. Doing individual Mother's Days for each mother and mother-in-law will take additional time and efforts and cannot be undertaken on a single day, namely on the real Mother's Day. It takes a semi-magician to get all the involved parties in one location. So they decided to hold the party in the park. A restaurant or any one's residence is not large enough to accommodate all and keep the kids entertained, happy and under control.

So the event and celebration took place in the park. But it was no ordinary municipal park with large expanse of greens and trees and picnic tables. It was an urban park – a recent phenomenon in Southern California. Though it is more prevalent in Europe – some urban parks are being developed here also. It was Americana at Brand in Glendale, California. It is a mixed residential - shopping - recreational complex with large open grassy and landscaped area with dancing water fountains, public ornamental statues,

and open area dining with soft music wafting in the air, large clock tower, open food courts, high-end shopping and luxury condos. The architecture is low-key Mediterranean. I also think this kind of development is good for all. In American way of thinking, we tend to compartmentalize everything. Work, recreation, dining are all different and distinct entities - to be set apart and treated separately. Thus we shop in shopping malls with all shops under the same closed roof. Then for dining we go to different commercial zones, and then of course for shelter we go to another residential zone. It is open and clear segregation (no Martin Luther King on this please), and does not generate the wholesome feeling that alleviates stress. This kind of segregated thinking creates lot of urban stress without the urban folks being aware of it. A seamless approach may not be hundred percent good for business, but definitely creates more harmony in life. So I salute Mr. Caruso (the developer) for his thinking and I think the mixed-use urban development will be the trend in future – where life openly meets each other with a respite from the usual urban stress. A little oasis of solace in an urban chaos is definitely a good diversion.

Before writing this blog on Mother's Day I was debating where to draw the separation line between personal and public details. Then I thought whatever we do in public is open and visible , so taking a keyboard tour of the events that we enjoy and that influence our lives cannot be out of bounds of appropriateness or common interest. So I will let my mind do the wandering on this topic. So here I go. First thing I am not sure about is whether it is Mother's Day or Mothers Day? Then I saw that US Congress had really passed a resolution that it would be commemorated as Mother's Day and not Mothers Day. On surface it may seem superficial, but it contains a message. Mothers Day means everybody celebrates all the mothers (no mother in particular) of the world. It is not so. Mother's

Day is meant to be very personal. It is a one to one event with each child celebrating and linking with their own mothers. So nothing can be more personal than a Mother's Day to a mother and her child. It is kind of reaffirming the bond of love, and acknowledging that mother's love in their beginning played a big role to make them the wonderful adults that they have become.

Where and when I grew up, we did not set aside any particular day to honor our mothers. Mother was always with us. We respected our mothers and they took care of our wellbeing all the time. So I think, at that time, if we did set aside any day for the mother, she would have been insulted. She would say – 'What about other days? Are not you going to love me on other days? And what is this phony greeting card proclaiming that I am the best mother in the world and you love me so much that words cannot describe it? Real love is not expressed in words. It is a feeling, it is a silent bond. If somebody loves you – you can sense it and you can feel it. Your cards and flowers cannot substitute or simulate any real love. Real love does not exist for only one day and then vanishes in thin air for rest of the year. You don't have to honor me when I am alive – you do that when I become a past tense. Just hug me today, tomorrow and day after tomorrow. Don't confine your exhibition of love to a few hours only – your love nourishes me, thought of your well being consumes all my waking hours, your happiness makes me happy. Your smile makes my day. You are mine and I am yours. The bond is eternal. Don't squeeze it in a few hours ... . My mother really did not say that – but I kind of intuitively sensed that. But if she was alive, I would have sent her a beautiful Hallmark card anyway that would say she is the best mom in the world. I don't know how much more happy she would have felt – all she was looking for was a big hug, an encircling hand of love and embrace, a moment of deep intimacy that only a child and mother can have. Probably she would have sighed.

But I think another thing is happening. There has to be a story of genesis how the card and greeting substituted for the real stuff. But, before that, I want to say a few words about the 'nuclear family'. Though practiced widely in the west, the concept of 'nuclear family' is not a paradigm of happiness and not a good model to emulate. Nuclear Family is two-dimensional and is always changing. Thus today's nuclear family dissolves after twenty or thirty years and another nuclear family starts when the kids are on their own wings. Then the tie to the older nuclear family gets weakened and the older nuclear family is destroyed. The mother of today's nuclear family will become a distant entity to the newer nuclear family. The newer nuclear family creates its own barrier to promote its own comfort. But this additional comfort does not create additional happiness. This barrier then makes the personal world very small. Everybody gets bogged down in the shallow depth of one's own interest and care. Real happiness comes from participation, involvement and sharing, and not from aloofness. It creates a selfish breed that only tends to go after its own pleasure. Actually I see this ingrained in western thinking. I don't know whether progress and happiness can co-exist. Probably it is a catch-22. If we think progress (that is more money) means more pleasure, then more progress can only bring more isolation. But life is much larger and intertwined. The participating elements should be coordinated and honored, and not disregarded and dishonored. Looks like I am getting off the course – so back to what I was talking about.

 I was just thinking how the 'Mother's Day' got started. 'Mother's Day' indirectly (may or may not) connote that other days are not my Mother's. I think it all started with industrialization and economic prosperity. When industries pulled away people from their families, newer families had to be formed for survival. The physical distance can only create more mental distance. Congress and President Wilson got alarmed that the larger consequence of this distant living can only destroy the family bond. The youth would go after their own enjoyment, and the older parents would get neglected. So they proclaimed the second Sunday in May as 'Mother's Day' in 1914. If it could not lift the death threat to a familial bond, at least it would alleviate the pain somewhat. So 'Mother's Day' was created. Mr. Joyce Hall sensed that cards could soothe out some pain that the parents might feel from separation of their children. So Mr. Hall started 'Hallmark Cards' in the card greeting business in Kansas City, Missouri around that time. Now it is so ingrained in our habit, we tend to delegate the responsibility of maintaining bonds between two humans to skillfully designed greeting cards.

This writing is getting long. But, no matter what I say, I realize that if I did not use Mr. Hall's cards today I would be judged a sub-human bore and a disgrace to human society. So, no more on this subject.

***

Slumdog Underdog *(5-22-2009)*

I did think about writing a blog on the movie `Slumdog Millionaire' sometime ago. Finally I get around to it. This blog is not about singing praise of the movie as others have already done it. It is more about things I did not understand. Many things confused me, so I don't know where to start. First of all, there is no word like 'Slumdog' in the dictionary. So somebody who wanted to know the meaning of 'Slumdog' (as the title most of the time condenses the theme of the story) was lost. First I thought probably this was a movie about a dog that lived in a slum. Then again I am no fan of dogs, so I thought the movie was not for me. Then I thought that it is probably about slums in India that also did not interest me. But how can the word millionaire be associated with a dog that lived in a slum in India – that also did not help me a bit. The dictionary did not help me, the title did not help me - so what was the movie about?

Then I also read it was a screen version of a book named 'Q & A' by an Indian author Vikas Swarup. Then it dawned on me that it could be about 'Who wants to be a Millionaire' – the popular TV game show in US, which has become popular all over the world. Then when I saw the movie I understood that it was not about a dog, but about an underdog. The movie producer had taken liberty of coining a new word, which is sometimes commercially allowed, though it is frowned on severely by academicians. Thus the expanded theme of the movie is really 'An underdog slum dweller that became a millionaire in a game show'. It is really a dream story, a fairy tale movie – probably more of a Disney genre than a regular main stream. So I was confused again. But I know now that the director gave birth to a new word that will soon appear in Webster and Oxford dictionaries.

Later on we shall forget the people behind the story, so it is a good idea to encapsulate the people and facts about this artistic creation. It is a story about Jamal who lived in the underbelly slums of the affluent city of Mumbai (Bombay). He always dreamt of riches, but had no idea how to get there. As most people do, they buy lottery tickets but he did not have money to do that also. So joining a game show that was giving away millions of Rupees to the winner could be a path to wealth, but the odds were a trillion to one against him. But dreams and creativity take over where rationality ends. His grit and isolated information acquired from chance encounters with unlikely important people always gave clue to him about winning answers in every round. The other contestants from higher levels in society had more knowledge, but then sometimes knowledge creates confusion as to clear-cut answers. This is the skeleton of the plot – now add a flesh of romance, police brutality, concocted situation comics, bureaucratic conspiracy, lost love and lover's reunion – you have got a beautiful cinematic story. A cinematic story need not be a true story as it is not exactly as written by a novelist - but it is enhanced by other creative team members with visual, audio, technical and acting skills. So it was the fictional creation that got the award, not the story nor any other single talent in any particular field. It is more like an orchestra – nobody can claim all the honors- all the participants have to share the credits. But as a conductor in the orchestra, the director gets the most credit. It should be rightly so. At first I thought the best director award went to somebody else as that happened many times before. So I checked the list of awards garnered by Slumdog and found that it won eight Oscars, one of them was for 'Best Director' also. That made me happy for Danny Boyle – who showed tremendous courage and thinking out of the box of the closed Hollywood mind set.

I read that many Indians were irked by the word 'Dog' in the title, as the first impression one gets is that the Indian slum dwellers are being looked down by the West as dogs or wretched pitiful sub- humans at best. Thus many people took it as a personal (or even a national) insult. I cannot blame them entirely about this sensitive mentality. For a long time the West looked on India as a country with a begging bowl. I know in 1979, when we went to Rome I saw a big fund-raising event collecting money for India's poor (though there was no national calamity at that time). Though this was an act of generosity still it always created a sense of aching inferiority complex among educated Indians. Even when Mother Teresa died – the West focused more on the poverty than on the wonderful saint with merciful compassion for the most wretched, disregarded and unfortunate human beings. Even I saw one well-known TV News anchor went inside a poor man's kitchen and showed the whole world what meager stuff they were cooking for their own family. That blatant poor taste and lack of sensitivity had also irked me. Though Indians are well aware that Americans are the most compassionate and kind people that world has known – still that choice of the word dog supposedly associated with India's poor did trouble many Indian journalists also. I think their pain has been superseded by pride when their Slumdog won the most coveted crown in the world of show business. So I am happy for them now. When I first saw the movie 'Slumdog' I thought it was an ok movie – but not any extra-talented movie.

The story line was more typical Hindi film, the songs and scores were typical Hindi film, the acts and acting were typical Hindi film – so in my estimation it was a typical Hindi film with an English title for an English-speaking audience. I did not rate it very high in my own mind. But I must also admit that I am not a movie conno-isseur and cannot be a consummate judge of an artistic creation namely cinema. Hollywood knows best. But I cannot stop thinking what Hollywood was really looking at? Is it the theme that corresponds with our present state of mind and affairs? A bleak, desperate time has befallen us all, a dark veil of economic doom is threatening us and many of us are not really too sure about the future. Are we now the Slumdogs who are desperately looking for better times and trying to get solace out of our dreams? The Indian poor masses are the real benefactors of the Hindi movie juggernauts that spin out impossible storylines – with romance, songs, dance and happy endings. We (the supposedly educated) in our youth scorned at these movies as they were so far out of the realms of reality. But the poor, uneducated masses liked those as it made them forget the dire reality and hopelessness they were mired in. To them it was a pill of happy feeling. It is just a guess, probably Hollywood did not think that way.

What then it was thinking about? I think probably it was a commercial move to extend the boundary of Hollywood and merge itself with the glamour of Bollywood. Bollywood is already an established powerhouse in the movie business. They make more movies annually; they have more global spread (population wise); glamour and talents are plenty. What they really lacked was acceptance by west. Movie-wise I still think Satyajit Ray's 'Pather Panchali' is the most sensitive beautiful movie I have seen. More people in the world (in Asia and Africa) know the names of the Bollywood heroes than the Hollywood heroes. I think Russians and Middle East people also watch plenty of Bollywood movies. The might of Bollywood is spreading out more and more. Probably this Oscar was an award to Bollywood and bringing it out on the stage for acclaim by the entire world to see. Probably it was more of a Lifetime achievement award for Bollywood than for a singular movie named 'Slumdog'. Or maybe it dawns the era of a commercial marriage between Hollywood and Bollywood. We will see.

Another thing I like to comment on is whether it was an English movie or an Indian movie. I think it is a moot question now. As the world has narrowed down, information and intellectual exchanges are not limited to one national boundary, when commerce has no national boundaries. Global participation in everything is more norm than before; it is now harder to isolate the country and its contribution. So instead of thinking of the country, let us think of the people who contributed. And that is a complex and multiple cast. So credit goes to all. But I shall credit the director Danny Boyle more than anybody else. So if that means it is a British movie – so be it. If you think it was an Indian movie – so be it. Who wants to take any side on this debate? I am not one for sure. What I saw was a merger of two forces which can only bring more variety and more flavor to the world of cinematic creations, namely movies.

***

A Visitor from India *(6-5-2009)*

L ast week we had a 'male cooking day' in our movie club meeting. In other words on that day the wives decided to stay away from the kitchen with their hands and mouths idled, so that husbands could prove how good they were in that women's specialty. It seemed the male cooking was super hit as the wives unanimously applauded the level of excellence and did not find anything to pick on their husbands (for a change). So it was a day off from blog. As blog is nothing but a random journey of mind, and events are nothing but footprints in time, so mentioning some out-of-context things are not really that irrelevant. So what is happening now also needs be narrated. Now President Obama has completed four months in his job. He had been very busy last few months – trying to prevent collapse of the banking system, collapse of American icons like General Motors and Goldman

Sachs, trying a new path of energy independence, reclaiming American honesty and leadership on the world stage, bringing back trust and transparency in the administration and myriad other things. Last Thursday he gave a very scholarly speech in Cairo University addressing the Muslim world (it is unfortunate that Muslims think they have another world) to build a bridge of understanding between Muslims and the west. I have not seen or read about such outreach by any political leader at any time in history. Sometimes it seems surreal that one person has so much energy, so much charisma, so much popularity and so eager to fix all the wrong and have welfare of all people on earth (except the wrong-doers and the terrorists), to put everybody on a more stable path towards a better sustainable and a less hostile future. I just pray for his success. It may not be so easy against a determined opposition of rich and powerful. In his success lie our future and our children's future.

The visitor that I am going to write about now was a very dear distant relative of us. He and his wife visited us in Los Angeles around late sixties. At that time we did not have many friends and did not know many people. So we were always excited if somebody came to visit us. One has to know the mindset of people at that time to get a proper perspective. At that time India was still struggling to stand on her own feet. Nobody seemed sure whether capitalism or socialism was better for them. There was too much poverty, too much illiteracy, too little foreign exchange reserve to play an even game with other developed countries. Going or visiting other countries was mostly out of question for most people. It was very unlike now a day when everybody seems to have some of their children or friend's children somewhere in the States. Also the parents and relatives seem to come here on yearly (or more frequently) to visit their children or relatives or just enjoy a change of pace. In other words in the late sixties when we were here, there were not that many Indian people to relate to or to say as our own.

 Even if we wanted some relative to visit us we had to pay for their fare, write letters of sponsorship for their visa and be a total host to them, entertain them, take care of their food, lodging, medical, entertainment and almost everything else. Some people of modern mindset may think either we were crazy or stupid, but almost all of us were like that. So Guests were not a bother, but their company was a pleasure and joy for us. Most Americans also knew very little about India. They used to think India was an exotic backward place of snake charmers, monkeys and the Tajmahal. Indians also knew AAvery little about America and thought anybody who lived in America was very rich, and we all had machines to do all our domestic chores like cooking, cleaning, washing, drying, calling on phone etc., and everybody had cars, refrigerators, TVs and what not. So America was also an exotic land for them and visiting America was a dream for most of them.

 To go back to the hospitality context, I had a friend's friend in New York. I visited him once. He did not keep any furniture in his living room - as he did not know how many people might be visiting him at any time and without previous announcements. Suppose the Air India flight arriving in New York was late – where were the pilots or other crews going to spend their night. He used to have his phone next to his pillow at night. What if any of his friends get in trouble and call him in the middle of the night- then? What were they going to eat? He used to keep all kinds of cereals and milks – eating a few bowls were as good as having lunch or dinner. Well I was not hospitable to that extent – but we were also very hospitable. And if some unknown visitors ringed us (figuring out from the last name in the Telephone directory that we could be from India) for help, we would do our utmost to help them. We were that backward in our mindset at that time.

Anyway, the preface seems to be getting larger and larger than the content, so no more on our mind set of the sixties. The dear relative (visitor) worked in an British Airline and he used to get free tickets to travel abroad as a fringe benefit. So when we knew that he and his wife decided to visit us and stay with us for a month we were excited. When they came here, we picked them at the airport and were very happy to have guests staying with us. He and his wife were very pleasant and they were also very appreciative of what we were doing for them. He would admire the beautiful landscaped lawns that every house had in front of their house. They were amazed at the speed the cars were traveling on the freeway, and obedient mindset of drivers to the traffic light and traffic lane. (In India they said nobody followed any traffic rules.) They were amazed that you could pick up the phone and ask for another line and next day you had another line. They were amazed at the size of the supermarket, with all the foods in neat packages on display on shelves. No dirt on the floor, nobody had to carry the produce in their own bags. They would amaze at the size of potatoes and onions. No bargain, no haggling- everybody paying whatever the clerk was asking. Nobody had any questions; nobody was bargaining or asking for concessions etc. The gardeners came at fixed time and did their job without somebody shouting out instructions to them. They really appreciated the discipline of ordinary people, work ethics, and they were also sure that this quality was very helpful in

America's progress. India would never match America as Indians talked too much and did very little. Indians were mouth-pundits but bone-lazy. I told them once that this quality helped Indians to stay in India unlike Blacks in Africa who talked little and worked more. As such the Blacks (and not Indians) were brought in as slaves here long ago.

Our visitor was a very curious person and was always correcting his own information and gathering new. He would ask me what was the biggest river in California, what was the highest peak in California, what were the names of the mountain ranges, where did the native Indians live, what were the mining products in California, when were the freeways built, when were the supermarkets built, was America this clean all the time etc. Most of the time I did not know the answer – then he would give me the missing information. He would ask for milk when we traveled and we did not know how to order milk in the restaurant. He told us that with age, bones lost calcium and must be replenished by calcium in milk. Without any other calcium source he would drink the milk that would come as creamer for coffee. He told us about the good and bad things about eggs - between the yellow part and white part etc. We took them to show Las Vegas and Grand Canyon. I had read about Grand Canyon from the pamphlets in the Visitor's center. Told them Grand Canyon was so much old, so much deep and even showed them the ragged edges of the canyon that had names of Hindu God's like Brahma and Shiva. He had also read about Grand Canyon and thought that was also a nature's wonder. Then he told me that the canyon did not look like the Grand Canyon he had seen in the movie 'McKenna's gold'. And he seemed to doubt whether we had come to the right place. I knew that I did not know much, but never thought that somebody would question me as to which one was real Grand Canyon.

Actually that was an exception. He believed me in everything I said. I had told him that California was an Earthquake country. I told him about the San Andreas Fault and numerous other faults all over. I told him that earthquakes were kind of commonplace in California and not to worry too much if he felt any trembling of the ground. We lived in a two-bedroom apartment – we used one bed room for ours and the other one was for their use. I did not really expect any earthquake during their stay here. But as it happened at that time the Sylmar Earthquake (Magnitude 6.8) in the morning (around 6 am in the morning) shook us all up. I myself had never experienced such big temblor before. I got very nervous, and thought it was prudent to go outdoor for safety. Before going out I frantically knocked at their door to wake them and tell them to come outside.

Without getting their response my wife and I went outside. There was a four-story apartment house nearby. That building swayed like crazy. The palm tree was shaking like crazy. The temblor was getting more frightening. I thought that was the end of world. I knew one day everything would come to an end, and I thought that time had come now. I had never been more frightened in my life. Everything seemed unreal to me – all buildings were shaking, all trees were shaking, we were tottering on the ground – I was also sad that they were inside and end would come to them in their sleep. After a while the temblor stopped – I could not believe that we were still alive. When we were sure that the temblor was over – we came in. We knocked at their door again. At that time they got up from their sleep. I asked them if they felt the earthquake that just happened. He said they felt it, but did not pay any attention to that. That was because I had told them that Earthquake was very commonplace in California and not to worry about that.

They amazed me, and I was really dumbfounded that somebody had so much faith and assurance from something I had told them. By this time I have forgotten about the Sylmar Earthquake, but I have not forgotten that visitor from India.

***

A Long Voyage Long Ago III *(6-19-2009)*

There was no blog last week as too much was going on and also I could not think of any new subject to write on. Then I thought why not finish the subject that I started some time ago and almost forgot about. The subject topic was previously blogged and posted in June and July of 2008. The previous blogs talked about what motivated me to come here about 40 years ago. It was partly the adventure of youth fuelled by ambition of getting ahead in life. Now as I reflect back I see many mistakes were made, and see that one's final orbit is limited by the power of thrust of the propelling rocket. I did not get much help, did not have any worthwhile connection, did not have a total understanding of things and people around, and did not have any wisdom of my own or from others to borrow. So it was basically a solo effort, a solo journey powered by the dare of adventure and will, and impeded by lack of ability and resources. But I wanted to give it a try – stand up or fall down.

Now my view of life is not negative at all, but I think I am lucky that I was able to undertake that adventure though it could be termed as a daredevil adventure of youth without any safety mat. We can look at life as a glass of wine half full (optimist) or half empty (pessimist). I look at life as 'half full'. I know it could be fuller if there were more available resources, connections, personal talent and people skill. But I am happy with what little I had and what little I have now. I realize now that reward of today is the result of yesterday's work. And every day, every moment counts in life. When I don't have the experience I would like to be enriched by other's experience (to save a misstep or two). Life is a river of learning and a flow of subjective experiences of different individuals towards a common stream that makes life interesting. I also realized when you achieve the wisdom your strength is almost exhausted and when you have the strength then you don't have enough wisdom. If philosophizing is a bad habit of the idle, probably I should not philosophize any more. So let me get to the topic in hand.

My journey started with getting admission into the Graduate School of Engineering in West Virginia University in Morgantown. I also arranged for the student visa, health clearances and abided by other numerous regulations (excessively bureaucratic) of that time. I also managed to procure the dollars that would take care of the necessary expenses to carry me through the Master's degree. I did not think any more beyond that. Like, whether I wanted to stay in US after the degree or go back or do what. Like I was saying youth does not deliberate – it only does. I was no different. It was just the allure of a better future without any particular shape of any kind. Probably it was a romance of the unknown.

My journey to destination was not straight forward, nor was it simple. At that time there was no trans-pacific or long non-stop air travel. I think the air travel range was around 5000 mile. So coming to America had to be in a few steps. So the itinerary could be all air with stops and changing flights on the way or it could be a complex combination of airplane, ship, train and bus. I chose the later. I don't remember the total thought process. But it had to be a mixture of economic considerations and a desire to go through different lands. So I boarded the passenger cum cargo French steamship 'Marseilles Mariner' from the Bombay port. I must confess I had no travel experience what so ever even in the Indian subcontinent except a small trip to a coastal city of Puri and another small trip to Darjeeling, a hill station in the Himalayas. But I was not nervous and was excited to get on the board of the ship. I felt somehow liberated from the shackle of my country, and was excited that all the places I read in Geography textbook would come alive in front of my eyes. Now a day, thanks to television, satellite and numerous niche cable channels – one can see the whole world in the living room. One can be a world traveler with a bag of potato chips and a few bottles of beer or wine or soda. Now I find the curiosity of adventure and passion to get to know the unknown are much lessened than what we felt when we were young. I had to see the world – not through other's eyes, not through other's writings – but with my own eyes and all the senses. It is a different feeling of euphoria. When the steam's siren announced the start of the journey – I felt boundless joy.

I think the ship had three stories above the deck (in contrast to modern 24 stories above the deck). Slowly the shoreline got smaller and smaller, and finally out of view. What I saw now was big waves all around with that little ship sailing like a small boat in a turbulent ocean. At that time water travel was considered safer than air travel. A little inconvenience – rocking and splashing of water on the deck was to be expected. I don't remember many details – but luckily my roommates were two students who were going to Oxford and Cambridge in England. We got to be friends and hanged around together. Also there were other assorted passengers on the board – but we did not know how to start a conversation with people we did not know. The ship sailed for seven days without any sight of any other boat or any other island on the way. All I saw was big waves and more waves all around. I think man being a land animal, tends to get sea sick when they are away from land for a prolonged period – I also started to feel a little sea-sickness (no big deal). I think the first sight of land was Aden at the south-eastern tip of Arabian Peninsula. The very sight of land seemed like a loaf of bread in front of a hungry man.

Next day the ship berthed in the port of Djibouti. I used to think it was in Somalia (where the pirates are now hijacking unarmed cargo ships) – but not so. It was a separate French enclave – the Republic of Djibouti. It was eight o'clock at night, and most of the passengers were happy to disembark for a taste of walking on the land again. Every port of call was important. All the mails from home were delivered to the ship's address in the port. And all new letters to home could be posted there also. So every stop was important. Next phase was journey through the Red Sea and eventually sailing through the fabled Suez Canal. The sight of the Suez Canal cannot be forgotten. It looked like numerous floating houses on water with all their lights on were in slow and silent procession in one long line. It looked like many candles were lit on the ocean like blazing needles in dense darkness. I think it was a 24-

hour sail through the Suez – then out to the big Mediterranean Ocean. By this time it looked like almost towards the end of journey. Total trip on water was about two weeks long. Next stop was in Barcelona. There also we landed and disembarked briefly. All I remember now was a big and imposing statue of Columbus right at the entry. I don't know whether he was welcoming us or he was looking at the distant sea. The final stop was in Marseilles at the southern tip of France.

From there we three (London being our destination) scrambled towards the waiting train to take us to Calais. I forgot all the details. But I now wonder how we managed to know which train was going to where, as the locals did not speak English. But we managed nevertheless. From Calais, we took the ferryboat to Dover – a port across the English Channel. I regret now that I did not have any camera with me – because it was so exciting at that time. In England it got little easier as we could now read the signs and directions. From Dover to London was another train ride (I think it was about 80 miles).

This writing is getting big. To make it short – in London I had a distant relative (a doctor) who was living in London. He picked me up at the train station. I stayed with them for seven days in London. As the host was busy with his job – I took it on myself to see London by myself. I forgot the details. But I managed to see Piccadilly Circus,

Trafalgar Square etc. London looked such an Architectural city with a regal and polished look. I did not have much money – so did not take any tourist bus etc. It was mostly by subway. Surprisingly I did not find it difficult to navigate to different area. I had always heard of glowing description of the city of pride of the British Empire, and considered myself lucky to see it firsthand.

From there the air flight took me to New York. From New York I took the Greyhound bus to Morgantown (a distance of may be 200 miles). From the Greyhound bus station took a taxi to reach my final destination – the Foreign Student Welcome Center in Morgantown. I don't remember all the details. But I am amazed now that an inexperienced person could connect all the different dots to arrive at the right destination, and that also on time. At that time I did not have time to think. Then was the time to go to the Engineering Department of West Virginia University to let them know of my arrival.

Like I was saying – if anybody now gave me that little money to go that far with everything unknown on the way - I would never take that. Nor would I advise anybody to take that because I am wiser (and less adventurous) now. But youth does not listen to caution of wisdom, That is why they are agents of changes and not us who have grown older and wiser. I don't remember all the small details, but I should have kept a diary then. That would have helped me now to write this blog with more clarity.

Last Respect to Mother-in-Law *(7-24-2009)*

Last few weeks there was no blog. Time was going fast. I noticed after a few weeks my pen is rusted. I always wondered why the basketball players (or any other players) spend so much time practicing their skills before a game, even as they play every day. I also know the Olympic swimmers spend about ten or twelve hours a day during practice. I used to think that was in excess. But now it seems to me the bottom line is to keep one's reflexes sharp as all our activities depend on the agility of neurons in our brain. Keep them field ready all the time if one wants to perform. That was just a side comment. Only professionals or who earn from their activities they need to do that. For others it is for leisure and pleasure, it is not a must, not a do or die.

Looking at the global political landscape, it seems things are a little ho hum. Healthcare, nuclear threat, local unrests, media hypes etc. President Obama is trying to prove that he is a man of words- but finding that it is not always so easy to solve all problems when you listen to everybody's concern and try to cross all the t's and dot all the i's. To me personally it seems all problems are solvable (unless it is in God's hand), but they are made unsolvable by other parties with vested interests and long term agenda. I think the real game is a hurdle race. One may run on a plain field, but when the hurdles are put in - then the outcome becomes uncertain. So the hurdles are basically greed and power, planted by interested parties. As mankind is a creature with those twin viruses of selfishness and ambition, no problem seems easy to solve. Probably man's fate does not lie in an easy solution in any endeavor, as problems and oppositions will occur.

A couple of weeks ago, we got the sad news that my wife's mother passed away. She was 87, but not in bad health. So the news was a shock. We had to make all the quick arrangements for the trip while taking care of alternate arrangements for the businesses while away. I won't go too far in details on this – as it is very personal and private. So I shall limit myself to other things that I noticed. One thing that always intrigued me – how does one overcome sorrow or the pain of a personal loss? In India they have a Sradh (paying last respect to the departed) ceremony on the eleventh day. The closest relatives go through a period of mourning (that includes abstinence from meats and alcohol and other pleasurable activities) for a period of eleven days. Indians tie everything with God or God's wishes – so there is a religious rite performed by a priest. Basically apart from paying respect to all the concerned Gods (Hindus have numerous Gods as many as humans have activities), it is a final farewell to a soul on its onward journey. According to Bhagawad Gita (the most sacred book to Hindus) - the soul discarded its old robe and then moved onward to its journey. This journey goes on through recurring incarnations till one has conquered all the evil temptations on this mortal planet- till one becomes Godhead and is finally liberated from reincarnation. This is called Nirvana. Obviously the underlying thought is that life is pain and suffering that we cause to ourselves- so liberation (or the state of detachments) is the goal. (Needless to say – I don't see anybody liberated from the vices to end his/her reincarnation cycle - as such the planet is getting over-crowded). But we common folks are not concerned with the logic or philosophy of life and death. It is useless to argue whether that kind of thinking is logical or practical – but it is a working social rite that unifies all and tries to smooth the pain of a personal loss, and serves a real purpose of closure of the feeling of loss and helps the bereaved to return to normalcy of everyday life.

As I was wondering, does the pain of a personal loss really go away? I think it cannot go away if one always thinks it is a personal loss. It seems to me everything has a limited boundary or scope, whether it is tangible or intangible. We can count the number of birds or bananas – but when it comes to quantify our happiness or sorrow – we have no numbering device. Even then it is for sure that loss or happiness like anything else, is a limited entity. Some one's feeling may be more intense than others or less. Now when that feeling of loss is shared by many – it is definitely lessened. One feels lightened from the weight of sorrow. When we reached India to the place of ceremony – most of the relatives had gotten over that feeling of loss. They all have new problems, new concerns to deal with. Other events washed away the feeling of loss from most of the attendees. But my wife was kind of carrying the whole weight by herself – which naturally affected her very much. While mingling with all and sharing the feeling of loss she felt much better.

Now it seems to work for people who have lot of friends and relatives to share one's sorrow. But what happens – when someone does not have lot of concerned people to share one's loss – where does it go? I had noticed that in Nancy Reagan's grief and in also some other people's grief. Those who cannot share cannot survive for long and will wither away. I was reading a beautiful account of someone who was struggling with her loss of mother for eight years, and it was never going away. She just could not share it away and the feeling of loss was intense. Finally she took a solo journey through nature for some time. Unbelievably the feeling of loss started to go away. She could think of her mother hiding behind the leaves, and talking to her as they were fluttering in the wind. She would look at the night sky – see all the stars and could feel her mother was twinkling to her. The whole nature was vibrant and in animation, a sensation of life sizzling through everything. She realized she did not lose anything. It was all there – she just could not see it in its old form. But she could feel her mother's presence in everything – in the wind, in the stars, in the waves, everywhere in eternity.

Thus going back to Gita's concept of Life and Death – which emphasizes that death is not a loss. It is a transformation. It is a journey of the unidentifiable entity Soul. If one cannot see the form – she is still there in some other form. It is not a loss, not a negation – but it is a migration of an entity named soul. So all the rituals were not for a person who was not there anymore, but it was a farewell to a traveler (a departed soul) who had stayed his/her duration, and now has become one who would live in memory (not in sight) only. Everything in the world recycles. The water comes down the mountain, travels to the ocean and then comes back as rain and settles as snow again. The cycle goes on. Nothing comes to an end – the duration of its form only expires. There is another school of thought that says attachment always ends in grief when it is gone. So their solution is – don't get attached to anything or anybody if you want to be spared the pain of loss I think that thinking is too harsh. Life is love though it is temporary. Love is to be enjoyed and loss is to be shared.

Understanding Time's Top 100 *(7-31-2009)*

What does a Blog mean? As I under-stand it is an internet terminology and stands for Web Log. That means via blog anybody whoever wishes, can log on one's thought on internet web. Of course this dawns a new social revolution empowering common people to participate in all kinds of dialog – personal, societal, informational, political or anything else. Soviet Communism did crumble before Internet – but many regimes now find it hard to blindfold their own citizens from outside world. The case in point is Iran. One can always dispute the veracity of news sources – but when it comes from common people it carries the stamp of authenticity. The new social revolution ultimately has led to the invention of a tool that satisfies man's gregariousness. Thus Facebook, MySpace etc are bringing more people together and Twitter is helping them to mass communicate instantly. But Blog's function is a little different; it can also mean that blog is just a log of one's thought. It can be fund-raising, consciousness-raising, or it can be a simple diary of thoughts. So Blog's horizon is basically unlimited. It may also mean a depository of thoughts of an individual at one particular time.

My thought is running like this. Most of the time what we talk about is what we need around. So mostly it has transient value. It has no permanence, though it has a direct or indirect relation with events happening at that time. Books are different – they are more meant to be permanent embedment in the memory of time – be it for knowledge, enjoyment or anything else. It is more than transient. When I read that Newspaper Industry is finding it hard to survive in the Internet age, I see mode of transient bites of information trying to destroy the age-old bastion of man viz. books and novels. So I thought why not dabble a little bit into things that are little more than transient. That is what leads me to look and comment on Time Magazine's Top 100 for 2009. That lists the top 100 people who t have influenced our lives most.

Before that a comment I cannot refrain from. This is about the brouhaha of racial altercation between Professor Gates (of Harvard) and Policeman Crowley (of Boston). Seldom do we see President Obama losing his cool in public. But on first chance on this incident – he termed it as evidence of embedded bad race relation in this country and termed the police officer's action as 'stupid'. Probably he should not have commented on a single incident as reflecting all policemen's racial attitude. But then again, who ever thought that a house-owner would be hand-cuffed even after he showed his identity and proof of living there. If nothing else happened, then of course the officer's action is personal misbehavior and personally racial, and if the professor provoked and insulted the officer, then it is not racial at all. I think both party's behavior is not clean, and it makes no sense that the President got involved in this. And the President called it a 'teachable moment'? I did not see any special teaching value of this incident other than a stupid misbehavior.

Going back to topics of top 100 influential people, Time magazine has made 5 categories of twenty top people each. The categories are:- 1) Leaders and Revolutionaries, (2) Builders & Titans, (3) Artists and Entertainers, (4) Heroes and Icons , and (5) Scientists and Thinkers. The first four categories are easily recognizable as they are highly visible on media. Definitely they influence our lives, behavior, future and security. But whoever cares to think how a scientist made our life different? We just talk about Newton and Einstein and some other profoundly notables. We seem to acknowledge they are genius, but our interest ends there. That does not seem right. Even in early ages we always had leaders, builders, artists and heroes – but progress of civilization does not owe much to them. They did not raise us from the dark ages. It was done solely by the dedicated scientists who by their work, dedication and intuition extended our frontier of knowledge, made us understand our relationship with things and harnessed nature's attributes to advantages of all. I don't think we pay enough respect to them appropriate to their contribution. So Time magazine's issue was important to me to get to know who and what of the world of science. This gave me an opportunity to understand them a little better. So I shall briefly go over them. The numbering does not mean any order of importance.

1) Nouriel Roubini (New York University Professor): A macro economist, who saw the

impending collapse of the housing market about a decade ago. While the Fed, Alan Greenspan etc were jubilant about the growth of US economy- Mr. Roubini was skeptical. So definitely he is outstanding.

2) Amory Lovin (Rocky Mountain Institute); A green visionary and environmentalist. He was fighting against our improper habit of wasting natural resources and was exhorting all to go green in the direction of renewable energy. He has been doing this for the last three decades. So definitely he is outstanding.

3) Jon Favreau (Massachusetts): Obama's chief speech writer. At age 27 he is the director of speech writing of the panel of White House speech writers. Though it is an outstanding achievement at a very young age – still I don't see how he can be so influential.

4) Dambisa Moyo (Zambian): She is an advocate of Foreign aids to Africa to be channeled through private sector. She argues that the corrupt Governments are the cause of Africa's backwardness. It is definitely a leadership issue but of a limited scope.

5) Dan Barber (New York): A chef of organic food. He was awarded $30 million for developing organic foods by the Rockefeller foundation. He has been an inspiration to other chefs around the

world. Though highly laudable, I don't see him to be of great importance.

6) Yoichoro Nambu (University of Chicago): A physicist and Nobel Laureate. He has continued where Einstein ended. Einstein was looking for a Unified Field Theory – where all the forces of nature including gravity and electro-magnetism could be correlated. This subatomic physicist came up with the theory that new subatomic particles are born when one form of energy transcends into another form. He termed the particle as Higgs Bison. The giant colliders in Texas are trying to find this subatomic particle. (My understanding is very sketchy on this). This is definitely on the outer edge of human knowledge. His contribution in understanding nature must be of great value to all.

7) Roland Fryer (Harvard University): A social economist. He has looked into all phases of lives of African-Americans. His study has focused and illuminated the disparity, standards and vulnerability of black Americans. Thus he can be applauded for bringing a coherent understanding of the blacks in US. This is great and a contribution of science to human welfare of living better.

8) Martin Lindstorm (Danish): He is a world renowned brand consultant. His book 'Buyology' took a bold step in neuroscience to figure out how

we choose and decide things. I should read more to understand it better.

9) Barbara Hogan (South African Health Minister); She is an Aid-activist and made Aids control a duty of the Government. That is good,

10). David Sheff (Author): His book 'Beautiful Boy- A Father's Journey Through His Son's Meth Addiction'. This is a book about a parent's loss of a child to drugs. It definitely will help other parents., but I don't see him in top 100.

There are twenty more people in the top 20 list. This writing is getting long,

***

8			4		6			7
						4		
	1					6	5	
5		9		3		7	8	
				7				
	4	8		2		1		3
	5	2						9
		1						
3				9		2		5

He Liked Sudoku (8-14-2009)

He was just another bored passenger- waiting for the announcement to board the plane. But the plane was delayed for another two hours. All waiting passengers seemed fidgety. The flight was a midnight nonstop flight from Los Angeles to Taipei – a long stretch of 16 hours. Most of the people I know get nervous when they think of the long immobile confinement in the plane up at 36000 feet high in the sky. They say the prolonged immobility can cause hemorrhage. Then when you add another two or three hours of waiting in the terminal (another form of mobile confinement) - then that extra straw can always break many ordinary camels' backs. I had taken some books to read on the plane. I am not that kind of person who will complain at everything - meaning anything that causes inconvenience. On the other hand I take it as a great opportunity to experience the convenience of a no-sweat high speed air travel undisturbed by any traffic (hopefully no other errant planes come on the way), and thank God to let me participate in the unimaginable short duration of travel that used to take months even sixty or seventy years ago. I think planes are like a genie's magic flying carpet. Even then the confinement (lack of body freedom) bothers me. But nothing seemed to bother this gentleman.

I was just curious what was he doing. He had a small book in hand which he was not reading, but studying with great intensity, and lifted his pencil every now and then to mark something on the page of the book he was on. It was not a crossword puzzle, where players close their eyes to come up with the right word. Sometimes a smile flashed on his face – sometimes the forehead was wrinkled with worry. He was not looking at any one or anything, but only at the book in his hand. Finally we got on the plane. Everybody got in the plane and got seated. After perfunctory ritual of the instructional video showing how to get off the plane if the craft lands in water, the hostess told us that if anybody sitting near the emergency exit door felt inconvenient, can report to the airline hostess for another suitable seat. It did not seem anybody cared at all. Then the hostess gave us hot wipes to wipe away our sweats probably caused by the long discomfort of waiting in the airport terminal. Then the pilot turned off the main lights in the cabin to induce a proper sleeping atmosphere for the weary passengers as it was after midnight. Many passengers already applied themselves to a serious slumber and some passengers got inebriated to forget the long confinement in the plane. But not this gentleman. He had his reading light on, and he was immersed in the book with his pencil in hand.

There was another old lady in the plane – she was checking her sugar level every so often by pricking her own finger. I don't know what she was monitoring. I never heard of any body's sugar going up in the plane – as she was not eating anything. I had an aisle seat next to my wife. I always ask for that because I want my emergency passage to the rest room unobstructed. I did not see that gentleman to get up to go to the toilet or bothering to take a nap. My curiosity was pricked about this gentleman, and I wondered what kind of book that was that made this gentleman oblivious of everybody else around. Then I fell asleep. I am a happy sleeper on the plane without any external aid of alcohol – which sounds unbelievable to many people.

The flight was kind of smooth except in the China Sea area, where the plane bumped quite a bit to the dismay of all. Then the plane landed at Taipei International. We were on transit, as it was a flight from Los Angeles to Bangkok. We got down from the plane and saw many people running towards the rest rooms. I think it was probably due to too much drink and too little activity in the plane. And the rest room was full of smoke. It was probably meant for 30 people, and all the gentlemen were happily puffing their cigarettes after tasting freedom on land. It must be said that at that time 'No Smoking' rule was not everywhere and not for everybody. We had seats in the plane at the border of Smoking and No-smoking zones – where we were subject to heavy cigarette smokes drifting from the Smoking zone. We also watched a big altercation between two passengers. The smoking passenger (a bulky heavy weight) was emphasizing his right to smoke and freedom, the non-smoking passenger (a small wrinkled woman) was emphasizing her right of clean air and freedom. While the noisy clash between conflicting rights was going on – we were subjected to the obnoxious cigarette smell. But nothing did seem to bother that gentleman who was intensely focused on his book in hand. Anyway when he sat down, I passed by him and noticed that he had a book in hand named 'Sudoku Puzzles'. I was really impressed at the Sudoku puzzle that took away all the worries from that gentleman. And I wondered how many were there like him.

I found out there were millions like him around the world. Since then I have taken to Sudoku puzzles – but my intensity is nothing like what I saw in that gentleman. For those who may be wondering what the Sudoku puzzle looks like - it is a game of single digit numbers that must be placed in the right location. It is a simple game with simple rules, does not need any special knowledge or word power to solve. It is a 9x9 square with 9 subsets of smaller squares. Like a Crossword puzzle one does not need a dictionary to check out the answers. I also read tidbits about Sudoku and how it affected many lives.

I heard from BBC radio that an Australian jury was dismissed in a criminal case as the jurors were playing Sudoku while testimonies were going on. The jurors were put on trial. Their defense was that the testimonies were boring repetition of trivial matters and they were tired of it, and also they were keeping themselves awake. The judge had mistakenly thought the jurors were taking notes while actually they were filling blanks in a Sudoku puzzle. By the way the Sudoku-playing jurors were sentenced to four years in prison for contempt of court and for showing little respect to the honorable civic duty of deciding whether any crime was committed. Sudoku puzzles are now published in 400 newspapers in 58 countries, and their popularity seems on the rise. It is a modified form of Latin Square (I don't know the detail), and was modified by a New York architect in 1979. It used to be published then in some US newspapers, but really became viral in 1994 when a Japanese game maker modified it further and named it Sudoku. Sudoku means 'single digit', because the game is confined to numbers between 1 to 9. Now they have World Championships with prize money every year in different countries.

I was even surprised to see an article about fighting dementia. It prescribed 'Sudoku' along with Google, Antioxidant foods, Exercise, Friendship and Meditation, Avoiding alcohol and Tooth brushing. Wow. Rubik's Cube puzzle came in the market in 1980, and is still popular but not a craze. Now I realize that gentleman in the plane knew something about Sudoku that I did not know then.

***

End of a Kennedy Dynasty *(9-4-2009)*

Actually this blog is not a paean for Senator Ted Kennedy. I don't write political blogs, so there is no reason why I should pick a topic of a political person like Senator Kennedy who just passed away recently. Somehow the Kennedy clans mesmerized me like many others. What was it that made people look up to them, listen to them and believe in them in spite of their many moral lapses (by conventional standards)? This writing is about the mist, about the siren, about the halo they seemed to possess. He was the last one of the fabled four that has captured our nation's adoration and imagination for more than half a century.

Even if we don't resort to hyperbole, we have to admit that he was a phenomenally productive Senator and was an activist for the poor and have-nots. Activists are not mere benefactors; they try to cure the system that leads to poverty. I see lot of political activism on behalf of the rich and greedy CEO's as if they are the true custodians of capitalism and many people believe our progress is due to their pragmatic running of our Capitalism's business machine. But not many fight to cure the causes of the less fortunate average Joes and plead for a fair share of the enormous riches of this country. When someone stands for the less fortunate, then he is stamped as a dim-witted liberal. And the liberals are portrayed as gateways to hell. We let the greedy CEOs rob our jobs and gamble our future, but if someone believes otherwise then he is a disgusting liberal and almost an enemy of the State, as if their causes will usher communism like in Russia. Well I don't belong to that school of fear and nihilism, so I think his causes were noble and humanitarian. Anyway, what I am getting at is that he may not be great but he was definitely a voice for the common men, those who are left out of the sunshine of prosperity that we all seem to bask in. But I think even then he probably would not have made much mark on our minds. But he being a Kennedy seems to make him larger than he probably was. That was the Kennedy myth, Kennedy charisma.

If I am neither a political person nor think that he was a great one – then why I am writing about him? This is something that perplexed me also. He was definitely privileged; he enjoyed all the advantages of being rich. His infidelity, love for booze and women were well known. Even then they seemed so adorable, so polished, and so classy as if they were characters in a romance novel. Were they real and bigger than us, or were they just polished poster boys of an imaginary American Royalty? America is a land of common people, where common people have risen to great heights by their own hard work, ambition, ingenuity and idealism, and that made USA a defacto leader of the world. The Americans are no royalties, but they rose by their own bootstraps from being penniless immigrant settlers to become the wealthiest nation on this planet. They don't like to be dictated by any individual – good or bad. They knew that evil lurks everywhere, and if not under constant vigilance the evil will take over. They hated any kind of ruler – benevolent or otherwise. They drove the Royal masters out of this soil. So here Royalties were suspected. They were deemed parasites, living off common people's sweat and toil. They are not like the British, who know Kings or Queens are not to be trusted to be their leaders and arbiters of their fate, even then they could not shake off the Kings or Queens. As if they were the virtual fathers of the nation. Their Royalties are adored, decorated, respected with royal honors and shows of royalty. Without any virtual parents they would feel like orphans. That is why the British have the showcase Royalties. But America is not like that. Americans don't feel orphans without the Kings and Queens, as they have termed their founding leaders as fathers of the nation. So Americans don't feel like orphans. Then what is the attraction to a family that looks and behaves like royalty but are not so actually?

Probably, because the Kennedy story has all the ingredients that capture our interest and sympathy. They had wealth, bravado, patriotism, passion, ambition and empathy with a dash of tragedy, lapses and tremendous personal losses. All the elements of fiction shaped their lives. Thus they always attracted us, though they have repelled us on occasions with some racy shenanigans. It seems somehow destiny blended their success with tears, made their achievements on a platform of tremendous personal loss. Ted Kennedy was the youngest of nine siblings. Four were boys. They were the ones that composed the Kennedy saga. The eldest brother (Joe) was the brightest and their parents dreamt that he would become the president one day. But tragedy struck him in 1944 while flying in a combat mission. The family hope then centered on John – not hundred percent physically perfect, suffering from back pain and living on pain-killers. John took on the highest crown of the land by defeating a pragmatist and seasoned Nixon. Somehow he was probably the youngest president in the nation at that time. He exuded youth, vitality and hopes that captured nation's imagination. I remember the pictures of his children playing below his desk in the White House. White House was meant for guys with white hairs, we had to rub our eyes to believe what was going on. Then also he had a beautiful wife, elegant life style and really seemed of royal bearings. He was made of things that dreams are made of. He did not succeed in everything he wanted to do, but life also did not give him much time to implement his dream. He was struck down in 1961 in Dallas.

Next to fall in 1968 was his next brother Robert. That was also in the run for presidency. He also inspired, he was also full of passion and idealism. Whether right or wrong, nobody could challenge his patriotism and he was also a shoo-in for the democratic nomination for the presidential candidate. How much would any family sacrifice for the well being of the nation, how much tragedy would finally take their quest for the presidency away? The answer was simple. No obstacle was strong enough to stop them. Because they were born to be different - different enough to make an impression forever.

Overall they captured our imagination. I remember vividly the presidential inauguration speech of his elder brother John. He inspired all, he built up hopes, gave us promises, built a bridge of friendship (with goodwill ambassadors) with the rest of the world, broke down his adversaries with steely resolve, and promised a newer and braver world where we all stand to help each other, share our success, and join hands to defeat the challenges. He promised us landing on Moon (an almost impossible dream it seemed at that time), he looked straight into the eyes of Khrushchev and tamed him down.

After Joe, John and Robert the baton was passed on to Ted. He also strove to soar high, but his personal lapses and irresponsible behavior in the Chappaquiddick incident in 1971 barred the door to Presidency to him forever. Barred by destiny, he rose to great height as a Senator from Massachusetts. He has been elected a record 9 times as a Senator. He became the champion for the causes of common people. He made his contribution in many major legislations (like Americans with Disability Act, Family Leave Act, Labor's Safety Act in creation of OSHA, Aids Legislation, His crusade on Immigration Reform and he conscientiously voted against the Iraq war etc). Above all he was a dreamer. His brother John had the vision, Bobby had the passion, and Ted had the dream. His support for Obama clinched Obama to get democratic nomination and prevented a sour division in the Democratic Party. Above all he belonged to the band of four that sailed and steered the nation through most difficult times. He may be a down soldier, but his fists were up even when he was struck by brain tumor, and he defiantly proclaimed that 'Hope again rises and the Dream lives on'. I also think so. So the Kennedys are not really gone – they will be with us all the time to inspire us and give us

the resilience and fortitude to tide over any
challenge that the nation may face.

***

A Book is Published (9-18-2009)

Somehow as usual I am not getting much
time to write blogs recently. Probably
the reason is my preoccupation with having my
first book published. *A Random Journey of Mind*
(published by Lulu) is kind of self-published with
very little coaching. Though Lulu has published it,
still I had to go through intensive editing of about
450 pages. Being not a person of literature or
journalism, I had no background in syntax and
formatting etc. I did not even know the difference
between Emdash and Ellipsis; did not know how
to make a TOC, nor knew about page numbering
nor linked and delinked pages. I did not know the
workings of ` pdf` formatting, embedded fonts,
did not know about the `pdf` incompatibility
between Word 2003 and Word 2007. Did not
know that pdf by Adobe and by other software
vendors don't mesh with each other. In other
words my editing effort was kind of groping in
darkness, finding obstacles – then resolving the

obstacle by reading and participating in community forums. There are real nice people in community forums, who are very kind and helpful. I think these people are the lubricants of the society - without them the society would not move in the right direction. When I reached a brief spell of success my ignorance led to another obstacle. I don't know if everybody can understand what I am talking about - except may be those who have suffered firsthand. Then also there were time gaps in communication between publisher and writer, the lack of direct conversation, exchanging questions and delayed answers through e-mail. Finally everything seems to be resolved. But due to its volume of 450 pages, cost of printing and retailer's cut – the sale price is a hefty $30.00.

Finally the book 'A Random Journey of Mind' is born. Google was gracious to link the book to their search machine so that anyone can find the book right away when queried by the name of the book. As I know every creation has birth pang, I don't mind all the pains. Now though, I don't have much hope of selling a lot of copies. Marketing is a different ball game. It is not for the shy and low decibel people. Yet self-publishing is like fulfillment of a personal goal, one gets the satisfaction of expressing oneself. Not really any great absolute achievement and it definitely does not matter to anybody else. There are millions like me and their sale basket is still untouched by any buyer. I just have done mass emailing to my friends and relatives of about 80 people – exhorting them to spread the news around. I know in my heart that not all friends feel the same tender way I do. Also most people think they are the last destination of my sales effort. They don't realize that they can be another link to their friends, who in turn should ditto- till the book clicks with the right person with right interest. So I just have to wait and see what is in fate for this book. My goal was not to sell a lot of books to make money, but to leave a footprint of myself for posterity. If anybody is interested they can now get the book at Lulu.com (either as a paperback or an e-book). Amazon, Barnes & Noble and other major retailers are also participating as a retailer. This book is a POD (Print on Demand) so it is going to be available as long as Lulu lives. and never would be out-of-print when the shelf copies are gone. I just wish good luck to myself and I don't know how many others care to join me.

***

A Grandparents Day (9-18-2009)

I was trying to find the reasons of my inattention to new blogs, which have become more infrequent than before. But I hate to neglect blogs altogether. It is a snapshot of current failings, current accomplishments and current thoughts of mine and others as whole. That is why I also don't like to have too much gap between blogs. The current topic is Grandparents Day. The Grandparents Day this year fell on September 13th (the first Sunday after Labor Day). In my last blog about 'Grandmas' on December 21, 2007 I mentioned about Grandparents Day. I don't want to repeat all that. But to recap briefly - Grandparents Day was officially proclaimed as a National Day of Celebration in 1978 (by President Carter). Margaret Mead (anthropologist) found out that almost all cultures except the Western cultures incorporate Grandparents in their daily lives. So the approaches to Grandparents Day are not identical everywhere. It seems the Western Culture thinks that one day in 365 days is enough to say thanks to Grandparents. So really the rest 364 days are not Grandparents Day, meaning that they may not to be seen and can be forgotten during all this time. My thoughts are really different. I think the concept itself is faulty and artificial. It has not much meaning or soul into it. But that is not why I am writing this blog.

I am writing this blog because we were invited to our grandson Shaun's preschool. He is three years old now. My wife and I were happy to be invited as such. Time allotted for the visit was one hour – from 10 to 11. When we came in Shaun was sitting near the teacher who was reading a book. He knows a lot compared to others of his age. But he is kind of shy around others. But in his home he is a completely different hyper person. He knows the numbers, alphabets and possesses a very good vocabulary. His brother Trevor (almost two years younger) is always in awe of him. Shaun is a completely different persona at school. The teacher served us cold drinks and cookies to share with our grand kids. They had done some coloring of sketches of grandparents. It was a very nice gesture of the school to bring in the grandparents to share some moments with their grand kids. I understand many communities in East Coast celebrate Grandparents Day in more elaborate fashion. They have community activities, many projects involving the grandparents and grandkids. I was looking at the guideline of suggested activities on that day. Most of the guidelines suggest Grandparents day to be a whole family day so that the bondage between generations become more intimate. They also suggest that as Grandparents are links to the past, they can narrate about events of past and can bring life to old days gone by.

I don't want to say much on all this. The whole thing seems so hollow and artificial (though I acknowledge the good gesture of the school). A 'thank you' means nothing if it is not connected to deeper feelings. I think the paradigm of family structure is at fault here. Usually a normal human life span covers three generations – with one generation going out and one coming in. So each family should have a three generational structure. But over here what I see is a two generation family structure- with parents and their kids only (with grandparents left out). That means the structure is good for a fifty or sixty year span of one's life. By the time the present parents have finished raising their children, the parents themselves will be superfluous. When they become fifty or sixty there is a good chance that they will be marginalized as grandparents themselves and will be remembered only once a year. They will be victims of their own self centered narrow thinking of what My Family means. The bond between grandparents and grandkids are too deep to be trivialized and cannot be ended with a single day's smile and a thank you bouquet of flowers. It is not one person's fault or blindness, it is a societal error.

Actual family structure is three generational. Margaret Mead said that, and most of world (so called less advanced nations) maintain that structure. Yes that creates additional responsibilities to parents, but that is more natural, humane and practical. I also think that way. But I am not finding fault with anybody here in particular. Because they are products of the environment they grew in. It is a systemic fault. But I guess we all have to live with that unless the society changes. Whatever that is, we were very happy that the school did something to cheer up the grandparents. Many of them truly are very lonely and love-deprived. Society owes to you much more than what it acknowledges. Happy Grandparents Day.

***

A Wedding at Bellagio *(10-2-2009)*

Last weekend we attended the wedding of our friend's daughter in Las Vegas. It was a beautiful ceremony, well attended by friends and relatives. The wedding took place at Bellagio in Las Vegas. I shall come back to it later. But I have to unload some confusion inside me about the famed Polish director Roman Polanski. He committed some illegal sexual crimes on a minor while she was drugged into semi-consciousness. It was back in 1968. I remember those days. It was traumatic for all in Los Angeles. The crime was committed shortly after Polanski had lost his wife Sharon Tate in a gruesome random murder spree by the Charles Mansion clan and nobody knew who the killers were. Charles Mansion and his clan were apprehended in desert probably six months later when one of them was boasting about their own heroic exploits. So Polanski was charged with the lewd act while he was still in shock (?). He fled US to avoid sentencing, though he confessed about his illegal sexual activity. He fled to France and became a French citizen and avoided extradition. He probably thought everybody had by this forgotten what he did 40 years ago – now that he is an old man. But lo and behold he has been caught. This speaks very highly of the vigilant LA police detectives. But what got me is that many people now are saying that he has suffered enough (escaped Nazi holocaust etc), and contributed enough (won some Oscars). Though I am an admirer of his films (I liked Rosemary's Baby), still my cerebral noodles are totally scrambled on this. Does it mean that the punishment can be forgiven if somebody has earned enough credits by one's contribution in arts etc? So does that mean that society is willing to give a punishment-free license to an artist, who has danced, directed, acted, wrote, painted or won Noble Prize etc? Then also when does the statute of limitation expire for major and minor crimes? I think it never does, as Law defines the boundary of acceptable behaviors in a society. Law by necessity has to be impartial to be effective and enforceable. But the victim can probably allow some concession from the level of punishment. I know it is a thorny issue, and not for me to solve.

A wedding is always an exciting event to attend. On top of that it was going to be a Las Vegas wedding. And for that matter a wedding at Bellagio. I know Las Vegas is for the rich and Bellagio is for the richer strata of society. Then again it was a sweet occasion and it was a splurge of luxury on our part. We felt very happy when we heard about the marriage in Las Vegas – because she had lost her dad (a dear friend of us) long ago while she was in school, and now she was in love with a smart and sweet man, and they had decided to start their life's journey together with hand in hand. She also has a son who is very smart and sweet. I think Kyle is only eight years old. It was amazing the way he was integrated in the whole thing. The new groom also exchanged rings and commitment to the boy. The whole party took place on a terrace facing the inner yards of gardens and swimming pools. Kyle was amazing, he clapped, danced, emceed, sang to the merriment of all. He was so happy to see his mother going to be happy. I have not seen so much maturity in a small boy like him. Amazing he knew most of the names of everybody invited (about 120 people or so).

Our job was twofold. One was to participate in the merriment of the party, and second was to take care of our 22 month old grandson Tejas when needed. My daughter was the bride's best friend and was very involved in the whole thing; naturally a little extra help did not hurt. Tejas does not speak complete sentence yet, but he has an amazing storage of vocabulary and amazing expression ability. Like when I am babysitting him, he is playing with me as if I am his best friend. But when somebody else comes to him, he holds my hand and guides me to the nearest door signaling my time is up and I can leave now! It was a party for the grownups with drinks and dances. But Tejas was made an exception, and he handled himself so graciously in his suit as if he understood the whole function and what was going on. We were living on the same floor though in different rooms at a distance. But Tejas's babbling and practicing of abbreviated sounds, loud dictation of his ever changing new wishes (like dictating which show on TV he wanted to watch – Elmo etc - and what snacks he wanted to eat etc) kept the decibel level on the floor high (not too high). That was a distinct advantage to us to figure out which room Tejas was in. He also went to the swimming pool with his mother, but he preferred land to water, so he kind of walked all over the inner yards of four fountains and six swimming pools etc. He seemed like a true *Bellagionese*.

Though it was a one day only stay there, we enjoyed it very much. For those who may not know, Bellagio is one of the four top luxury resorts on the strip. The others are Venetian, Wynn, and Trump Tower. Bellagio is named after a village on the beautiful lake Como. I read it is one of the most beautiful places in North Italy. Luxury is the game, price is no bar. A few drinks and some snacks can hit our modest pockets very hard. Steve Wynn and his enterprise own five of the prize resorts (Mirage, Venetian, Wynn, Aladdin, Caesars Place) from what I read. Bellagio is stocked with famous and rare paintings of mediaeval European artists. It has a fantastic upscale shopping gallery. It has a museum of statues in dynamic poses. It's dancing ballet of fountains, light and music is famous. It also has a botanical garden and also an avant-garde residential-commercial living complex next to it. I don't know about all the resorts, but Bellagio has a look and feel of luxury. It has world famous sommeliers and very inventive cuisines. I know wealth flies on wings of luxury.

One thing that strikes me is when somebody says it has a class. What does it mean really? I heard many of the Silicon Valley millionaires have no class – as they have their board meetings with hamburgers and cokes in their garages (though they have plenty of dough), whereas the people who have class dine with vintage wines in fine crystals. So wealth does not signify class per se. Class probably denotes a prerogative that one grows up with. The class concept also probably fosters a sense of exclusivity proclaiming oneself to be on a higher level of living (not in thinking or in humanity though). But if one does not have the inborn prerogatives – can he never achieve a class? Yes one can. All one has to do is go and live in Bellagio or other similar class resorts. So we all enjoyed the class by living at Bellagio though for a very short while. Our trip was very nice – because we attended a very sweet event and saw a sweet future in the making. And I think that was a class wedding in a class Bellagio.

***

Jia Your Mom is calling you *(10-23-2009)*

I don't know Jia or who she is. Only thing I know that she is a little Chinese girl. She caught my attention from a newspaper article I came across in the Los Angeles Times recently. Jia is kind of a cultural phenomenon in China. But this kind of thing is not uncommon now in the internet age. I shall come back to this later. But before that I have to note what else caught my attention during the last two weeks. During the month of October (I think before the winter sets in) the Noble Selection Committees announce the names of the awardees in all the different disciplines as per criteria, benefactor Mr. Noble had ordained in his will. The Noble selection committees do not pick up names out of nowhere and anoint anybody with glory and fame. They have to choose from many contesting candidates whose names have been submitted to them. And who submitted the names? They are not ordinary people like us. They are distinguished people themselves who are also Noble Laureates, by those who are in the highest echelons of the society across all the nations of the world. So the Noble Selection Committee, in their cool deliberations, had to choose the most likely candidate amongst names submitted. When it came to selecting the Peace Noble Laureate they came up with the choice of President Obama. What surprised me is the lack of decency of the Republican Party spokesmen, who criticized the selection. According to them President Obama has not really achieved the peace and they suggested that the committee should have chosen somebody else who has done actual peaceful work, and not someone who is only trying to get there. What I cannot grasp is why everything has to be political. It is not the American voters that were making the selection. Why cannot they acknowledge and honor the fellow American who is being honored by a distinguished group of people who are not under the spell of American politics? I am not going to debate the decision, but just want to be proud of the award they bestowed on another American. Why the partisanship has to be so mean? If one of their own had won the prize they probably would have applauded? May be President Bush and Vice President Cheney did not make the cut in their decision, though they did whatever they could to establish permanent peace on this earth. So? All I can say is that any honor cannot be demanded, it has to be achieved. As for Peace, it is ever elusive; one can try to achieve it by peaceful means only. Anyway...

Back to Jia. Her name is Jia Junpeng and everybody is saying that her mother is calling her for dinner. Hence the catch phrase '*Jia Junpeng your mom is calling you for dinner*'. It is now an internet craze in China. Everybody is talking about Jia and her mother. The Automobile dealers are putting up billboards saying Jia your mom is calling you to drive their car to go for dinner. It is a buzz word. In cartoons even president Obama interrupted his speech to remind Jia that her mother was calling her for dinner. Why is the whole nation obsessed with Jia and why should they worry if her mom is calling her for dinner? Researchers dug deep into this and found only 14 girls have the unusual Chinese name of Jia. I also read that it is so viral that it has infected all the Chinese population even beyond Internet. I had no idea that such silliness can engulf a whole nation – specially the Chinese people, who are considered relatively serious in their behavior. I know over here Americans enjoy their goofiness. They have TV shows of funny videos. They came up with You Tube videos showing silly dog jumps, babies tumbling, cats singing etc. The Chinese Communist Party officially analyzed the pheno-menon and classified it as 'a demonstration of collective boredom'. It means the teen agers or young people have no exciting places to go, or exciting things to do, and also they do not want to be parted from the computer or internet. Hence they created imaginary Jia Junpeng and having some laughs about the somber Chinese society which abides by whatever their elders ask them to do, even when to eat. Whatever be it, it has happened before. These kind of viral quips are not new. They belong to a genre of fictitious imagination, which are products of the internet age. The Internet can propagate the silliness among all the internet denizens with a lightning speed. The genre is called 'Meme' (it rhymes with

Cream). It is a new coinage of word in English vocabulary.

Since I did not know anything about Memes I had to look into it more. I remember the TV show Ally Mcbeal (1995) where there was a Dancing Baby on the screen. Though I did not know what was that really, now I read that it was a meme that was very popular at that time. Now the study of memes has become a discipline called 'Memetics'. It studies the Memes and how they spread across the population. They theorize that meme is a postulated cultural unit (like a gene) that is transmitted from one mind to another through internet or paper or books or movies or any other cultural media. Then the unit goes through a process of variation, competition and mutation amongst its users. Basically the process follows the Darwinian evolution model. Some memes survive, some perish. Actually I don't want to go deep into the theories, but I thought it was an interesting finding. And memes are not idle creation, but they are a real product of the desire for levity in human minds.

So what are my thoughts? We know all living things evolve. Living things procreate, evolve, multiply and then perish. So memes are also living things except that they propagate through human minds. Thus in Internet an idea or a catch phrase is born, and then that is transmitted to other users who transmit to other users and the small catch phrase becomes viral. It is always true that ideas are living entities that propagate from one person to another person, propagate from one generation to another, mutates during the process, and ultimately loses its longevity and falls out of public favor. That has happened with all religious ideas and social customs. In other words memes are little units of entertainment created by human mind. It may also carry a message, a frustration, a gripe etc. Memes spread faster in the internet age– some may jump out of internet and become part of social verbiage. Some are better known than others. So, who is Jia Junpeng really? It seems Jia represents a Chinese stereotype that does things whatever their superiors want them to do. That struck a chord in the Chinese society, and made that catchphrase so viral. And where can we find Jia? She is not in the physical world, but we can find her as a meme

**

A Seminal Decade *(1-15-2010)*

My pen is kind of rusty. But I thought no matter how rusty it is, it is time to reminisce the past year. Blog is one way of marking the events of our lives and history. So the first order of business should be to wish A Happy New Year to all. But my thoughts are a little different. Instead of reminiscing on the events of last year alone that just ended why not ruminate a little bit about the decade that just ended. I see last decade was a seminal decade in modern human history – a decade in which our utopia was broken, our limitation was exposed and we were confronted by a realization that no matter how powerful we are, no one is strong enough to conquer all enemies and no one is rich enough to solve all problems. Many things happened in last decade that will change our lives forever. But while I was thinking along that line, I also see that one of our neighboring countries (Haiti) has been devastated by a humongous earthquake of magnitude 7.3. It is too tragic to overlook the suffering of fellow human beings though they are not exactly our problems. The more organized and advanced nations might have fared better, but this impoverished neighbor was not equipped enough nor advanced enough nor lucky enough to survive this catastrophic event. I am talking about the Haitian Earthquake that struck the tiny Caribbean island on January 12, a few days ago with casualties estimated to be around 200,000.

As I am aware of my limited knowledge in history and geography I had to do a little search about Haiti. All I knew before was that Haiti was a very impoverished, tiny Caribbean nation - not enough info to form any understanding. Now I know this country is the western half of a Caribbean island, the eastern portion being Dominican Republic. It is about 10000 square miles and mountainous. It is in a chain of islands south of Cuba, followed by Haiti and Dominican Republic, then Puerto Rico etc. It is the only other French colony in the Western Hemisphere besides Canada's Montreal regions. United States had occupied the island briefly in the early part of the last century. It has a population of about ten million people. The earthquake struck their capital city Port Au Prince, a dense population center of about one million people. About three-quarter million Haitians live in United States who support their relatives back home. It is the first Black Country that gained independence from France. The island is French speaking on west side and Spanish speaking on eastern side. It is so because the French pirates used to operate from the west side and the Spanish pirates from the east side. Later on the pirates became settlers on this Caribbean paradise and imported slaves from Africa and started plantation. It is also kind of commercially isolated from rest of the Latin American nations. After a long reign of the Duvalier family, Haitian people finally overthrew the dictator and established a People's Republic in 1987. People are very impoverished and live on an average income of $2 a day. (I know this averaging business is tricky – as statistically US families produce 1.6 children per family. Figure out that fractional child!).

I just mentioned a little bit about Haiti to remind us that they also do have some history, had struggled for independence and do exist alongside us, and we are all bound by a universal brotherhood. They have political problems, economic problems, development problems. Most importantly their problems are also human problems. When a person in distress is attacked, when a child cries in agony, when a nation is thoroughly shaken up, shattered and slammed on the ground, it definitely needs help. We cannot just close our eyes and pat ourselves in smug contentment. President Obama has come forward and stretched his hand of help and promised to do whatever US can to help this hapless brother in the Caribbean. The problems are enormous, and it needs cooperation from all countries. Starvation, epidemic, hopelessness etc are going to strike next. I am also happy to see that doctors, nurses, fire fighters, rescue squads, army engineers, hospital supplies etc are already in Haiti to help. I know natural disaster is nothing new to Haiti. They were slammed by three hurricanes last year. I don't know what a small person like me can do, except to make a donation to Red Cross, who will be the Angels at work. I also know the Americans are broad hearted. In spite of severe economic duress and personal hardships they will open their wallets and help as much as they can do. And I heard about millions of dollars pouring in from all sides. America is good and noble, we are there when any nation is in distress and their people suffer.

I also heard many countries (including Dominican Republic and many other small countries) have come forward with money, goods and rescue efforts. This is as it should be, because we are all bonded and bounded by our common humanity as we share the same planet. But I did not hear any rich Arab nation (flush with godsend unearned oil money) to come forward with help and donation. They probably would have come forward if it was a Muslim nation to preserve Islam. They spend their enormous wealth to spread their religion. As if their world is different. Nobody can dictate anybody, but it kind of pains me that's why I mentioned it.

Going back to the events of the last decade, many events occurred that impacted lives of their countrymen. Indian Ocean Tsunami in 2004 perished more than 200,000 people. The Bam earthquakes in Iran shattered a whole town and killed upward of 20,000 people. In 2008 Sichuan province earthquake demolished a whole town and about 10 million people had to be relocated. Pakistan survived a major collapse when their popular leader Benazir Bhutto was assassinated, that raised the specter of Taliban control of nuclear armed Pakistan. Then there were terrorist attacks on numerous occasions on different targets in India (including the parliament). And there were other major events that I cannot recollect now. But those incidents are not seminal. They are deadly serious and jarred the bones of the affected countries, but life or life styles won't be changed.

So I shall categories the incidents that I think are seminal (not in order of importance).

1. Terrorist attack on World Trade center in 2001: this exposed the ubiquitous threat from the terrorists. That changed the way we travel and created a chasm between the militant Islam and rest of the world. It seems like a Third World War, except that not a single state is culprit here, nor is the enemy visible and stationed in a war zone. It seems the bad elements of the militant Islam have declared war on the rest of the world, disrupting normal lives of common people everywhere. I don't see the terrorists have any single aim; all they want is to spread terror by indoctrinating innocent and probably illiterate or overzealous jihadists. This war is going to be waged with no end in sight. That's why I consider the terrorist attack as seminal. It did one thing good by uniting most of the world in their common objectives of confronting terrorism. Stupidly the terrorists have awakened the giant

and they will be eternally on run till they are driven away from all civilized countries of the world. Hopefully things will get better when this generation of Jihadist leaders becomes extinct.

2. Collapse of big western banks and financial centers in 2008: this decade marked the time when our way of life of easy credits and living beyond our means got jolted. The capitalism as it is practiced got mortal shock. Common people felt the crunch after losing jobs due to widespread failure of businesses and collapse of credit system. The whole world got sucked into recession with the younger generation's dream of a bright future in jeopardy. Governments had to pitch in as Big Brothers all over the world. Seems to me a new era of Capitalism 201 has started. Before combustion of greed sparked motivation and progress. The underlying principle has to change to moderation and living within one's means. From an era of waste, we are entering an era of reuse and containment. Three R's now are Reuse, Repair and Recycle.

3. Global Pollution and Green Revolution. The scientists are convinced that something has to be done to prolong our lives and ways of living. We have to change the ways we live and think. This gave birth to Green Revolution. New sources of fuel need be invented that will be sustainable. Generation of power by wind, solar, hydrogena-

tion, biomass etc have to be developed. America has to unite with other leading nations in recognition of the fact that the planet is in peril. Global Pollution from burning of hydrocarbons has to be curtailed. All of these project a radical change in our ways of living and thinking.

4. China's rise as an economic super powe: it seems China is marching ahead at a dizzying pace of growth and probably will get closer to US in coming days ahead. That probably will end the *numero uno* supremacy of US. After the demise of colonial era probably this will regroup world's power balance. Also India's and China's growth will lift the standards of two billion people that will shift the consumer centers of the old era. Also the same pattern of economy will promote cooperation and enhance the awareness of our interdependence. All of these make the last decade as seminal, when lasting changes will take place with global redistribution of wealth and power.

5. The advent of Web 2.0: this evolution of web is already changing the way we do our thinking; the way we do our commerce and the way we socialize. Conventional TV journalism and print media are facing major threats from the powers of speed of Internet communication. Power of social networking like Tweeter has overcome censorship of suppressed people, made the people across globe to connect faster and

instantaneously. Google has brought the amassed human knowledge on our computer screen with a soft click on the keyboard. Google Earth has brought the distant places on the planet instantly visible. This is definitely different from the tools the older generation used to broadcast and communicate. President Obama showed the power of Internet by starting a grass root movement without large corporate coffers behind. Politics and faces will be more open books and there will be less scope for manipulation. So I think more changes along this line will occur.

6. Lastly but not least, the election of a black man as America's President is a seminal event. Though Mr. Obama fought the election on his own merit, but that loosened the iron grip of power brokers, where elitism, money and race played big roles. I don't know if other blacks can match Obama's ascendancy, but it definitely raised the hope of a neglected race to be equal. Not only the blacks, Obama also spearheaded the ascendency of the youth, smart and articulate, that smashed all kinds of barriers, and made the color or minority issues as moot. I just hope Obama's election does not turn out to be a freak show, but becomes a powerful agent of integration leading to equality of all.

***

Remembering A Good Friend (1-22-2010)

Hello Bhai (brother), tell me what is new now. Did you see what the communists are doing to the state of West Bengal...? I had been used to that friendly call for about 30 years now. This was almost like a routine weekend telephone conversation. Then I would tell whatever I knew was new to the best of my knowledge. Then he would say 'That is not all brother, a lot more is going on... . Then he would narrate all the political scandals and mischief going on in India. He knew a lot about what was going on. He read and listened to all the news about India. He would listen to BBC morning news, as he deemed that was very authentic and unbiased. He would read on Internet all the local Indian dailies. Then he would sigh - 'Brother, things have changed so much in India now, you would hardly recognize...' Then he would narrate some bad events that happened on his last trip to India. Time would pass by with this kind of exchange of our knowing and understandings of the world and India in particular. Of course he knew much more than I knew. He loved India in his heart. So any kind of disparagement or perceived deterioration in modern day attitudes of young Indian people would hurt him. I am talking about my dear friend Sankar da. His name was Sankar. But we called him Sankar da, as younger brothers customarily and affectionately call their elders in India, if they are not a generation apart in age. To our great pain and sorrow, he just passed away last month.

But he would not talk about himself or what was going on in his personal life. We know his family very well and are very close to them. We all share the deep sorrow and loss as his extended family. He was in very good health and was as productive as one could be, but then all on a sudden on a visit to his doctor for a small discomfort (about two years ago), he came to know that he had got this terrible thing – cancer (T-cell Lymphoma, a sort of blood cell cancer). He could not believe it himself. He was a non smoker all his life. He was very diligent about taking care of himself. He did regular walking, gardening, other health maintenance routine, a careful eater. He was an expert on nutrition. He himself was doing related research in the university. I was a routine smoker about twenty years ago- that hurt him. He told me – 'brother, you have no idea how smoking damages the lung. The lung gets to look pitted and black; we see it all the time in the laboratory. Try to get rid of that dangerous habit...' I had eventually given up smoking at his insistence and my doctor's insistence. But he had assured me that lung gets back to normal eventually if you give up smoking. He knew it well, because he was an accomplished researcher in the field. He got hefty research grants from sources like National Institutes of Health etc. He was a professor in Respiratory Physiology in UCLA. He published numerous papers on his research. He did not talk about that to me as I belong to a different profession. Probably I would have not understood the importance of his research. We used to hear that he had gone to Brazil or Sweden or India to present a paper. Though we were proud that he was so valuable to his profession, but as a brother our respect to him was not for being a scientist, but for being an affectionate older brother.

I did not know then, but I know now that his dream was to contribute to the science of respiratory physiology. He himself was a doctorate in Physiology and specialized in Respiratory Physiology. His dream was to work with Dr. Karl Wasserman, a renowned pioneer in that field who has devised Wasserman exercise and has contributed to a better understanding of human physiology in routine Treadmill Test (as practiced now). According to his son – the fact that his dad got opportunity to research with Dr. Wasserman was a dream come true for his dad. He co-authored many papers with Dr. Wasserman. Though I did not know about all this before

– now I wonder how come he never talked about this to me during our frequent conversation. I think this was probably due to his modesty about his own accomplishments. Probably because to me he was not a successful researcher, but a very under standing elder brother.

When he came to know that he himself had gotten the terrible thing he could not believe that. He fought within himself about the injustice. He would not even accept that he had got cancer. He would not tell that to anybody. Finally we came to know that he was going through all the different chemotherapy and he did not want it to be known to everybody. He was very vigilant about the treatment and his doctors knew that they were treating one of their own and showed him respect. The treatments were nerve wrenching and terribly painful. But he withstood all the pain smilingly as he loved life and he wanted to live to take care of his family. He even went through the fifth stage. He told me most other patients give up at fourth and are not willing to go through any more excruciating pain. Unbelievably, after the treatments he apparently came back to his usual upbeat cheerful mood, though he had lost weight considerably. Then he started to talk with us like before. He used to say – 'brother I feel so light hearted after I talk with you that I feel like I got a dose of fresh oxygen in my heart...'. I don't know what he meant really, but I used to feel much lighter also. He always enjoyed good laugh. And we used to share good laughs during our frequent light-hearted conversation.

He was also a gadget freak. His son says that his dad would have been a gadget salesman if he did not go to the research field. He used to go to Circuit City and Best Buy, and look at all the electronic gadgets that were on display. He had collected numerous clocks, including one atomic clock that he synchronized with the official scientific time. He used to say during changes to Daylight Savings Time – brother, these clocks turn me into a banana. But he would not stop collecting clocks and other gadgets. He was also very thrifty, he did not believe in any waste. He knew the gains in life are prizes of hard work, and should not be disregarded or belittled. That was probably due to his early childhood memory. He came from a large ordinary family in a small village in West Bengal. Success did not come to him on a silver plate. He fought hard all his life and cherished his achievements – not to be broadcast publicly but to be enjoyed privately. He loved his wife Dipali (Dipali di- to us) very much. She herself has a doctorate in Biochemistry and was a clinical researcher in that field. I under-stand he met Dipali di in college and they spent more than fifty years together. He always said – brother I want to live to take care of Dipali. A very kind loving man, husband and father – he was so much dear to us also. His passing leaves a big void in lives of everybody who came close to him. We all just pray (in Hindu fashion) that - may his soul journey through time in peace. And may his kindness and love be as nurturing in our memory as it was in his presence.

***

Facebook Phenomenon (2-12-2010)

With New Year came new problems. I saw the other day two TV anchors were debating how to say 2010, - whether to say it as 'two thousand ten' or 'twenty ten'. I did not have any problem for 2009 and called it simply as two thousand nine. But in case of 2010 it is much easier to call it twenty-ten. Anyway as it is not my problem, there is no need to think about it anymore. The economy is really terrible. It seems that no amount of incentives can create jobs and bring back people's happiness. I don't know who is to be blamed. I know that it could be a natural economic cycle with long frequency (like a frequency of 80-100 years) – as the last Great Depression was about 80 years ago in 1930's. In those days there was lack of data, lack of indicators. But now there are indicators - so many of them, so many indexes- there must have been some tell-tale signs somewhere. Probably it is partly political, partly inevitable and partly leadership. I just hope we see brighter days with more smiles on more people's faces.

Last few days I was thinking of writing about Facebook that looks like a phenomenon to me. How can a Facebook (though interactive) with personal profiles and pictures of people and accessible by friends can be so captivating that it is used now by close to half a billion people on earth. I don't want to be left out – so I am also there, but I don't find much worthwhile to share. So I only share jokes, albums etc. I am not a social scientist or a social advisor, but I read social advices meted out by social etiquette gurus. And very frequently I see people writing about how embarrassed one had become in Facebook. That kind of piqued my interest. There are lots of columns like 'Ask Amy' and others that encourage a social dialogue where one tries to share one's embarrassments in social behaviors and seeks some quick advice.

 I see that an aunt shared her memories of her niece's childhood on the niece's Facebook wall, and was embarrassed that her niece was so upset, as her peers started to tease her. Should any aunt write something personal and private things on the walls of her niece's house? That is what seems to be the problem. Many of the older generation thinks all the social networking devices are toys of a technical nature. There seems to be a mental divide between generations on the use of social network. Younger people don't want to bring in the elder folks in their lives. Probably they want to create their own virtual world where elders have a restricted entry. But one thing for sure – a physical letter or a picture can be shredded or destroyed, but any post in the cyber world is going to be there forever. So we all have to be careful.

I read that Mark Zukenberg was a Harvard student when one night he was very desolate after being rejected by a girl for a date. So he was looking at the Harvard Facebook (a book with the faces of all students) to find some other friend he could approach for a date. Necessity is the mother of invention, so he thought of creating a virtual Facebook that would be accessible to his friends only and thus was Facebook born.

I cannot imagine that such a simple beginning could start a company which would be valued at up to 8 billion dollars (now) and still going up. It is embraced by all people over earth. I know there are people who fill up their walls with updates on their babies, cats and dogs. I know it has become an impediment to productivity as employees update their walls with trivia on company time. I read that the Christmas bomber (the Nigerian student suicide-bomber) had expressed his loneliness and some indication about his evil intention on Facebook. There have been other similar stories. And there are nations that think it is a trivial pursuit and some rulers are worried that via Facebook any disaffected person can spread some anti- government buzz, so they wanted to ban Facebook.

This freedom of expression has also landed many in trouble. Like somebody (student or employee) bragging about their beach outings on a work day while playing truant, and some employees making jokes about their bosses did not earn them any promotion. Just like anything, guns don't kill people, people kill people. Everything depends on how it is going to be used.

There are other networking sites (like Twitter, MySpace, LinkedIn and many others) that are equally popular (or may be a little less). Twitter has been instrumental in spreading the news of oppression in Iran during their last election, and it has been instrumental in spreading the news of natural disaster much before the media got hold of it. Now many networks encourage people to twit them about anything unusual or tragic happening. So a simple pastime on an idle evening did give birth to a phenomenon. I have many idle evenings – so I can also wait for the days when I may have some great idea! As the great idea is not forthcoming, I just spilled out this blog.

When Graham Bell came up with the talking device that we call Phone - that was the birth of the first social networking device. Who knew that talk would generate billions of dollars one day, as billions of people talk with other billions? Now it seems if somebody sums up the wealth of all telephone companies – that would be the biggest revenue earners of all. Facebook and others are like the telephone was a social networking tool in the earlier days.

**

Mr.Toyoda (2-25-2010)

Coming to think of what to write today, I cannot refrain myself from commenting on Toyota's misfortune. Of course Toyoda family is the owner of the company and that name is the brand name which we have associated with quality. My wife drives a Toyota Avalon and I drive a GM car Pontiac. And we always think that the GM car is no match to such a brilliant car of a Toyota brand, and for any long distance driving

Toyota is an uncontested choice. Previously the word GM meant God Made and their Chevy brand was the backbone of America's heartland and the country's automotive pride. Now GM stands for Government Made – saved from the brink of failure by Government largess. That failure has been attributed to short-sighted leadership, inept management and lack of proper planning. Recently we also saw the prevention of the collapse of the banking system by heavy handed government intervention. That I also thought was brought on by banker's greed that had spread like cancer through American Capitalism.

But the same fate and ignominy are tarnishing Toyota! I could not think of that before. Before I always thought Japanese culture is a shame-based culture where personal shame (not greed) guides an individual. Though many eastern cultures are shame based, but mostly that is confined to morality and fidelity at a personal level. But I thought that the Japanese had extended that to corporate entities too, where a corporate failure is deemed culpable at a personal level also. Toyota was doing everything right that a responsible world citizen should do. They were building excellent, reliable machines of transportation, coming up with hybrid cars (Prius was their pride); doing commendable research on energy-efficient engines; building plants in America and all over the world to provide jobs everywhere. But how did the ignominy of callous and reckless behavior attack this citadel of excellence? The 'sticky gas pedal issue' has made Toyota to recall over 8 million cars and that has tarnished Toyota's pride beyond repair (at least seems to be so). It is of course very painful to Mr. Toyoda. Was someone hiding something from him or was it a deliberate financial planning and taking chances with people's lives? I don't think Mr. Toyoda would have allowed such a flawed product on the road if he had an inkling of knowledge about this. But I shall be eagerly waiting to see how it happened and how the pride is going to be restored.

***

Four Little Rulers (2-25-2010)

This writing is about four tiny rulers – all aged three and less, who have become de-facto rulers of our small world. I have read that Alexander the Great was a short man and Napoleon Bonaparte too. I can understand that – because height cannot be a determining factor in controlling people's lives. But these four youngsters do rule us – well kind of. The rulers in question are Shaun, Tejas, Trevor and Jinie. Of course I am not complaining about their rules – because it is a privilege and fun to be under their rules. Luckily though they are not together all the time. But when they are it is almost a 911 scenario.

First in line is Shaun (3.7 year). He now goes to preschool. I don't know if he enjoys the school and the confinement – but he does not complain nor does he like to discuss about his school. Any discussion about school turns him off. He is a great fan of Transformers (convertible robots in sci-fi). And he wants all of them in different sizes – big ones to play in home, small ones to carry in the car. Now I am learning which Transformer is Optimus Maximus, who is Bumble Bee etc. And when he tests my knowledge on the names of the Transformers and what each of them can do – I know he won't give me a passing grade on that. He sleeps in Spiderman uniform. He watches Spiderman movie in his Spiderman sleeping suit. He has all kinds of character toys, trains and cars with names (which I cannot keep track of). He knows the names of all the cars, all the characters etc. He is imaginative and very interested in hearing stories about dinosaurs etc. Once I was telling him a story (which I made up) about Spiderman. He said – what color is the Spiderman. To be realistic, I said the Spiderman was black and white. He corrected me –

Spiderman can never be black and white, Spiderman is always blue and red. After that I don't dare to make up any unrealistic stories – because chances are he would find fault with the storyline. When he comes back from school in his house, he is in charge.

His little brother Trevor sometimes wants to share his toys, Shaun does not like that. So he rolls up his eyes and brings that in close range of little Trevor's eyes and gives him a glaring look and warns him not to do it again. He is kind of jealous about Trevor as Shaun knows that both have to share the attention of their parents. He likes to mess up things, makes big fuss while being tooth-brushed, and anything in his hand can be ballistic any time. To enjoy some privacy from Trevor he has created a space of 4'x4' in his room barricaded by toys – where Trevor is not supposed to trespass. Trevor being as young as he is now – is now learning to say a few words. Once he said Mooon (meaning the moon). On hearing that Shaun warned Trevor that he himself would ride around the moon and cover it with a blanket so that Trevor cannot see the moon. Shaun definitely rules his parent's world. He has picked up all the adverbs very well, and sprinkles his talks with 'probably, may be, approximately, how much etc'. You better believe that, he knows what he is talking about.

Next ruler is Tejas (2.2 year). He knows it all. He is barely two – but a tall boy in his age group (90 percentile). Even a few months ago, he was not saying many words. But we knew that he was very attentive and knew exactly what was what. When he is watching his favorite Monster Truck or one of his thirteen or fourteen favorite shows on TV, he does not want any disturbance. So when any unwanted sound reaches his ear – he shouts 'top (stop) that Dadai – no no'. He knows his Dadai (me) is a trouble maker and always coming up with some strange and mischievous tricks that disturbs his attention. I think he was kind of shy – that's why he was not speaking much till he was sure that he picked up the words correctly. His mom is always expanding his boundaries of freedom and always checks with his liking before doing anything to him. He knows that he has the final say. His mama was saying that she took him to the local library to listen to stories that other kids were listening. Though reluctant to be so quiet, he sat quietly on his mama's lap during the story telling. To make the children participate in the story, the librarian mentioned 'Is not that a good idea – children?' Tejas could not take it any more – and shouted 'top, top (stop, stop) that is no good idea'. His mama thought it was better to leave that place before Tejas starts to express his opinions on other things. He knows that time has come for him to go to school. So to get used to that – he (guest status) is taken to the preschool two times a week. There he takes full command, instructing some teachers to 'go home'; to some he gives the broom to clean and others different tasks. The teachers say he knows too much and recommend him to be taken to the three year olds' class. I heard he behaved nicely and listened to the teacher in the senior class. The senior teacher said he did not find any disagreement with her yet. His house is full of toys – that is now occupying 75% of the house. He knows his toys very well, and amazingly he knows how things work. Once I was putting up a railway track in a wrong place, he said 'no Dadai, no no, here'. He loves the tools very much. He dictates when and how he would sleep – usually needs a 30 minute pre-nap cooling time in the car riding around. He likes to play with Shaun, and says 'Thaun (Shaun) come, come' – then they start to run around, over the sofa, over the chairs, over anything or obstructions that come on the way – alarming the adults nearby. He likes taco – and says 'dadai, get taco'. And I have to say 'Taco ako (okay)'. Then he becomes happy. He has been treated with all kinds of fancy foods by his mom, but seems to like the simple foods prepared by his Amma (grandma) and Aji (Dadaji). He is definitely ruling everything that he comes across.

Next one is Trevor (1.7 year). He has a different personality. He is happy and contented by nature.

It is like 'don't disturb me, and I will not disturb you'. He is a fan of the Australian band (Wiggles) and watches all their intricate dancing moves that include swaying sideways half body. When I come across them and their favorites I am always reminded of my minuscule knowledge of the children's world. Now I subscribe to Netflix, where I intend to watch all the kids programs to boost my knowledge level. The other day in the Toys R Us store, I was amazed that each popular character had their own aisle of shelves for display- of which I had no idea before. Trevor knows that Shaun gives him hard time. So he has come up with some tricks of his own. Like, when Shaun passes by him, he does a full body slam on the ground with accompanying cries which alert everybody that another injustice is being done to him by his elder brother Shaun. Many times I found that Shaun was completely innocent. He is addicted to mother's milk – and will ask for 'bapa'(his own coinage) anytime he does not get what he wants. His mother has to comply right away; otherwise there will be another Broadway show of body slam etc. Shaun may or may not like his school, but Trevor likes Shaun's school. He loves Shaun very much and affectionately utters Shaun's name all the time. It is very painful to him that Shaun does not allow him to trespass into his private space. So he sadly sits next to the toy barrier outside the space. Sometimes when Shaun lets him in – that makes Trevor's day. He becomes so happy. When daddy comes home, he talks incessantly. But he follows minutely Shaun's each move and wakes up the neighbors when he is being tooth-brushed also. He also definitely rules his parent's world.

Next one is Jinie (1.4 year). She came to visit us from India along with her grandparents and parents. She is very cute and very responsive. If you express a desire to see her pretty face – she puffs her cheeks, narrows her eyes to make sure that she looks her prettiest best. We saw her in India in July last year. She lives on the fourth floor with a view of the road below. She would listen to the crows' cacophony, watch the dogs passing by and the pedestrians in a hurry while she had her breakfast or lunch. Her parents and grandparents were very proud that she did not need expensive toys to keep her interested. But her brief (three weeks) visit here in December has changed her completely. She now picked up all the bad habits of the American children – like being addicted to Elmo etc. So his parents and grandparents scoured the toy store to pick up as many toys (along with bountiful gifts she got) as the travel allowance would permit. Now I hear she has become a toy-addict like American kids. While here, she being of a smaller stature, Tejas would take upper hand to stop her intrusion into his world of toys. But she picked up enough courage in a day or two, and was ready to combat with

Tejas. She would make sure that she had unobstructed entry even when Tejas was hiding in the play tent. She has picked up many words now – rapidly growing up. She knew all of us in her short stay here. Her parents are always thoughtful about how to make her more happy. She definitely rules her parent's world.

Actually one can go on and on, but this writing is getting too long. So more later.

(P.S: Now we have another granddaughter Kajal – she was born on July 2011. By the press time she is about 18 months old. She is always full of smile, does not cry for minor inconvenience, but always lets us know her likes and dislikes very distinctly. She is also another delightful dominating ruler in our house)

***

A Princess is born – Kajal *(7-19-2011)*

We are so excited that a princess is born. Her name is Kajal. She was born on July 13 (Wednesday) at 10:20 pm. Her weight on debut was a little shy of 7 lbs and her length was full 19 inches. She is coping very well with her new environments. She sleeps during day and stays awake at night. So it means somebody else has to stay awake at the same time. Naturally it makes it difficult for her to get a nap. But she is well up to her challenge and keeping up with the arduous task. Of all the grandkids, three were princes, so a princess definitely fills up the gender gap a little bit.

We were all anxiously waiting for her arrival. She was three days late from her expected day. Her little big brother Tejas (3.8 yrs) is all play for her. Yesterday when he came home from school at 2 pm, he was loudly knocking the front door- ' Biga, come on I am home now. Your big brother is home now'. Tejas is very articulate, does not do any baby talk and his running flow of conversation can match any adult. His breadth and depth of knowledge of things he comes across is amazing. When I take a turn that he has not seen before–he will remind me that was a wrong turn. He points out that he colored the mountain in front of his house and takes credit for many other things. He knows which things are sold in what stores, and knows that outside dirty shoes should be left at door and not inside. He likes Tacos on Tuesday, Hamburger on Wednesday etc. The other day he went to play with his plasma car in the neighborhood park.

There was a baby and his non-English speaking grandma. Tejas struck up a conversation with her telling her that – he was 3 and half, he goes to school, knows Chinese and can count in Spanish etc. (Of course everything he said was a little inflated) The other day when the teacher gave him some work to do – he nicely said he was frustrated (of course). His vocabulary may match an eight year old. He affectionately called her sister "Biga'- now that she is born he calls her by her real name 'Kajal'. He affectionately already shared with her many precious cars that he is owner of.

Kajal, welcome to a new world. I know you are occasionally peeking all around to see what it is all about and what is all around. When you grow up you would probably like to know how things were when you were born. So a little rambling about the state of Earth is not out of context. Now we are all going through a long and deep Economic Recession. Many, many people don't have any jobs. Nobody knows how long it will last. All the big economic powers in the west are getting severe beating. President Obama is in charge - he wants to do many things but does not get any cooperation from the Congress

Other sad events that took place were - the Japanese Earthquake and Tsunami that devastated parts of Japan and almost triggered the calamity of a Nuclear Reactor meltdown.

Tejas, Shaun and Trevor are your little big brothers and will give you plenty of company all the time. Disney-Pixar's new *Car2* movie was just released and we all went to see the movie. Now your brothers have moved over from Toy Story 3, and Woody, Buzz etc. Now they are preoccupied with Lightening McQueen and challenger Francesco Bernoulli. The earth's climate seem to be changing with more hot days in summer, more extreme weather like tornadoes etc.

But you have a bright future. You are born in a very loving family where everybody cares and everybody wants to excel. You are born at a time when new things are happening on the internet every day. E-mails are old fashioned; now most everybody communicates through Facebook and Twitter. You can access instant knowledge about anything by googling. To enjoy the world you have to love others also and stay connected with others – family and friends. World has many things to offer – so prepare yourself accordingly. Love, love, lots of love to you.

{ I am in a quandary now. Kajal' Annaprasan already took place on February12, 2012. This publication is going to press in April 2012. So for sake of completeness and for sake of Kajal I have to mention that.

About ninety people were invited. Kajal had something to say and I did that for her as she cannot talk yet as she is only seven months old now. But I am pasting the speech in toto for completeness.

Kajal's Speech

Hi everybody

I told my dadai to say a few words for me. I am Kajal, I want to greet all of you and give you all a warm welcome smile. My mama said not to hug everybody for health reasons or something like that. I understand almost everything but cannot talk yet. I am small, only one day shy of full seven months.

I have only three teeth now. I invited you all for my Annaprasan. In simple words, you will just watch when my uncle and others feed me solid food. My elders call it Annaprasan Ceremony and that is party time. My Dadai said - it is my Food Graduation Ceremony from liquid food to solid food. I have no idea what my Namma has prepared for me for the transition. But I am a good sport. I shall give it a try. I hope my Namma has not messed it up.

I get amused when somebody jumps. My brother Tejas, my Aji (Papa's papa), my Dadai , - they all jump to amuse me. Only when they do it well, I give them a big smile. Though that is one form of entertainment that amuses me but you don't have to do that. My mama said that should be done only with doctor's permission.

I was just trying to be funny. I have been told there will be two games – one to see what I am going to be (i.e. what I like- Money, Real Estate, Art or Education). The other game will be to see what profession I shall choose. The elders will try to figure out what I am going to be – (whether a lawyer like my mama or a tall professional basketball player per my papa's wish). My elders think they are very smart and they have figured it out already – but I am telling you it is not that easy, I will have my own say.

Oh, I almost forgot. The teachers and staff of Wonder Years Montessori School are here. I am glad they have come to see me eating solid food. I just hope they don't start teaching me right away.

There will be foods after the games. Because I am so small, my dadai said big talk does not fit me. So I won't try to say more. But I must emphasize the essence of this gathering, which is very simple. It is so that I know you and you know me. And I need your well wishes and blessings to grow up properly. Thank you all. Lot of hugs and kisses for you all.]

***

Gandhi &
(10-2-2011)

**Rabindranath,
Shantiniketan**

Rabindranath always thought that Vedic civilization was the highest form of civilization that mankind has seen. It is also true that Vedic civilization was not an urban civilization where humans congregate in large numbers. But it originated in nature and   is forest based. Thus when we call someone a Maharshi (Maha Rishi) the concept is implied that it is non urban or forest based. Rabindranath had nature ingrained in him as probably transmitted across generation thorough his father Maharshi Debendranath. Rabindranath was tired of urban civilization or civilization that is intrinsically influenced by stress , has violence embedded in it, and as such is not real but a little tainted and created under duress.(I also personally think that human system when in harmony with nature has natural rhythm and is devoid of stress and hence has more intrinsic potential.) Rabindranath wanted to unfold human potential through Vedic concept. Thus in a sense Rabindranath himself can be called a Maharshi like his father. He found the opportunity to implement his Vedic dream. The location he selected was Santiniketan, an estate left by his father near Bolpur in Birbhum district of West Bengal.

Rabindranath himself did not have much means to start the project in a grand scale. The estate's income was meager. He sold his personal belongings, his seaside residence in Puri, his wife's jewelry and all that. Even that did not amount to much. So Santiniketan started as a pathsala (Vedic elementary school) with a few students only. Another reason that thwarted participation of more people was the British suspicion that Rabindranath was giving birth to a Nationalist movement. Nevertheless his dream unfolded as a Vedic school in 1901. Rabindranath really did not want a parochial school. He wanted to build up a congregation of universal brotherhood where there would be free interaction of knowledge and ideas among world's cultures and inhabitants. So when he won the Noble Prize in 1913 he put all his prize money to the creation of a universal school and Visva Bharati was born in 1921. The campus that started with a few students now is a robust campus of 6500 students and a faculty of more than 500 with a world famous art division that outputted a staggering number of geniuses in their own fields. It is the foremost center of study of ancient Asian culture. United Nations realized that Shanti Niketan was a hallowed ground where a living saint and savant had his habitat, and was a place where a pioneering experiment in Internationalism took place. Some time ago UN declared it as a hallowed World Heritage Site.

For a real interflow of cross-cultural ideas
Rabindranath recruited many foreign academics
to staff his school of Vidya Bhavan (a Research
Wing of Advanced Study in International
Cultures).It was to be the center of Indological
studies, Buddhist Literatures and Vedic
Literatures in Sanskrit, Pali, Prakrit, Tibetan and
Chinese etc. It was no easy job to recruit and staff
this school of such unique experiment. Chancellor
and Founder Rabindranath (endearingly called
Gurudev or the Respected Teacher of all) worked
tirelessly day and night. (One may wonder how
he got any spare time to do anything else.) Syed
Mujtaba Ali was a student there for five years and
studied under the direct tutelage of Gurudev, and
has written extensively his recollection of his
days in Santiniketan. Interested readers will
enjoy tremendously his anecdotal recollections
presented in a light, awe-inspired and humorous
vein.

Rabindranath personally invited and recruited
the staff from all over the world. They were as
follows in the beginning. Here I am focusing on
foreign academics only; there were many, many
other illustrious Indian Academics.

1. Sylvain Levy (Indologist) from France
   1921-23
2. Sten Konow (Archaeologist) from Norway
   1924-25

3. Moritz Winternitz (Indologist & Sanskrit Scholar) from Austria 1922-23
4. Fernand Benoit (Linguistics) from Switzerland 1922
5. Arthur Geddes (Musicologist) from France/UK 192-23
6. Andree Karpeles (Painting Artist) from France 1922-23
7. Mary Van Eeghen (Musicologist/Theosophist) from Holland 1922
8. Stella Kramrisch (Art Historian) from Vienna 1923
9. Giuseppe Tucci (Sanskrit Scholar) from Italy 1925-26
10. Carlo Formicci (Religion Scholar) from Italy 1925-26
11. Arnold Bake (Musicologist) from Holland 1926-34
12. Igor Bagdonov (Persian Scholar) from Russia 1929-30
13. Mark Collins (Linguistics) from Ireland 1922-31
14. Tan Yunshan (Chinese and Buddhist Scholar) 1928- 38 .... Etc.

I don't think we can exclude influences of Mahatma Gandhi, Charles Andrews (from Scotland) and William Pearson (from Ireland), who were associated deeply with Santiniketan during its formative stage. Mahatma Gandhi also was a great admirer of Gurudev. In 1915 when Gandhiji was drafted from South Africa to pioneer the Indian Independence Movement he was debating immensely where to start. He had narrowed down to three locations – Rajkot, Porbander and Santiniketan. Finally he zeroed in on Santiniketan and started as a teacher in Santiniketan. Also he learnt Bengali real fast in

the Ashram. When the Independence Movement was going in high gear, Gandhiji would come to Santiniketan to get Gurudev's blessings as Gurudev's view was different from Gandhiji's view. Gurudev thought that human development and emancipation would lead to sovereignty and did not like extreme nationalism. And Gandhiji was a soldier in the field and pioneering non-obedience movement. Though the movement was peaceful, still it was confrontational. Rabindranath never vociferously supported that. But Gandhi could not morally proceed without Gurudev's blessings. So he would come to Gurudev frequently and their meetings used to be very private and nobody could witness that and no public accounts were to be released for that.

Charles Andrews was a confidante of both and he (and only he) was allowed to be present in their private meetings. Such historical meetings were going unrecorded, and artist Abanindranath could not take it. So he peeped through the keyhole and got a glimpse of the trio meeting and recorded that in his painting. It is said that painting is the only recorded meeting and was a gift to posterity. It is admiringly treasured in Santiniketan. Gurudev finally indirectly blessed Gandhi by composing – *jadi tor dak sune kau na ashe tabe ekla chalore*. That song was Gandhi's morale-booster and his number one favorite song throughout his life.

Rabindranath lived a simple life and so did Gandhi. But they were so different. Gandhi once announced that he would drop in at Santiniketan to meet the Gurudev. So Rabindranath, as he was in charge of everything in Santiniketan, asked the dorm manager to set up a suite for Gandhi. That manager knew that Gandhi was a returned-from-London Barrister and furnished the suite in latest English fashion. When Gurudev came to see the progress he was disappointed at the English décor. So he chided the manager and told him to refurnish the room with drapes in Indian decoration, put *'alpana'* (finger-painted floor decorations) on the floor and lotus petals at bedside etc. When done, Gurudev inspected the suite and was very happy that it was appropriately decorated for Gandhi. When Gandhi arrived and came to the suite, Gandhi was disappointed. He said it was too decorative and wanted to spend the night on roof on his 'khatia' (a rope supported wooden cot). Rabindranath, when he visited Gandhi in Gujarat had similar problems. Rabindranath's favorite dress was light *Panjabi* (a loose flowing attire) – but Gandhi did

not like anybody who did not wear desi (home-made) khaddars'(coarse cotton attire). I don't know how Rabindranath compromised that.

Going back to foreign academics, Rabindranath had a hard time to persuade students to come to the lectures of the foreign academics. To increase participation Rabindranath made arrangements with Calcutta University to bring the students to hear the lectures. Very few used to come, and those who came were more interested in sight-seeing than listening to the lectures. Once it was announced that Sylvain Levi, the noted French Professor and Indologist, would give a public lecture on ancient Sanskrit Literature and all were invited. But during the lecture time Rabindranath was disappointed that the audience consisted of only two students from Calcutta. So he himself sat down in the front row with his paper and pencil to take notes. Later on when Sylvain Levi was asked if he felt bad that nobody came, Prof Levi said that was the most satisfying lecture he ever gave, because the audience included Rabindranath. Prof Levi is well known for his 'Dictionary of Buddhism' etc. He returned back to University of Paris.

Prof Tan Yunshan regarded Rabindranath as a god-figure. Rabindranath appointed him as the Director of Chinese Studies when Prof Yunshan was only thirty year old. He founded China Bhavan. It was the first Indian Institution of Chinese Studies and Prof Yunshan had brought many archaeological documents from China and Tibet. At his behest Rabindranath visited China in 1924.Tagore's visit was a renewal of friendship between the two great countries. Rabindranath was the second ambassador from India to China after Emperor Ashoka sent twelve monks to spread Buddhism in China circa 250 BC. Chinese scholars thought that India was a paradise for 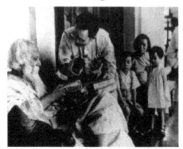 Britons, but a hell for Indians under British tyranny. Yunshan being a poet also left his memoirs about his days in Santiniketan. He wrote that the post office in Santiniketan was world's busiest post office when Tagore was alive. I think Yunshan was awarded India Government's Deshikottama award in 1948.

Moritz Winternitz (Indologist & Sanskrit Scholar) was an assistant to the famous Indologist Max Muller at Oxford University. He is best remembered for his work 'History of Indian Literature' (Sanskrit) and his critical edition of Mahabharata. He translated Rig Veda and wrote about ancient Indian marriage rituals. He went back to teach at Oxford University.

Sten Konow (Archaeologist) is noted for his compilation of Linguistic Survey of India and played prominent role in Indian Archaeological Survey. He later returned back to University of Hamburg.

Giuseppe Tucci (Sanskrit Scholar) was an Italian scholar of Oriental cultures, specializing in history of Buddhism and Tibet. He is considered one of the pioneers of Buddhist studies. He pioneered many archaeological digs in India, Afghanistan, Persia and Tibet. After spending many years in India, he went back to University of Rome. In 1978 he was awarded the Jawaharlal Nehru Award for international understanding.

Arthur Geddes (Musicologist) helped Rabindranath to translate his songs in

International notations. Mary Van Eeghen (Musicologist/Theosophist) and Arnold Bake (Musicologist) also joined in the same efforts.

Leonard Elmhirst (English) was Rabindranath's secretary and companion on travel. He helped Rabindranath in building up an agricultural and rural reconstruction in Sri Niketan, an adjacent facility. Same for William Pearson (English), who was very affectionate towards Rabindranath and gave his wealth and life to Rural Reconstruction in Santiniketan. Both lived in Santiniketan and died in India.

Stella Kramrisch (Art Historian) was an authority on Indian art. Her notable books include 'Indian Sculpture', 'The Hindu Temple', 'Indian Terracottas' etc. She spent her later life in the University of Philadelphia.

Charles Andrews (English) was not an academic per se, but played a big role in Santiniketan. He was a constant companion of Mahatma Gandhi and was a pioneer in India's Independence Movement. He was also a close confidant of Rabindranath. As Rabindranath and Gandhi had  different opinions about how to win freedom, he mediated many times between them. His contribution to India's freedom was tremendous. In 1935 Gandhi asked him to be behind the scenes so that Indians themselves could fight for their own freedom. He lived his later and last part of life in Santiniketan.

So we have to say that though Santiniketan was Vedic in concept, Indian in ideal and Internationalism as its mantra – the contribution of foreign academics and other associates cannot be forgotten in the creation of Santiniketan. Rabindranath in his last letter (1935) to Gandhi said 'Visva-Bharati is like a vessel carrying golden cargo of my life's best efforts and it may claim special preservation by our countrymen'. So Visva- Bharati was his **Sonar Tari** (The Golden Boat) that he loaded with his life's treasures.

Ajay Ray is a licensed professional structural engineer by profession with his practice in Southern California. He has masters in engineering and business, but his interest goes beyond. He immigrated to US in the sixties as a graduate student. Widely traveled across many countries, he lives with his wife in Southern California. His wife is a teacher and runs a preschool. His son practices in medicine and his daughter practices in law. They all live in southern California with their own families.

(His other book A Random Journey of Mind' was published in Sept 2009 and available from Lulu.com)

BLANK PAGE

A Random Journey of Mind
by Ajay Ray

It is about our daily lives, living and experiences - written weekly and posted as blogs. The journey is A Random Journey of Mind. As such it involves experiences, funny events, memoirs, thoughts etc on every body and every thing around us. So the range is as broad from Kennedy to French Fries, to Happy Cows, to Grandmas, to Maui Mishap and to Cairo Kidnapping etc. All presented in a light vein with amusement.

Lulu.com

BLANK PAGE

www.ingramcontent.com/pod-product-compliance
Lightning Source LLC
Chambersburg PA
CBHW051222050326
40689CB00007B/768